IMAGES
of America

MEDFORD IN THE VICTORIAN ERA

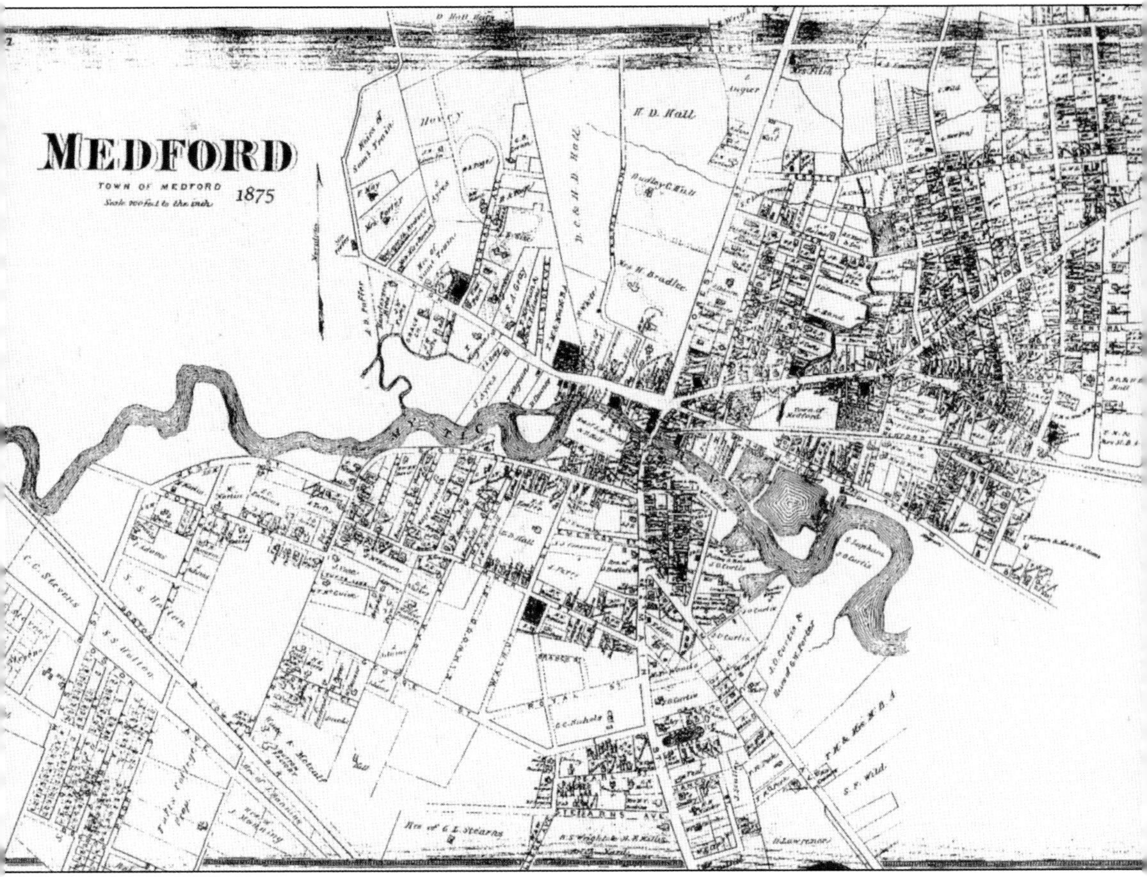

This 1875 map of Medford shows the town in the middle of its Victorian growth. Notice the densely populated areas off Salem and Main Streets and the more open spaces in West Medford and the Hillside area. The empty spaces would fill in within the next few decades as large tracts and estates were divided up into house lots.

IMAGES
of America

MEDFORD IN THE VICTORIAN ERA

Barbara Kerr

ARCADIA
PUBLISHING

ISBN 978-0-7385-3665-1

Published by Arcadia Publishing
Charleston, South Carolina

Printed in the United States of America

Library of Congress Catalog Card Number: 2004108187

For all general information, contact Arcadia Publishing:
Telephone 843-853-2070
Fax 843-853-0044
E-mail sales@arcadiapublishing.com
For customer service and orders:
Toll-free 1-888-313-2665

Visit us on the Internet at www.arcadiapublishing.com

This book is dedicated to Medford, because there is no place like it.

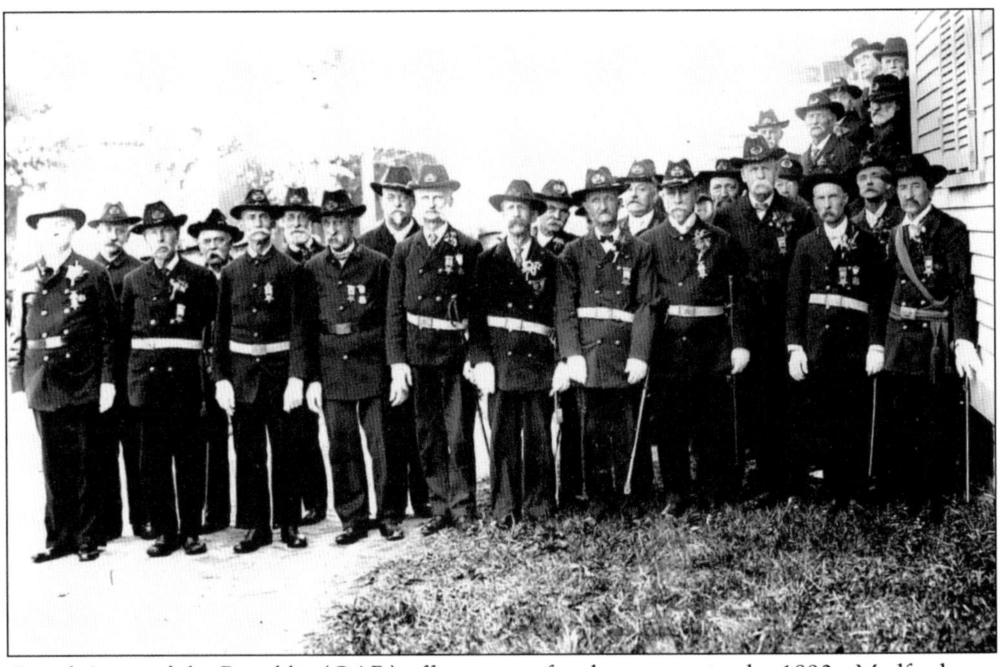

Grand Army of the Republic (GAR) officers pose for the camera in the 1890s. Medford sent 769 men to the Civil War, and the GAR post of veterans was a very active institution. The officers were photographed in front of the Grand Army Hall on High Street. (Courtesy of the Medford Public Library.)

Contents

ACKNOWLEDGMENTS

My gratitude goes to the following for their help and support: Brian Boutilier and the staff of the Medford Public Library, Michael Bradford and Ryan Hayward of the Medford Historical Society, Dee Morris, Nicole DeLaria, the Reverend Hank Peirce, Beth Fuller, Sharon Guzik, Joe McGonagle, Rob Dilman, Mary Kerr, Archie Kerr, Koko Kerr, and Samuel Crocker Lawrence.

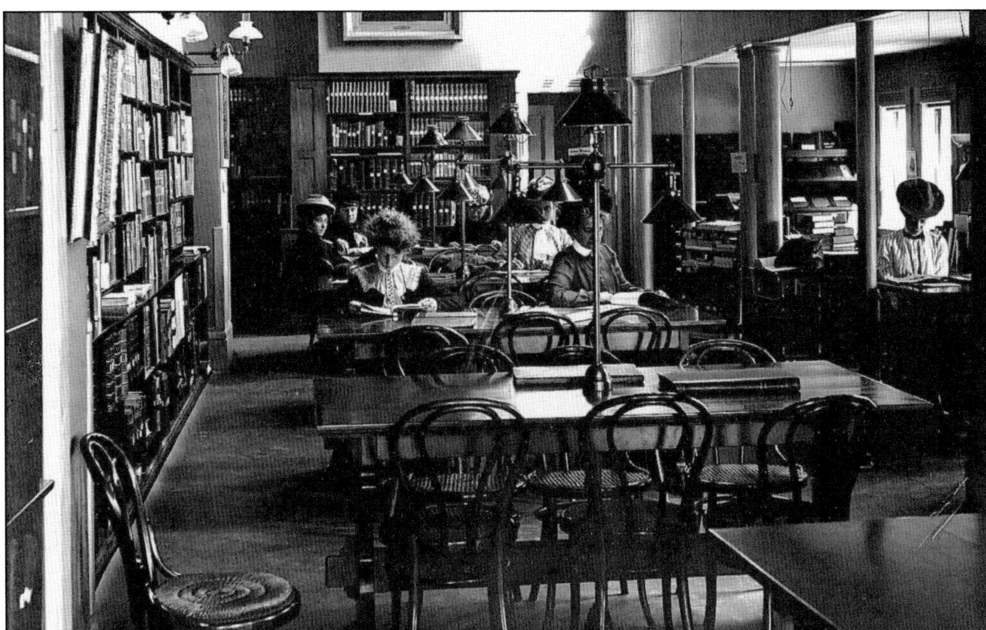

This was a busy day in the library reading room *c.* 1897. The library was housed in the former mansion of shipbuilder Thatcher Magoun. The reading room was refurbished in 1897 after the book stacks were moved into an addition on the back of the building. (Courtesy of the Medford Public Library.)

INTRODUCTION

In June 1905 Medford celebrated the 275th anniversary of its settlement with a great celebration that went on for days. During the festivities, many notable politicians and prominent citizens gave speeches about Medford. They spoke of the civic pride of the town's leaders and the religious spirit of its people; they described a town full of citizens who lived a fine and worthy public life in beautiful houses. They thanked Providence for the prosperity of the town and for the bounties of the natural beauty that surrounded them. They spoke of Medford's history, from its founding in the 1600s to the sacrifices of its citizens in the Civil War. They spoke of change and growth and development, and they spoke of a city that came to be because of the forces of change in the 19th century.

Although the Victorian era had ended by 1905, the men who spoke at the anniversary were Victorians, born and bred in the latter half of the 19th century, and the Medford they spoke of was a Victorian creation. At the beginning of the 20th century, Medford's residents could look back on an era of dramatic change, when everything seemed to be new. What changed Medford in the Victorian era was an influx of new people, and what brought the new people were two factors: the railroad and real estate development.

When the Boston and Lowell Railroad came through in 1835, Medford was a country town with a population of about 1,700. Once the railroad made the town accessible, however, the population began to grow, slowly but steadily. In the 1840s and 1850s, many wealthy Bostonians built houses in the town so that they could live in the country and commute into the city. In this period the new residents built large homes with ample grounds. After the Civil War, real estate developers began to buy up farmland and land formerly attached to large estates to divide into house lots. In the 1870s and 1880s, new residents arrived in droves, and new houses sprang up all over town. By 1900 the once quiet country town had grown into a bustling city of 18,000 souls.

As more and more people moved to town throughout the 19th century, the town government had to grow to provide the services the growing population needed. For the town of Medford, the Victorian era was a time of firsts—the first town hall, the first town fire department, the first police officers, the first public library, the first high school, the first town cemetery, the first college, the first water pipes, streetlights, sewer system, almshouse, savings bank, newspaper, telephone, and paved roads, among a multitude of other firsts. By 1892 the town and its government had grown so much that Medford officially became a city and elected its first mayor.

The nature of Medford business and industry also changed in the Victorian era. In the early 19th century, the primary industries were shipbuilding, rum distilling, and brickmaking. The rum and brickmaking industries continued to thrive well into the 20th century, but shipbuilding, which had been the Medford's largest industry, reached its peak in the 1850s and declined after the Civil War. The last Medford clipper ship was launched in 1873. When the shipyards closed, the face of local business changed. After the 1870s, small business rather than major industries dominated the scene. Medford's new residents needed services, and the new businesses provided everything from groceries, clothing, and wallpaper to hay for the horses. The growth of small business in turn promoted the growth of the town, as business districts and offices were built in many areas to house the new merchants and contractors.

Intellectual change was also in the Medford air in the 19th century. Before 1823 there was only one church in town, but new residents brought new ideas and new beliefs, and by 1900 there were 16 churches. The national conflicts over slavery and states' rights also influenced town life. Many Medford residents were involved in the antislavery movement, including the prominent abolitionists Lydia Maria Child and George Luther Stearns. The Civil War affected the entire nation, and Medford was no exception. In 1861 the first Medford soldiers went off to serve in the Civil War; by the end of the war, 769 men had served and 43 had perished in the conflict.

In the midst of all this history, Medford's Victorians lived their daily lives. They went to school and church, joined clubs and societies, rode horses, bicycles, and boats, and dabbled in everything from photography to amateur theatricals. The look of Medford changed as new architecture took the place of the 18th-century structures that had been the standard early in the 19th century. New homes, businesses, and public buildings sprang up, decorating the streets in all sorts of fanciful styles. The face of nature was changed, too, as Medford Pond became the Mystic Lakes and public pressure brought about the creation of the Metropolitan Park Commission to protect the beauty of the Middlesex Fells. And in the middle of it all were Medford's people—prominent and ordinary, new residents and old families—all sharing in the creation of a modern town.

Medford had come a long way by the turn of the century, and the speakers at the 1905 anniversary celebration extolled the changes that had turned a country town into a suburban city. In the following pages, you will see some of these changes and the people who made them. Medford's Victorian journey was a fascinating one, full of energy, industry, and innovation. The city that stands today would not be the same without the Victorians who passed this way a century ago.

One

Around the Town

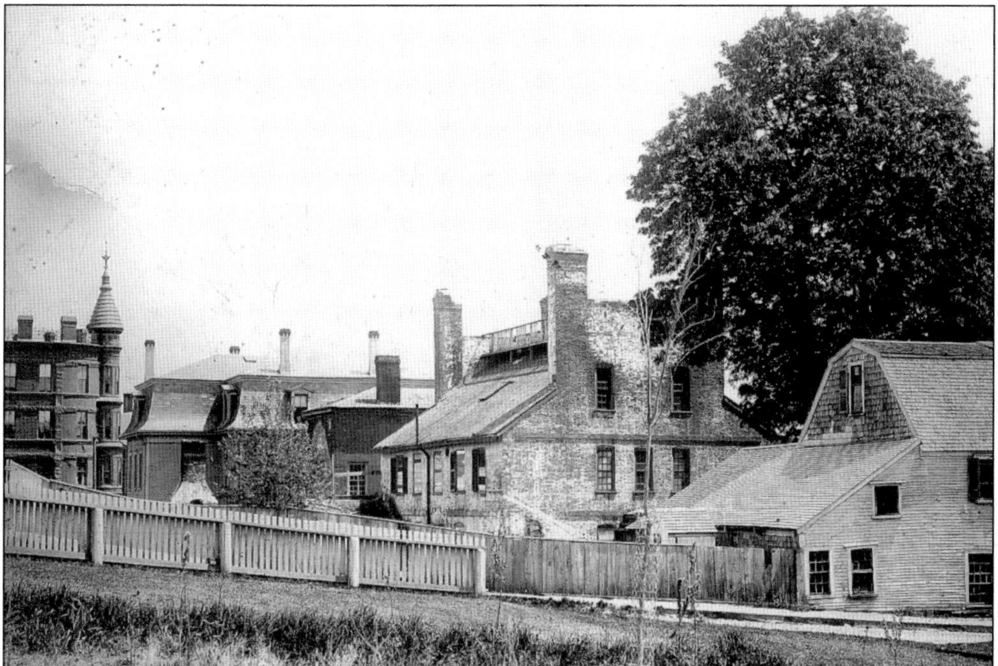

Old and new Medford are represented by two centuries of architecture along High Street. When the Thomas Seccomb House (second from the right) was built in 1756, Medford was a country town. By the time the Bigelow Building (far left) went up in 1886, the town was well on its way to becoming a city. (Courtesy of the Medford Public Library.)

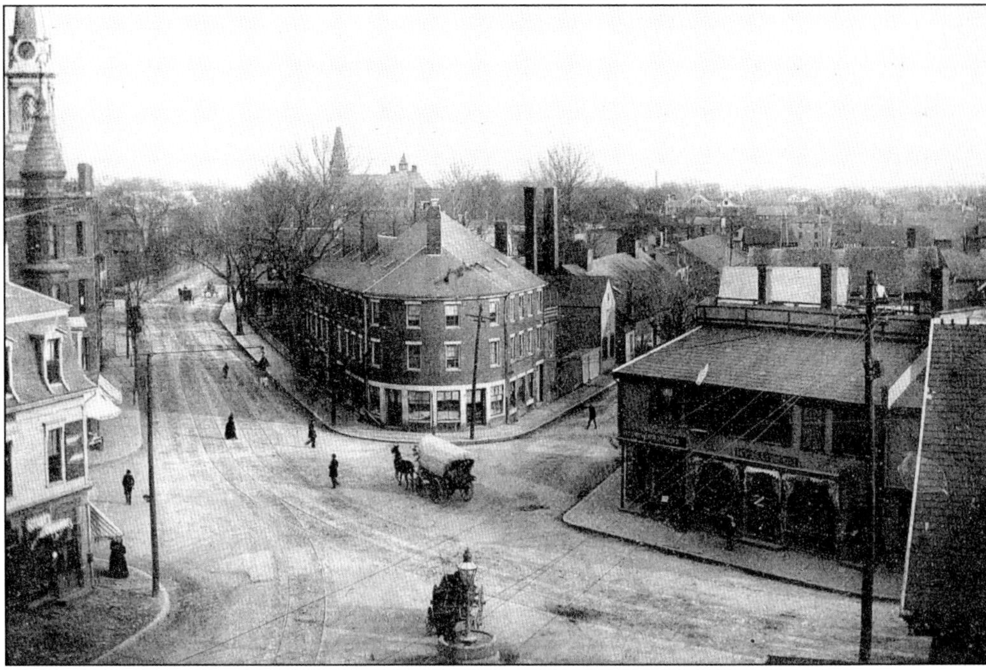

This 1890 photograph of Medford Square was taken from the top of the Medford Opera House on High Street. The town's major streets branched off the square. Seen here, from left to right, are Forest Street (to the left of the Bigelow Building), Salem Street (to the left of the Brick Block), Riverside Avenue (to the right of the Brick Block), and Main Street. (Courtesy of the Medford Historical Society.)

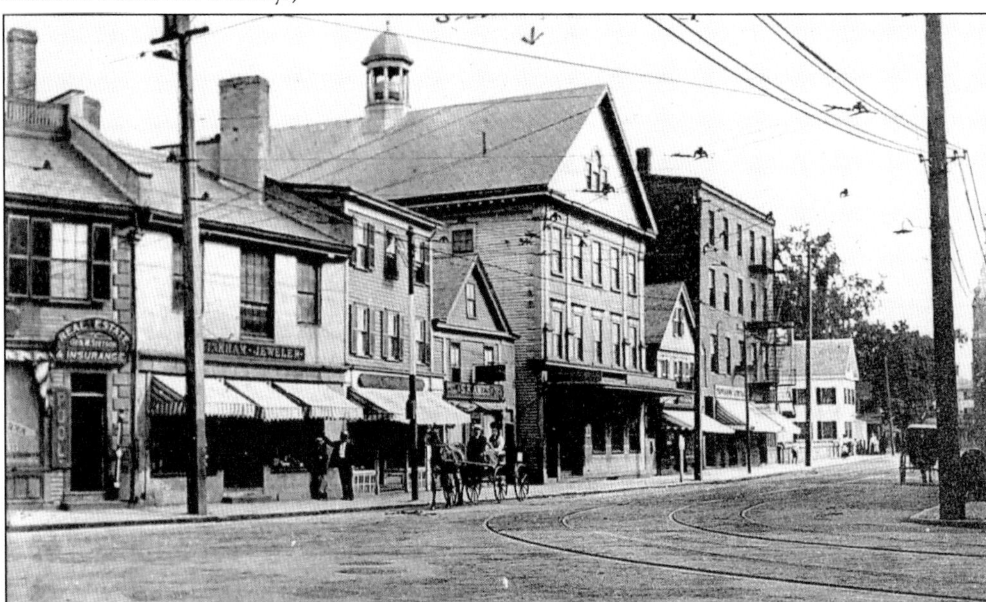

This is a view down Main Street in the early 1900s. The building with the cupola was the Boston and Maine depot. The brick building with the fire escape was the grain and storage warehouse belonging to flour and grain dealer George B. Green. (Courtesy of the Medford Historical Society.)

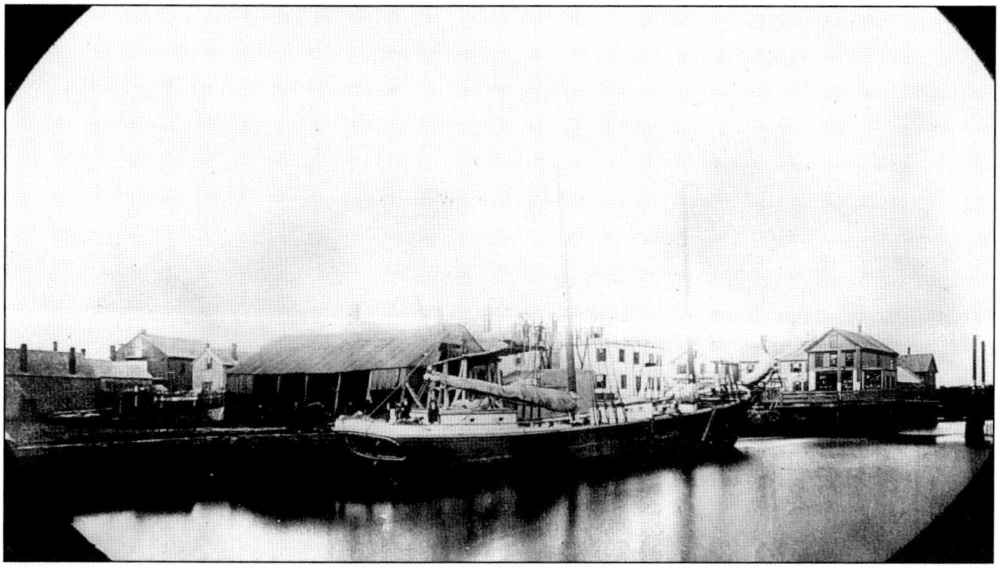

Shown here is a view of the Mystic River, looking east toward Main Street and Cradock Bridge. Before 1880 Cradock Bridge was a wooden drawbridge that could be raised to allow ships of many sizes to reach the shipyards farther up the river. (Courtesy of the Medford Public Library.)

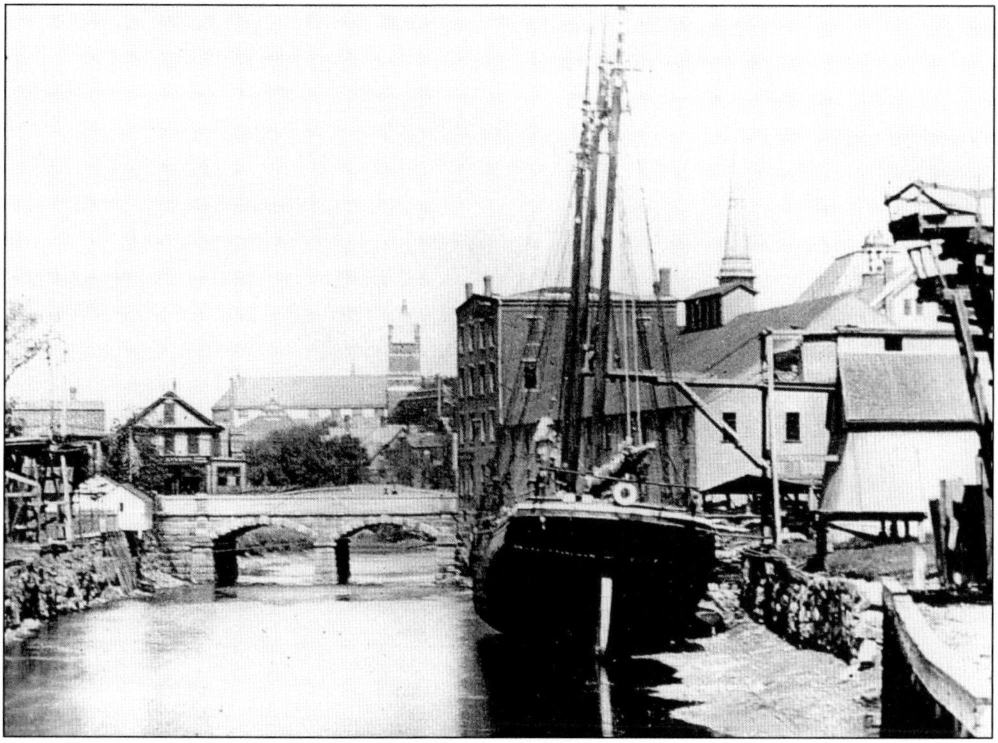

This photograph of the Mystic River, looking west toward Cradock Bridge, was taken after 1900. The drawbridge was replaced with this granite structure, completed in 1880. The town concluded that a drawbridge was no longer needed because the shipyards in the upper part of the river had closed. (Courtesy of the Medford Public Library.)

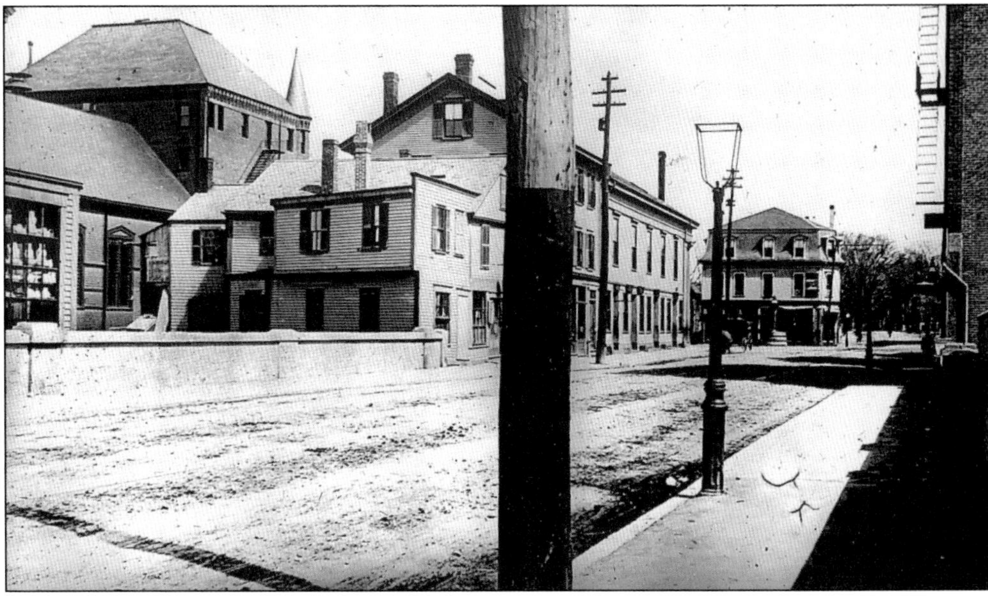

This photograph of Medford Square from Cradock Bridge was taken in the 1890s. Tufts Hall is directly ahead, and the city hall is on the left corner. Notice the gas streetlight on the sidewalk. (Courtesy of the Medford Historical Society.)

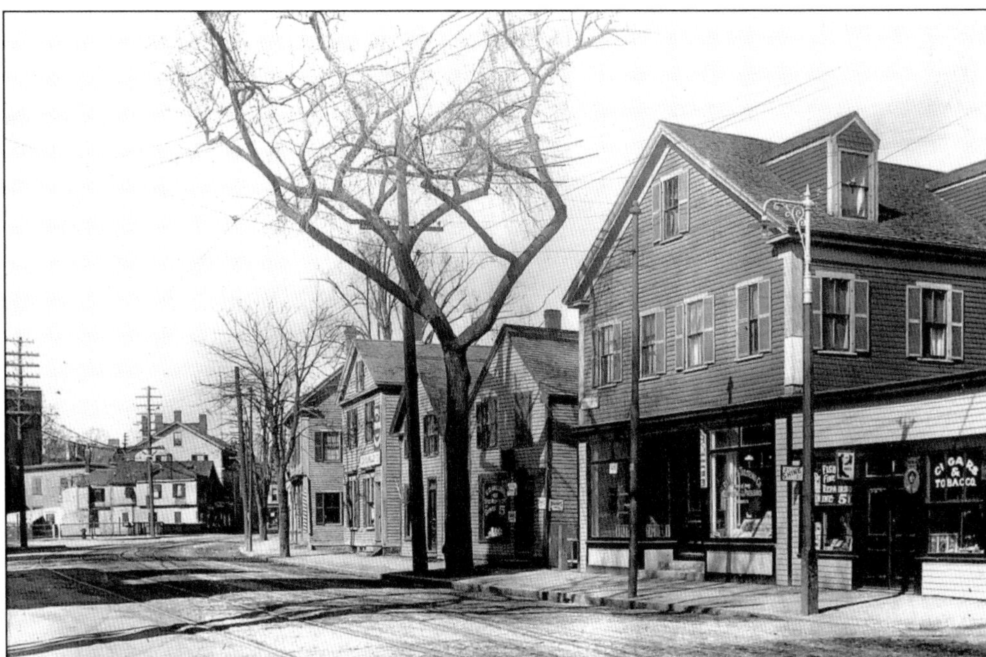

On the other side of the river, Main Street was a combination of business districts and residential areas. This photograph shows businesses on the corner of South Street in the early 1900s. Notice the electric streetlight on the pole at the right. (Courtesy of the Medford Public Library.)

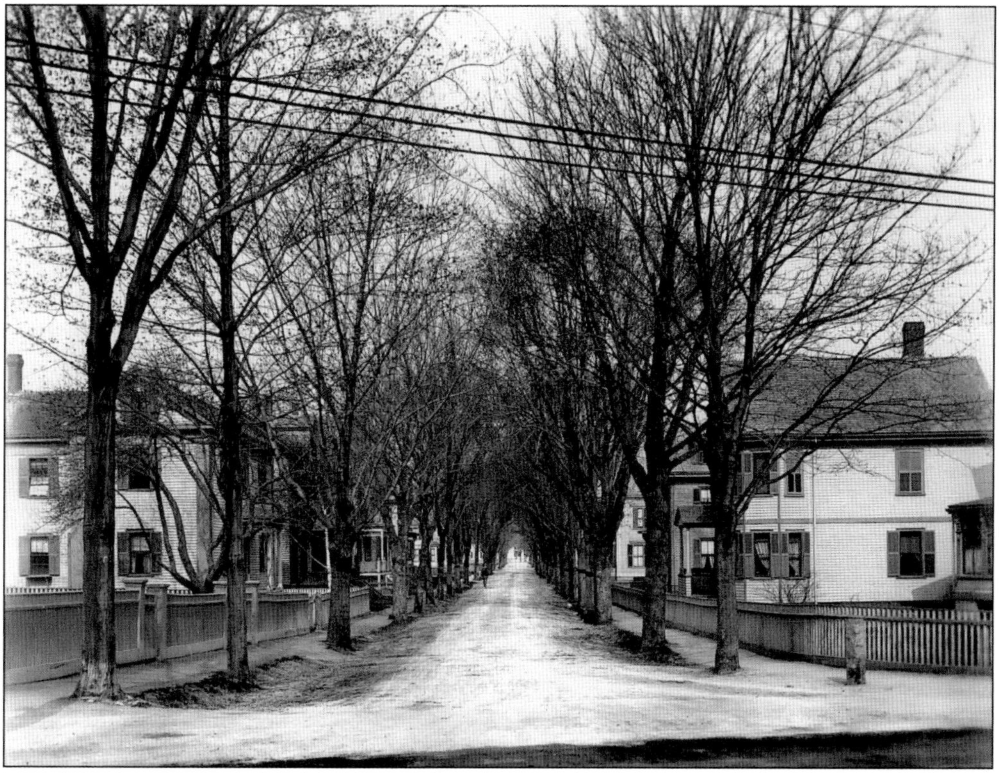

This photograph of Summer Street from Main Street was taken *c.* 1890. Earlier in the century, the Middlesex Canal, built in 1803, crossed Main Street at Summer Street. The canal, which was quite successful until the arrival of the railroad in the 1830s, ceased operation in 1852. (Courtesy of the Medford Public Library.)

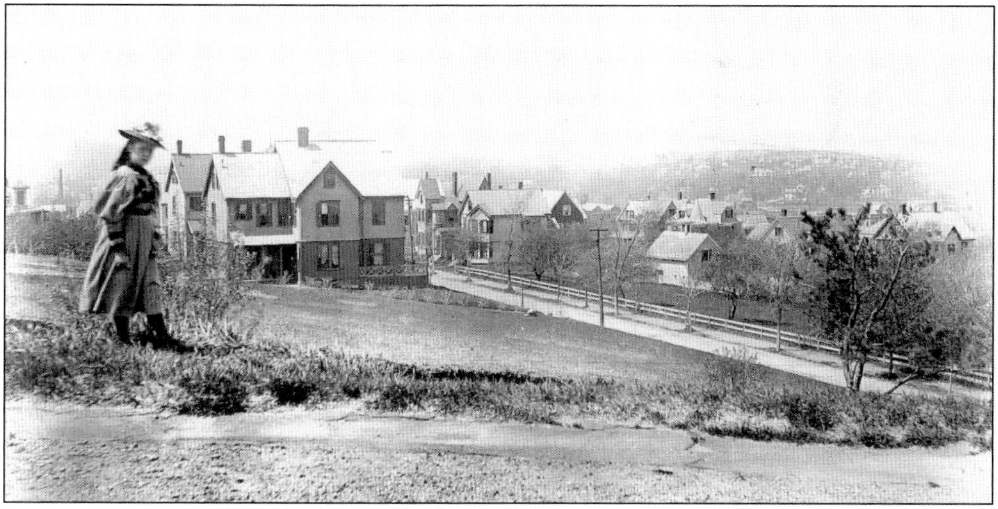

In this view of Medford from the Tufts College area, Capen Street is in the foreground. The site was originally called Walnut Tree Hill, but in May 1896, when this photograph was taken, it was known as College Hill. The girl in the picture is Flora Enright, whose family lived on Capen Street. (Courtesy of the Medford Public Library.)

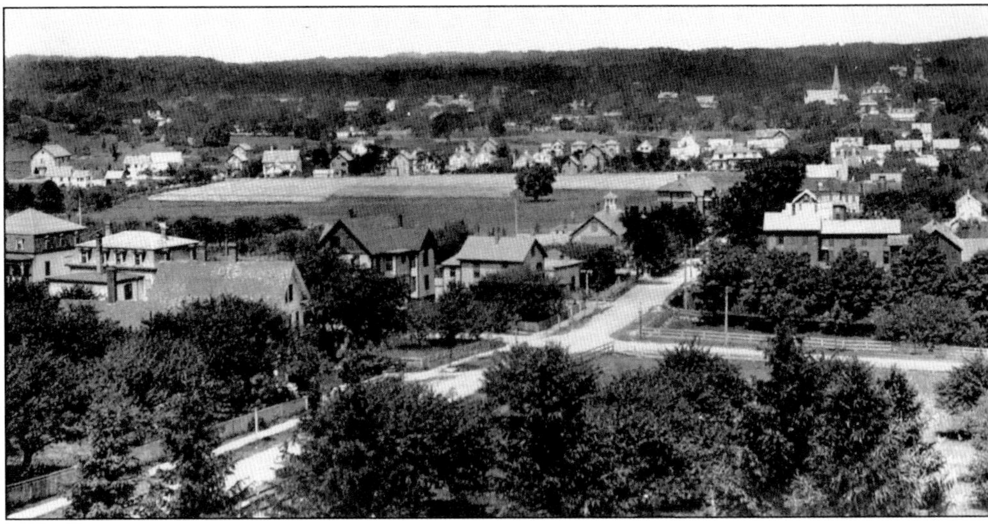

Medford's residential areas grew rapidly in the 1880s. In this 1885 view from the Hillside area down South Street, some open tracts can still be seen, but before long they would be filled with houses. In the distance are the spires of the Grace Episcopal and the Unitarian churches. (Courtesy of the Medford Historical Society.)

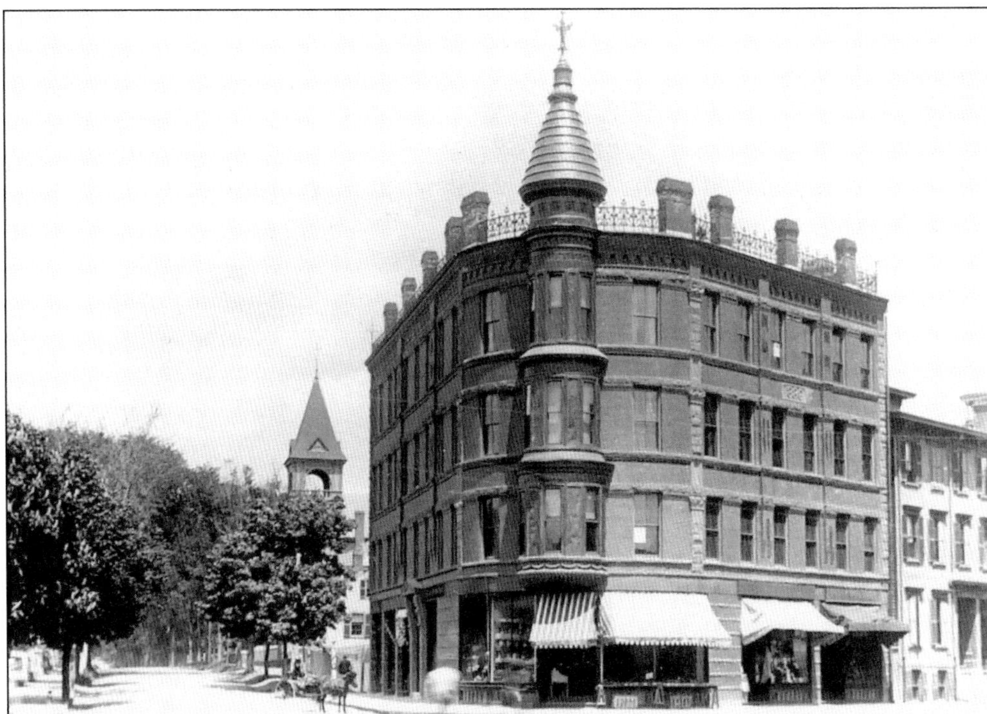

Back in Medford Square, the Bigelow Building (built in 1886 on the corner of Forest and Salem Streets) combined commercial space with some of the earliest apartments seen in the town. The architecture is distinctive red brick with a mixture of decorative patterns on the outside. Notice in particular the granite bands, the ornate roof railing, and the turret on the front of the façade. (Courtesy of the Medford Historical Society.)

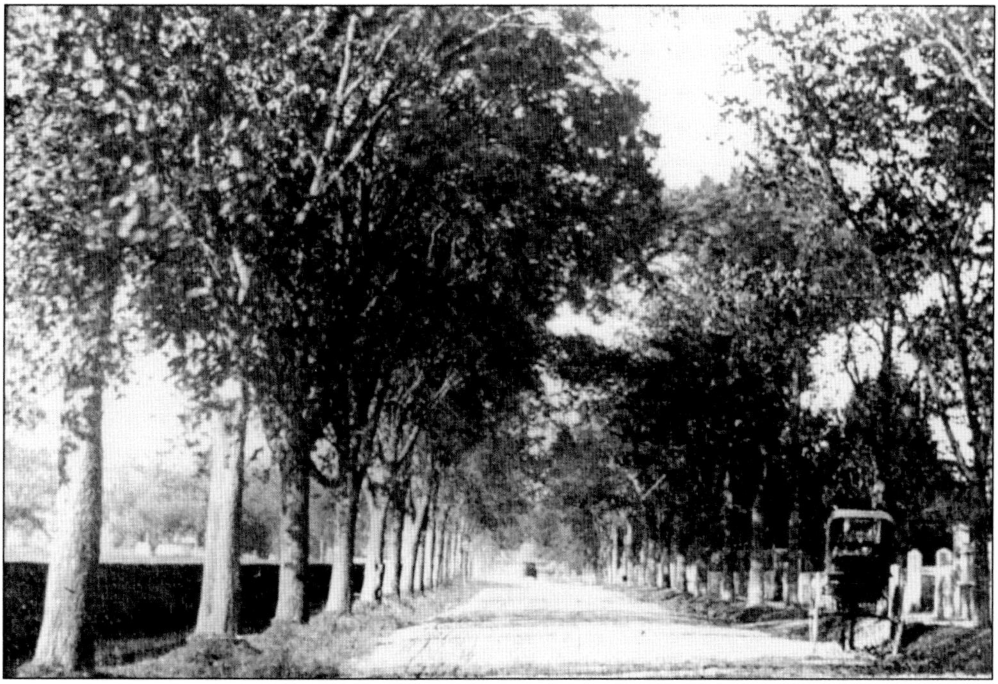

This view of the aptly named Forest Street dates from the early 1870s. The street was lined with elm trees planted by Turell Tufts, who died in 1842. In the early part of the 19th century, Forest Street was part of the Andover Turnpike, which opened in 1805. The turnpike proved unprofitable, and in 1831 it became a public road. (Courtesy of the Medford Public Library.)

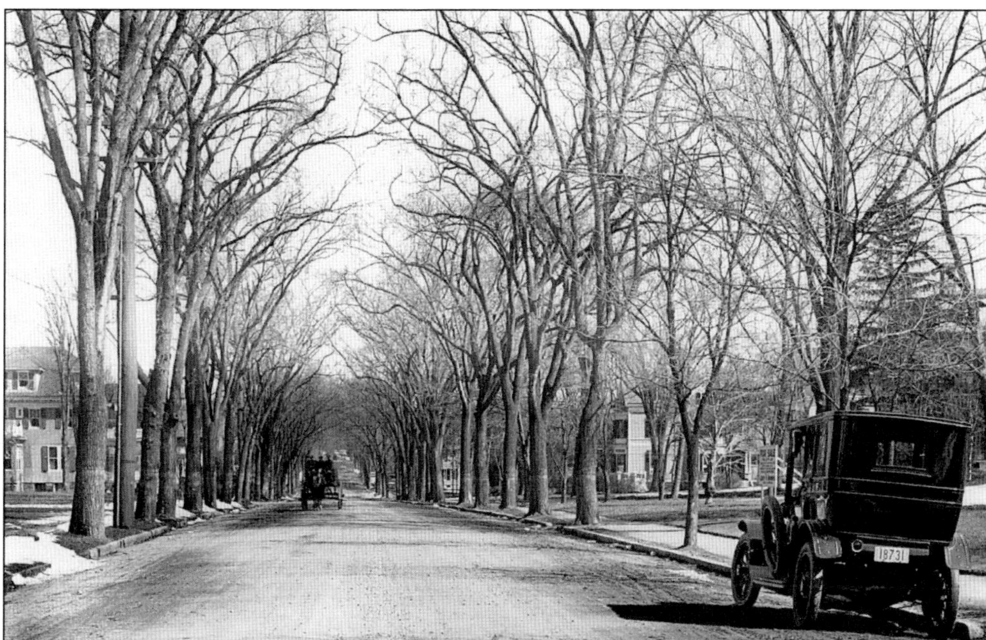

The era of the horse and the age of the automobile cross paths on Forest Street in the early 1900s. (Courtesy of the Medford Public Library.)

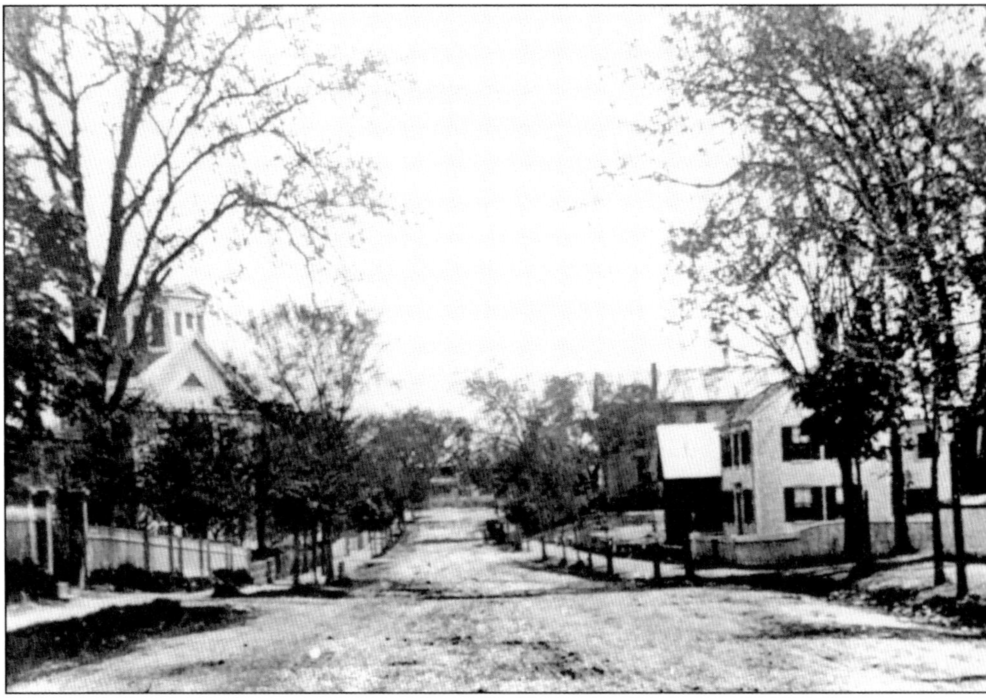

Salem Street, originally known as Salem Path, was one of the first streets in Medford. Like Forest Street, it was shaded by elm trees. This 1870s view into the square shows the Methodist church on the left. Many of the developing residential areas of Victorian Medford branched off Salem Street. (Courtesy of the Medford Public Library.)

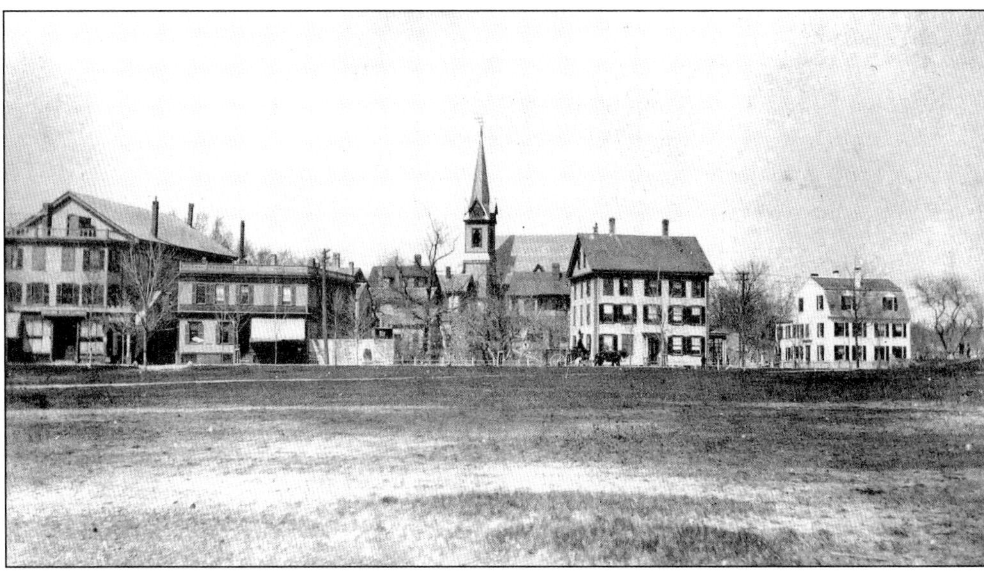

This 1880s photograph of Salem Street, taken from the railroad tracks, shows the Music Hall (second from left) and the First Baptist Church behind on Oakland Street. The Tufts Estate, at Salem and Forest Streets, was divided into house lots in 1844, and other estates soon followed as the Salem Street area was developed in the 1850s and 1860s. (Courtesy of the Medford Historical Society.)

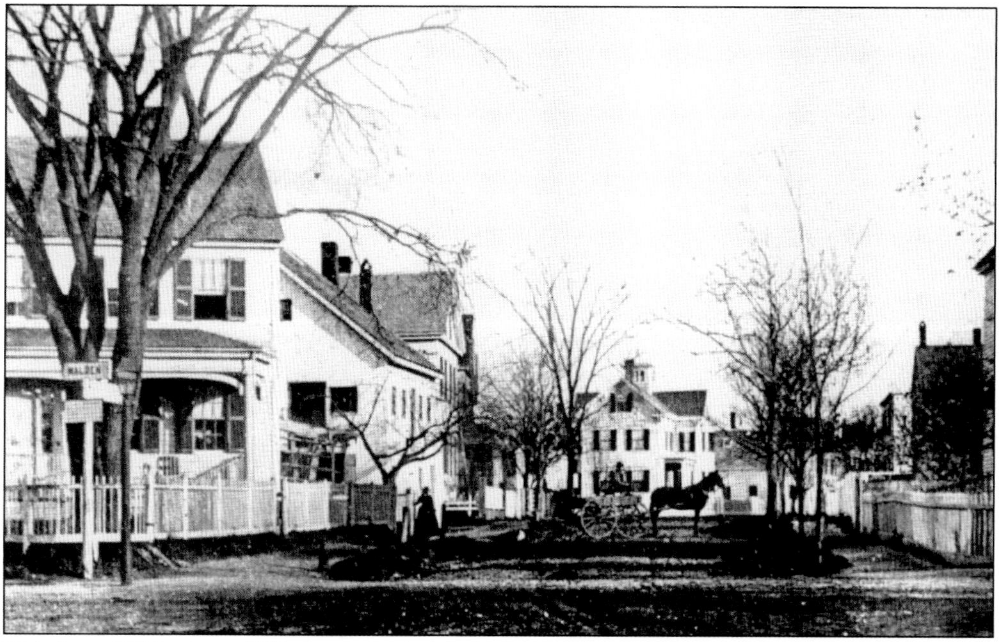

This is an 1870s view of Washington Street, looking east from Washington Square. The Jacobs House (left) belonged to a physician and was used as a hospital. (Courtesy of the Medford Public Library.)

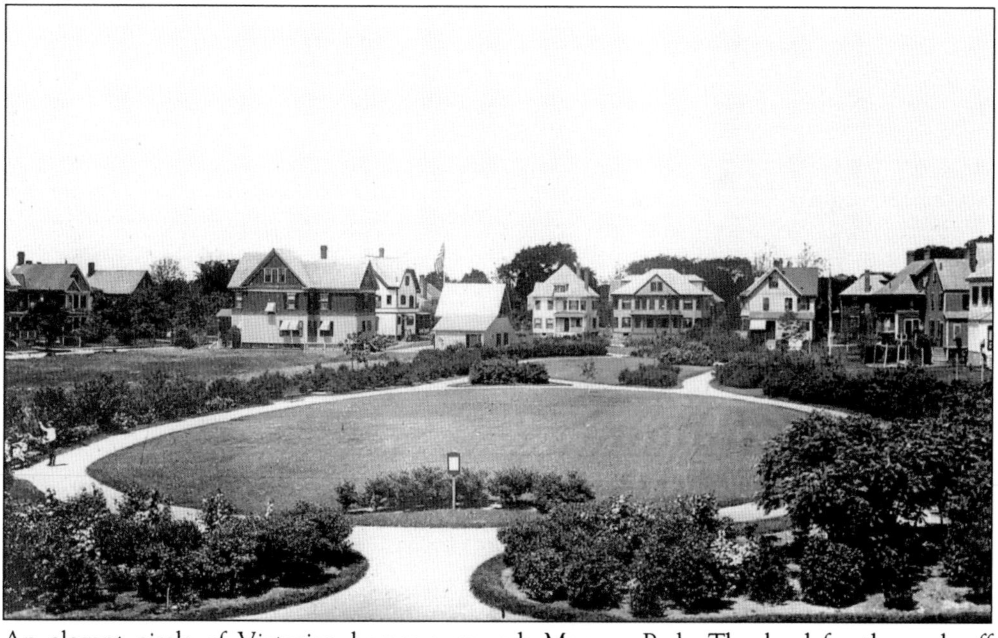

An elegant circle of Victorian homes surrounds Magoun Park. The land for the park off Pembroke Street was bequeathed to the town in 1894 by the estate of Martha Adams. The city named the park after shipbuilder Thatcher Magoun and hired a landscape architect to create green space in the residential neighborhood. (Courtesy of the Medford Public Library.)

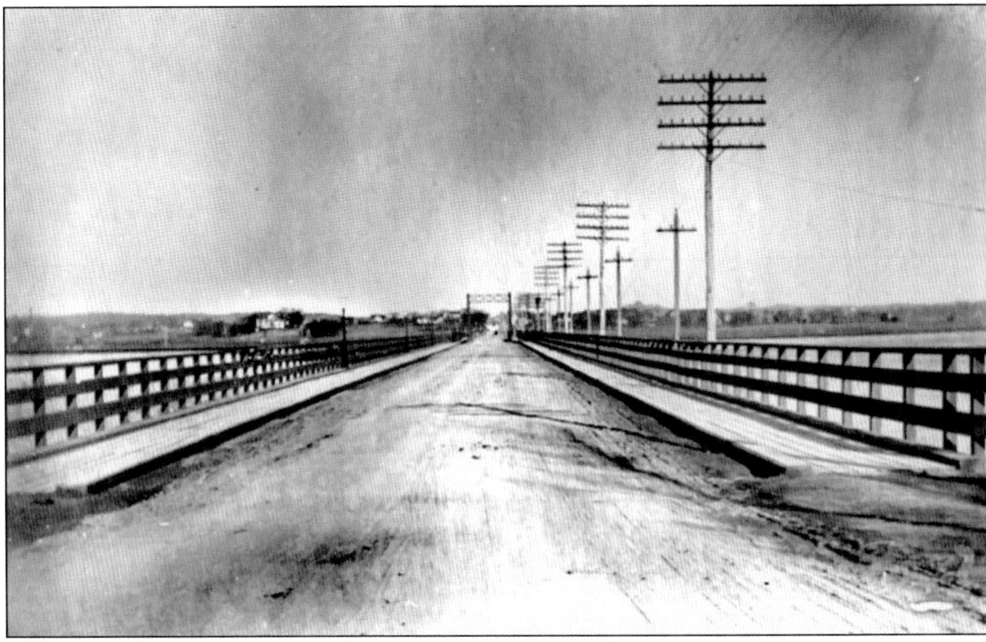

House lots became available in the Wellington area as early as 1854, after farmland belonging to the Wellington family was sold and divided. But the area did not begin to thrive until 1874, when the Wellington Bridge and a new road to Boston were built. (Courtesy of the Medford Public Library.)

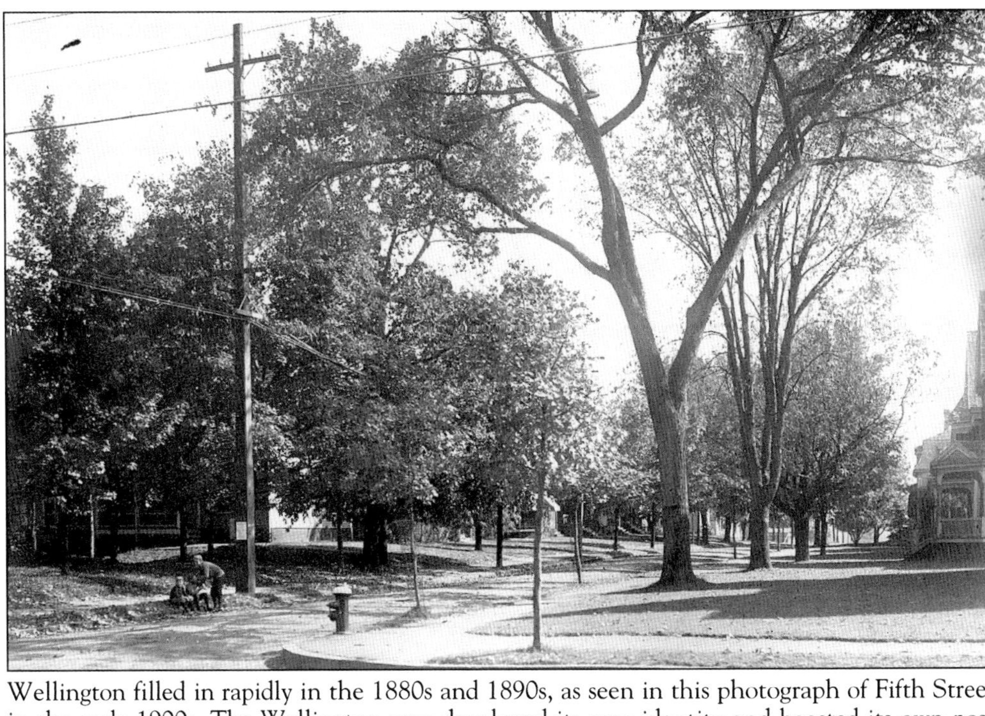

Wellington filled in rapidly in the 1880s and 1890s, as seen in this photograph of Fifth Street in the early 1900s. The Wellington area developed its own identity and boasted its own post office, railroad station, schools, and social clubs. (Courtesy of the Medford Public Library.)

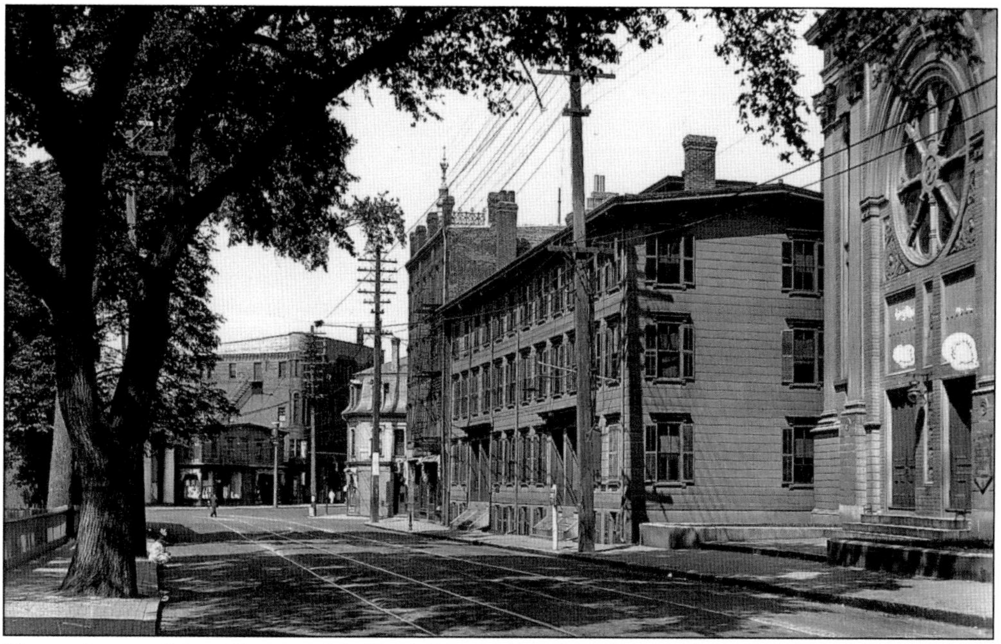

Shown here is Salem Street in Medford Square. The building in the center right was known as the Doctors' Block because it housed so many physicians' offices. For some reason, the majority of Medford's Victorian doctors either lived on Salem Street or had office space there. (Courtesy of the Medford Public Library.)

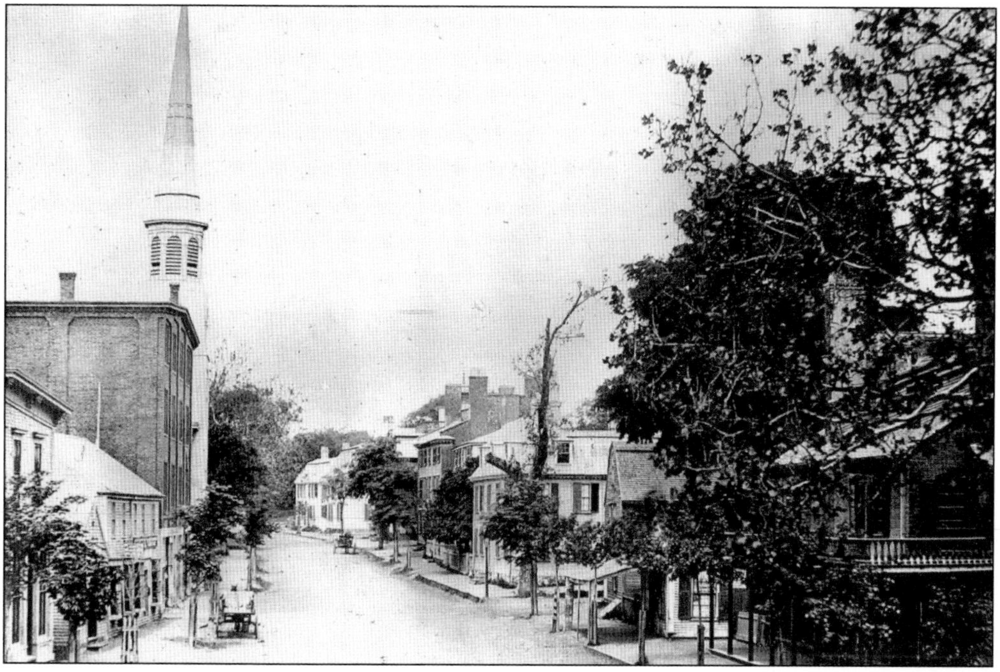

Seen in this photograph of High Street in the 1860s are, from left to right, the brick Masonic Apartments (built in the 1850s and owned by James M. Usher), the Second Congregational Church (purchased by the Catholic church in 1878), and the three Hall Houses. (Courtesy of the Medford Public Library.)

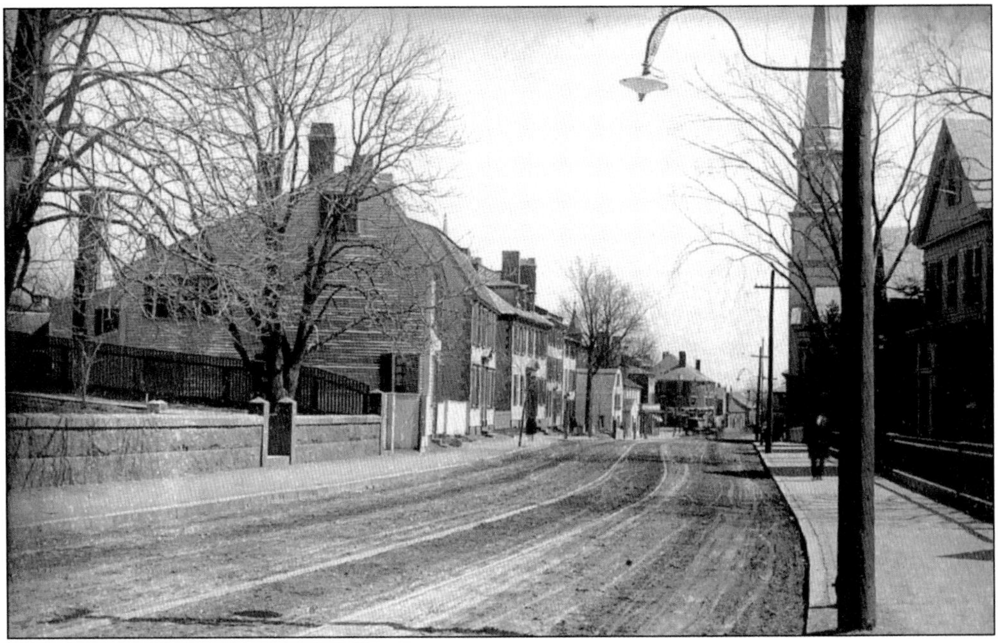

This late-1800s view of High Street looks east into the square. The three Hall Houses are on the left. Originally there were five Hall Houses, built in a row for five brothers, three of whom married sisters. Paul Revere stopped at the third Hall House on his famous ride. (Courtesy of the Medford Public Library.)

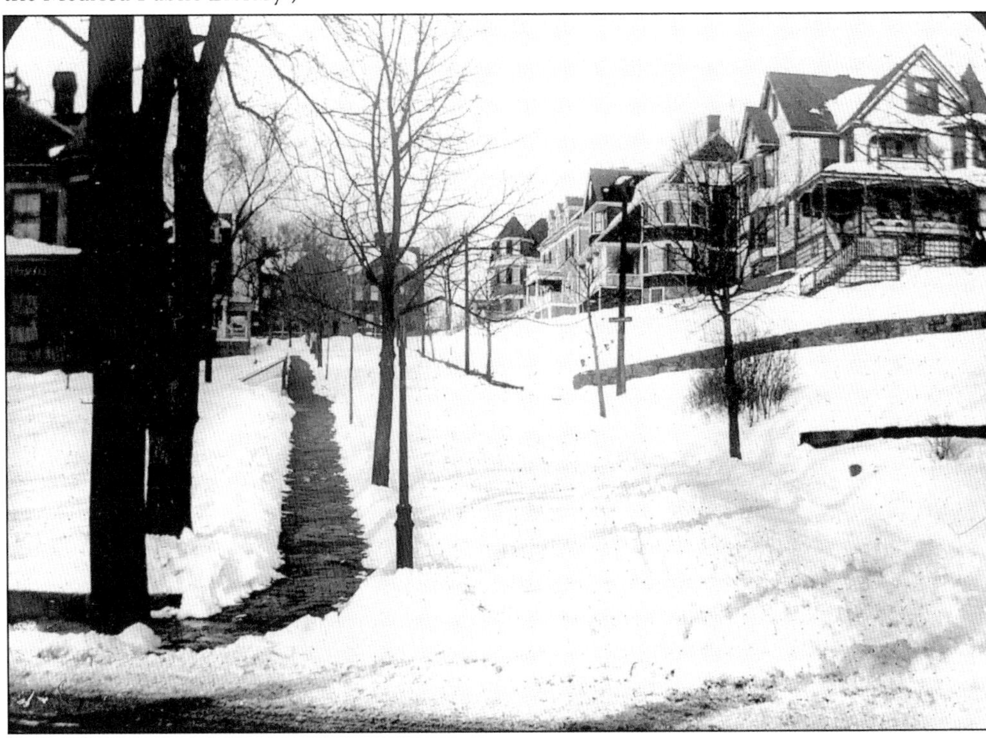

This winter scene from 1897 shows the houses of Hillside Avenue, which were built in the 1870s and 1880s, primarily in the Queen Anne style. (Courtesy of the Medford Public Library.)

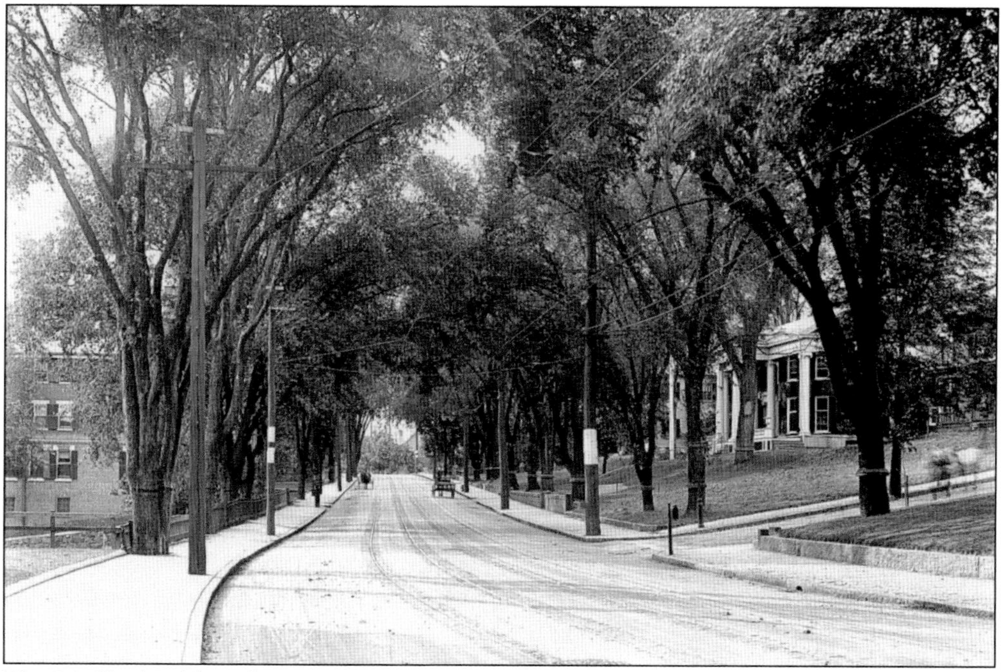

The Medford Public Library, formerly the Thatcher Magoun Mansion, is seen at the right in this view looking west along tree-lined High Street. Thatcher Magoun Jr. gave the house to the town in 1875, and the current library is built on the same location. (Courtesy of the Medford Public Library.)

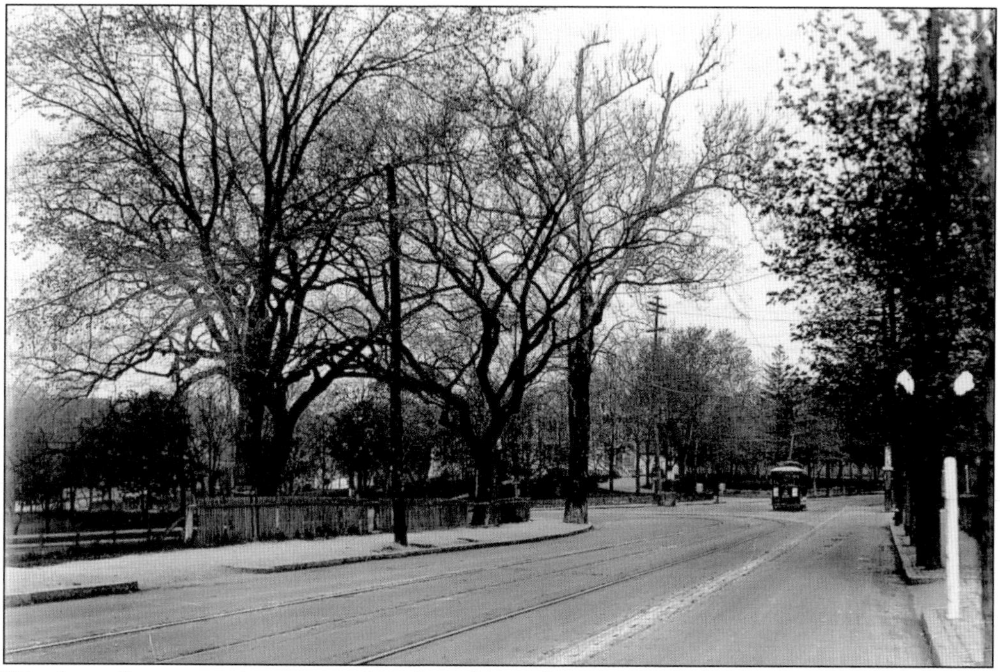

Winthrop Square, at the corner of High and Winthrop Streets, was earlier known as Turell's Corner because it was the home of Ebenezer Turell, pastor of the Unitarian church from 1727 to 1778. (Courtesy of the Medford Public Library.)

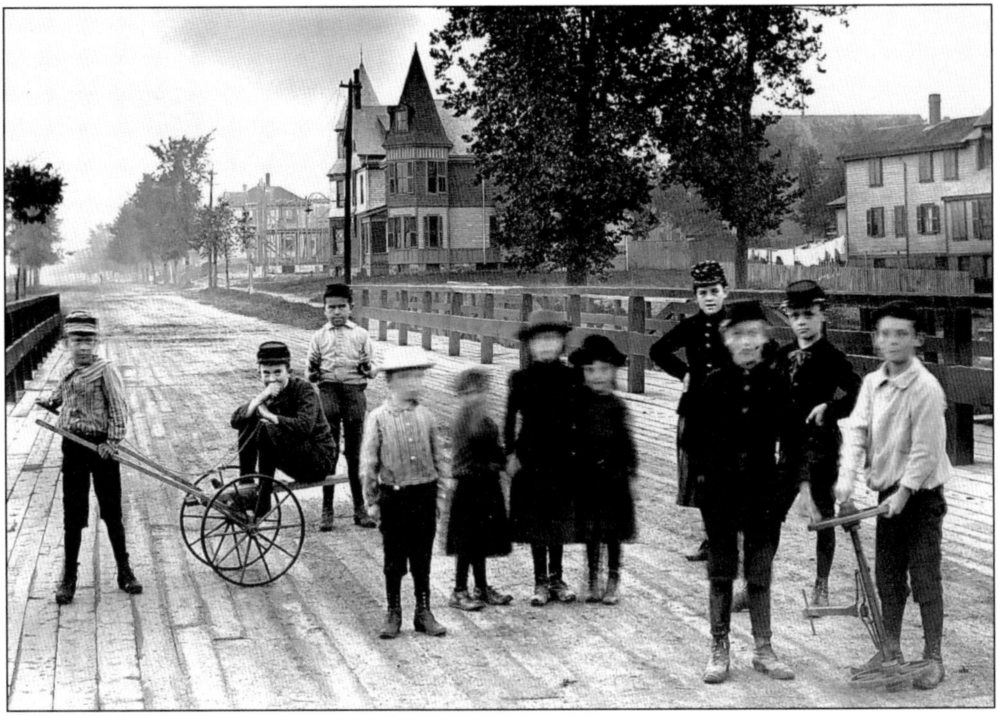

The first house on Boston Avenue was built for Samuel S. Holton Jr. in 1873. These children are posing on the Boston Avenue Bridge in 1891 against a background of new houses. The blurry children are the ones who could not stand still for the photographer. (Courtesy of the Medford Public Library.)

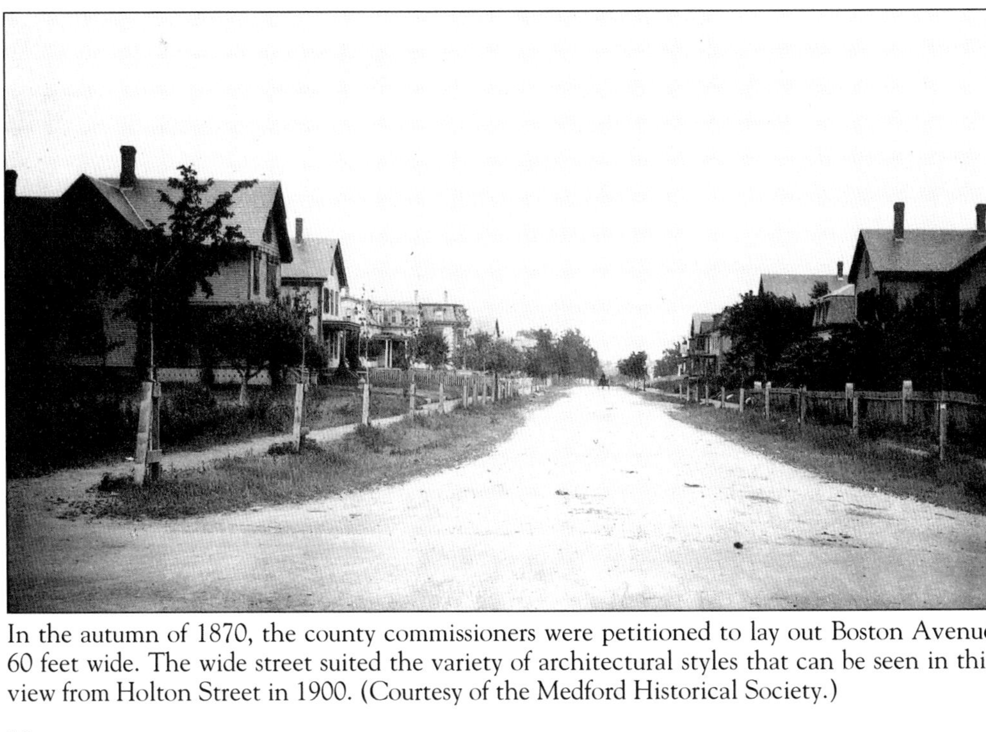

In the autumn of 1870, the county commissioners were petitioned to lay out Boston Avenue 60 feet wide. The wide street suited the variety of architectural styles that can be seen in this view from Holton Street in 1900. (Courtesy of the Medford Historical Society.)

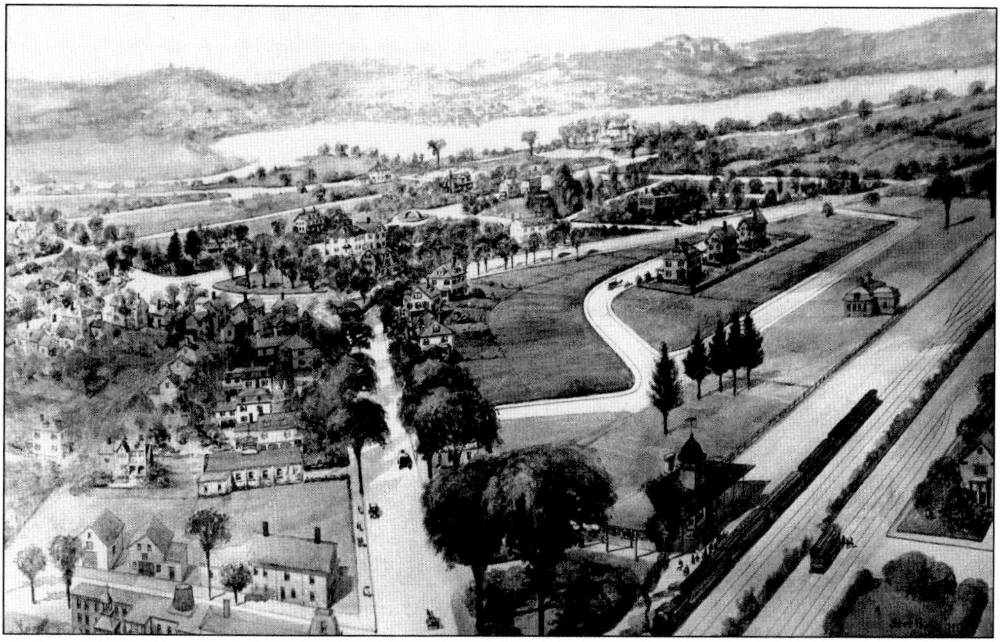

Before 1870 West Medford, west of the railroad tracks, had fewer than 50 residents. This painting shows West Medford as it may have looked in the 1870s, with few houses and much open space. (Courtesy of the Medford Public Library.)

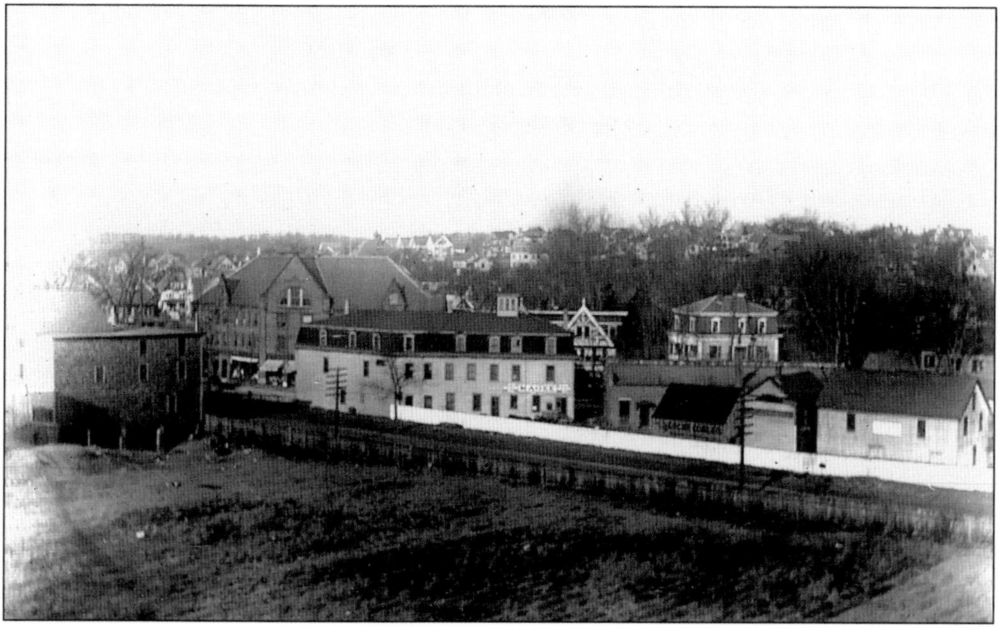

Many of the large estates in West Medford were broken up into house lots in the 1870s, and a great deal of house construction followed. This 1890s view from the tower of Trinity Church shows houses filling in the distant landscape and businesses thriving in the foreground. (Courtesy of the Medford Public Library.)

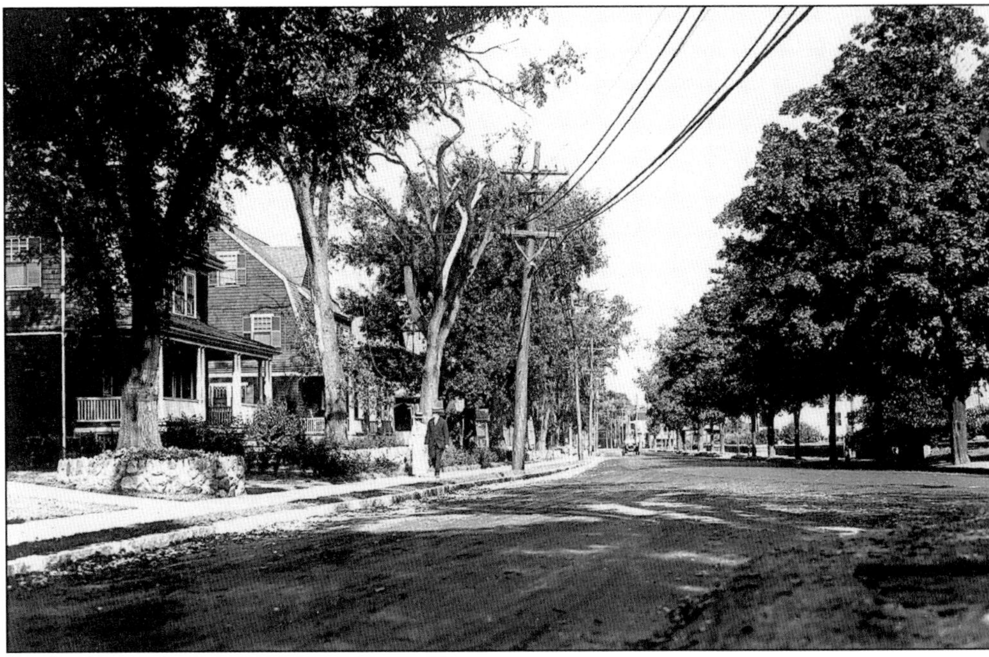

By 1887 West Medford had acquired its own identity, and its citizens petitioned the general court to create a separate town called Brooks. The new town would have encompassed all of the land west of Winthrop Circle, including this curve of High and Grove Streets. The court refused the petition and several appeals. (Courtesy of the Medford Public Library.)

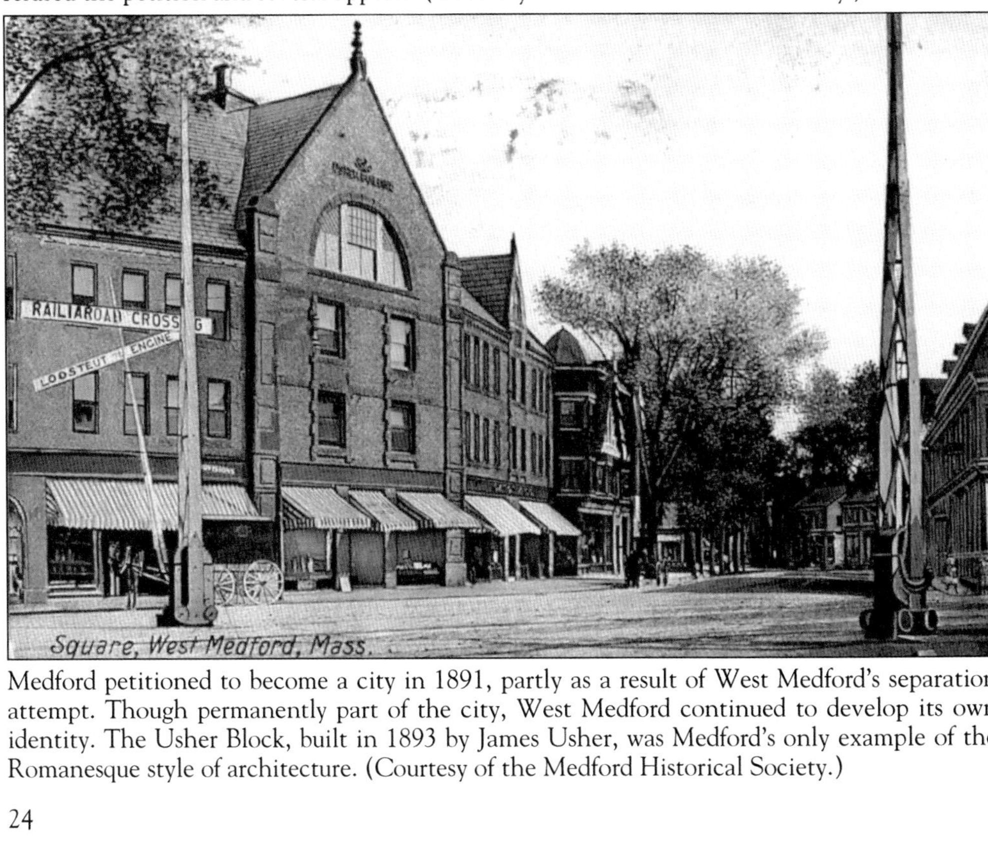

Medford petitioned to become a city in 1891, partly as a result of West Medford's separation attempt. Though permanently part of the city, West Medford continued to develop its own identity. The Usher Block, built in 1893 by James Usher, was Medford's only example of the Romanesque style of architecture. (Courtesy of the Medford Historical Society.)

Two

PROMINENT PEOPLE

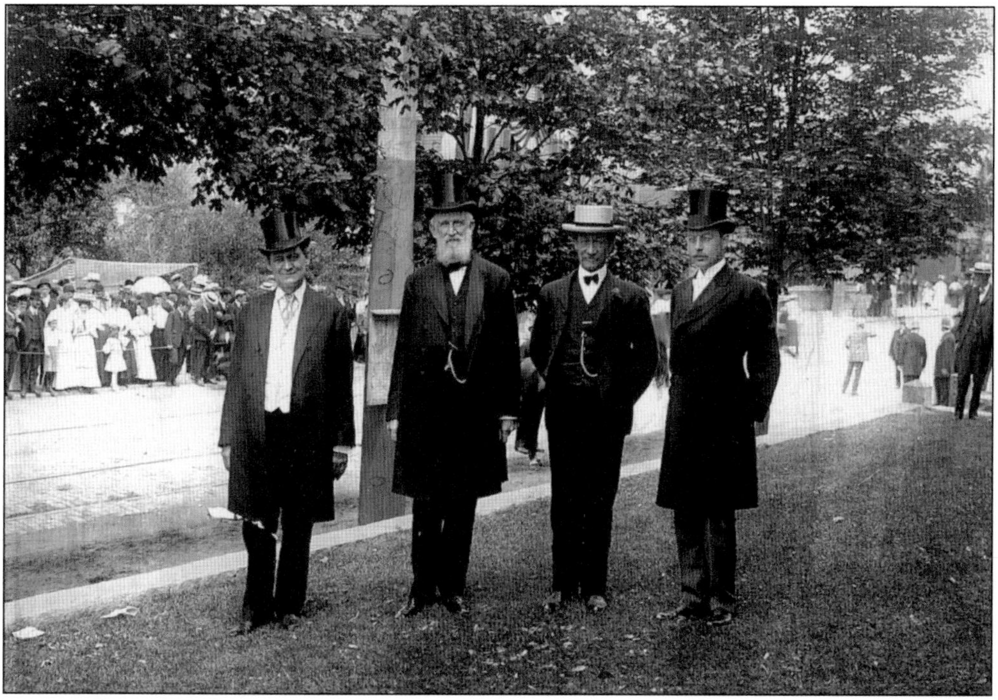

In 1905 four of Medford's first six mayors pose together at the 275th anniversary celebration. From left to right are Michael F. Dwyer (1905–1907), Samuel Crocker Lawrence (1893–1894), Lewis H. Lovering (1897–1900), and Charles S. Baxter (1901–1904). (Courtesy of the Medford Historical Society.)

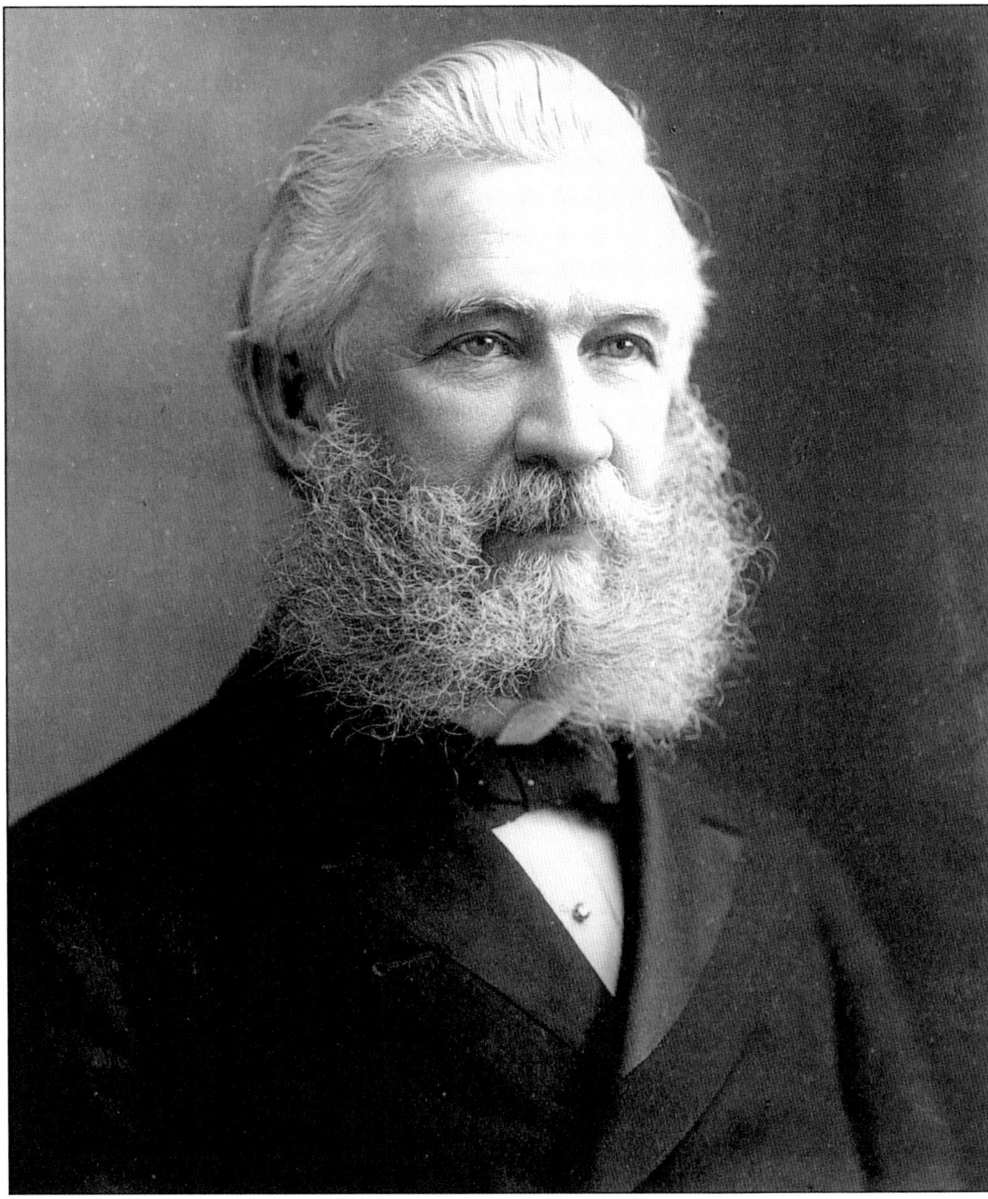

Samuel Crocker Lawrence (1832–1911) was the first citizen of Victorian Medford. Born into the Lawrence rum family, he was educated at Harvard and then went into the family business. He married Carrie Badger in 1859, and they adopted two children. He was colonel of the Medford Lawrence Light Guard in the Civil War, was wounded at the First Battle of Bull Run, and was mustered out in 1862 at the rank of brigadier general. Lawrence was deeply involved in civic life. He was trustee of the library, commissioner of the sinking fund, charter member of the Medford Club, and the first mayor of the city. In 1905 he spent $500,000 of his personal fortune to combat the gypsy moth infestation. He was also a prominent Mason and in the 1890s was appointed to the highest position in Masonry in the United States. In 1902 he built the armory on High Street for the Grand Army of the Republic post that he had founded. At his death in 1911, some 2,000 people attended his funeral. Lawrence is buried in Mount Auburn Cemetery. (Courtesy of the Medford Historical Society.)

Samuel's father, Daniel Lawrence, was the founder of the Lawrence Rum Distillery. He came to Medford from Tyngsboro in 1823 and joined the distillery of Bishop and Goodrich. He later assumed ownership of the distillery under the name of Lawrence and Sons. Daniel Lawrence died in 1879. (Courtesy of the Medford Historical Society.)

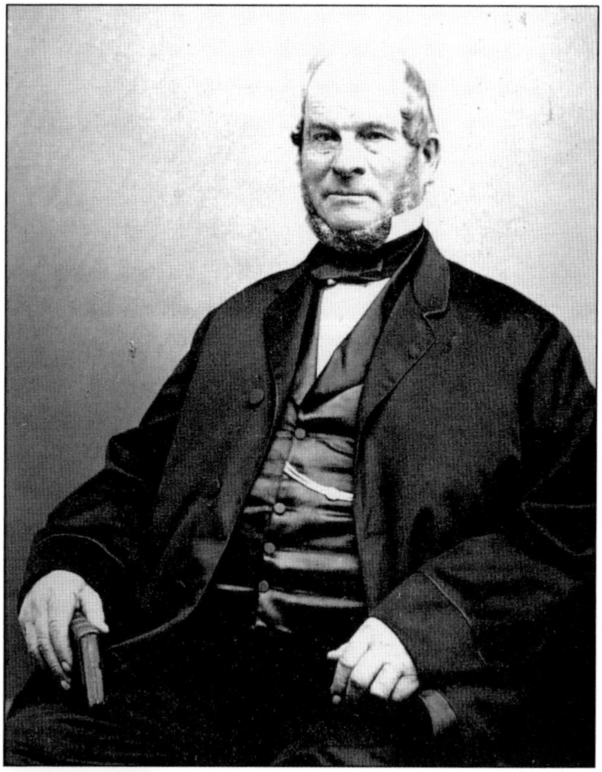

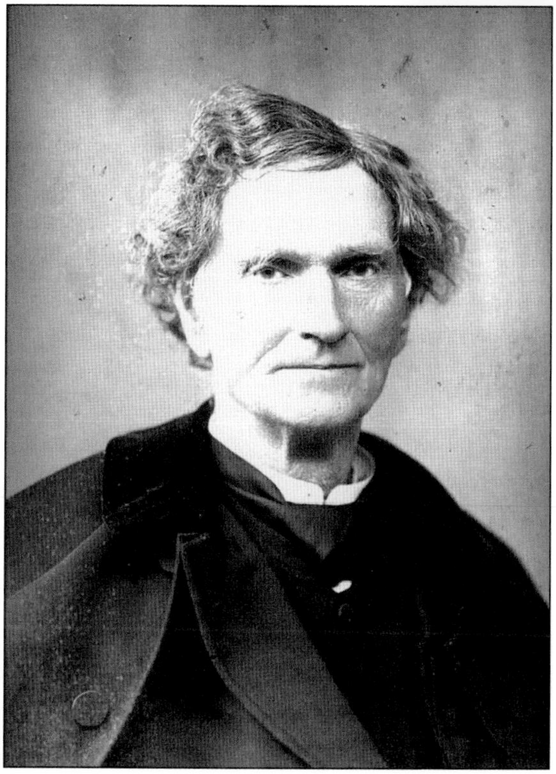

James M. Usher was an important force in the development of 19th-century Medford. Usher owned both the Bigelow Building and the Masonic Apartments in Medford Square. He built the Usher Block in West Medford, along with a number of other business establishments in that area. Also a literary light, Usher published Medford's first newspaper, the *Medford Journal*, and wrote the 1885 *History of the Town of Medford*. (Courtesy of the Medford Historical Society.)

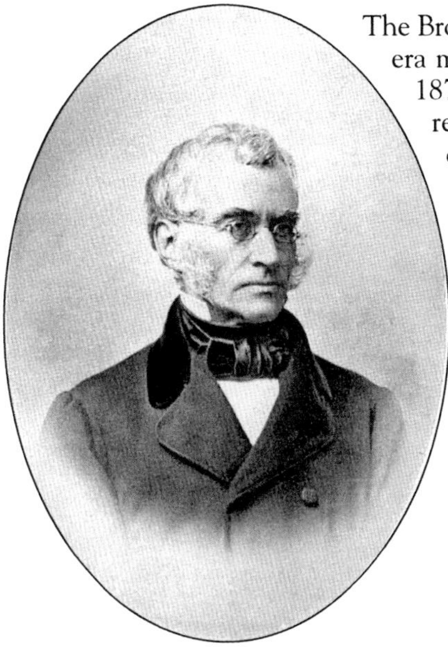

The Brooks family was one of Medford's oldest. The Victorian-era members of the family included Charles Brooks (1795–1872), who was a Unitarian minister, an educational reformer, and a professor of natural history at the College of the City of New York. Brooks published *The History of the Town of Medford* in 1855. (Courtesy of the Medford Public Library.)

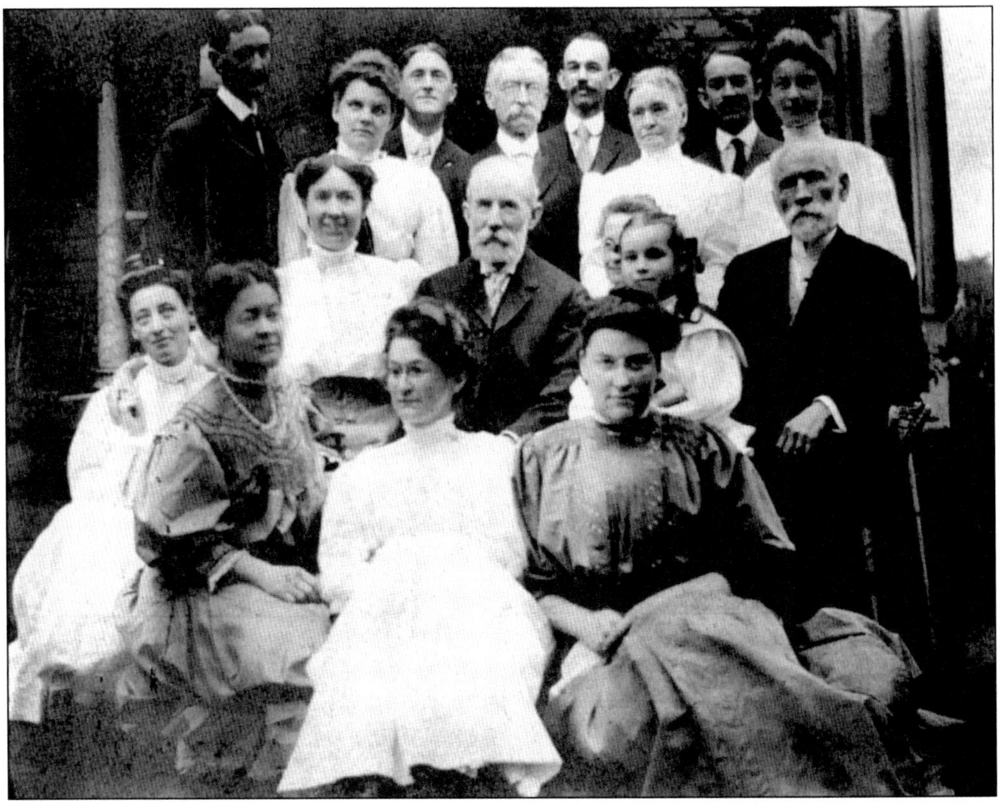

Peter Chardon Brooks III and Shepherd Brooks are shown with their families in a 1906 photograph. In the mid-19th century, Peter and Shepherd Brooks each constructed a summer estate in Medford. The families lived most of the year in Boston but summered in Medford. (Courtesy of the Medford Public Library.)

The Wellington area was named after James (pictured here) and Isaac Wellington, who bought farmland there in 1819. The brothers were influential in shaping Wellington. They donated land to the Boston and Maine Railroad on the condition that all Medford trains should stop at Wellington. (Courtesy of the Medford Public Library.)

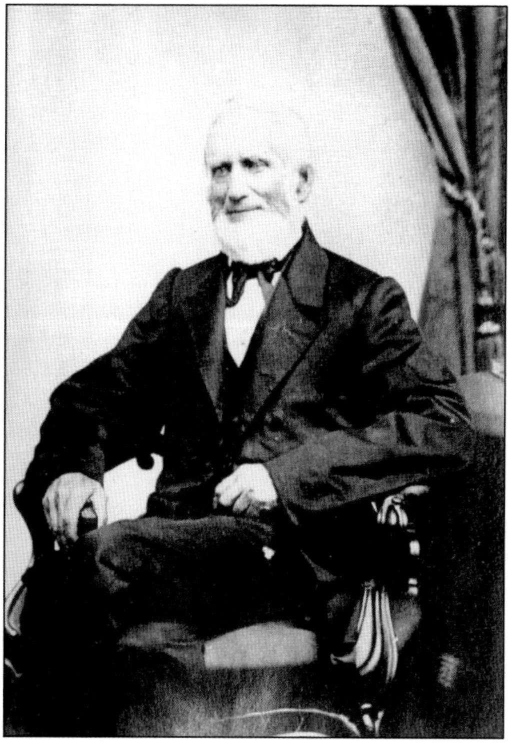

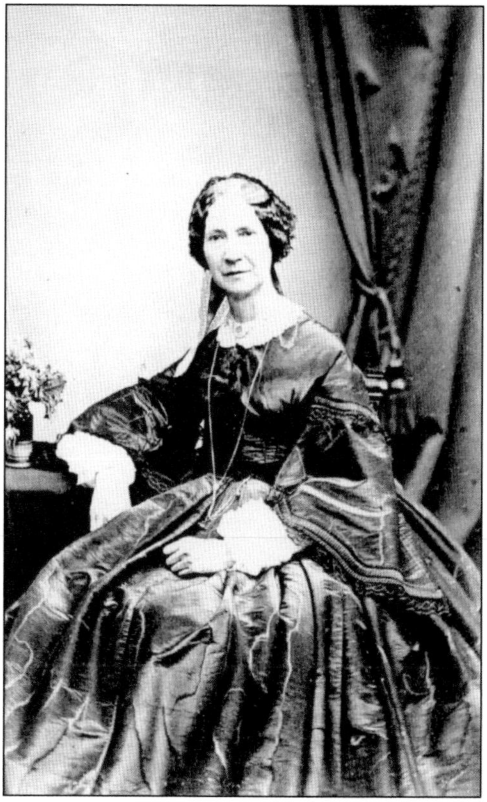

Lusanna Jacobs Wellington married James in 1821, and in 1823 her sister Mary married Isaac. The two sisters and their husbands shared a house on the Wellington farm for many years. Lusanna's daughter Angelina married Darius Crosby, who collaborated with James and Isaac Wellington on many community institutions, including the Amaranth Social Club. (Courtesy of the Medford Public Library.)

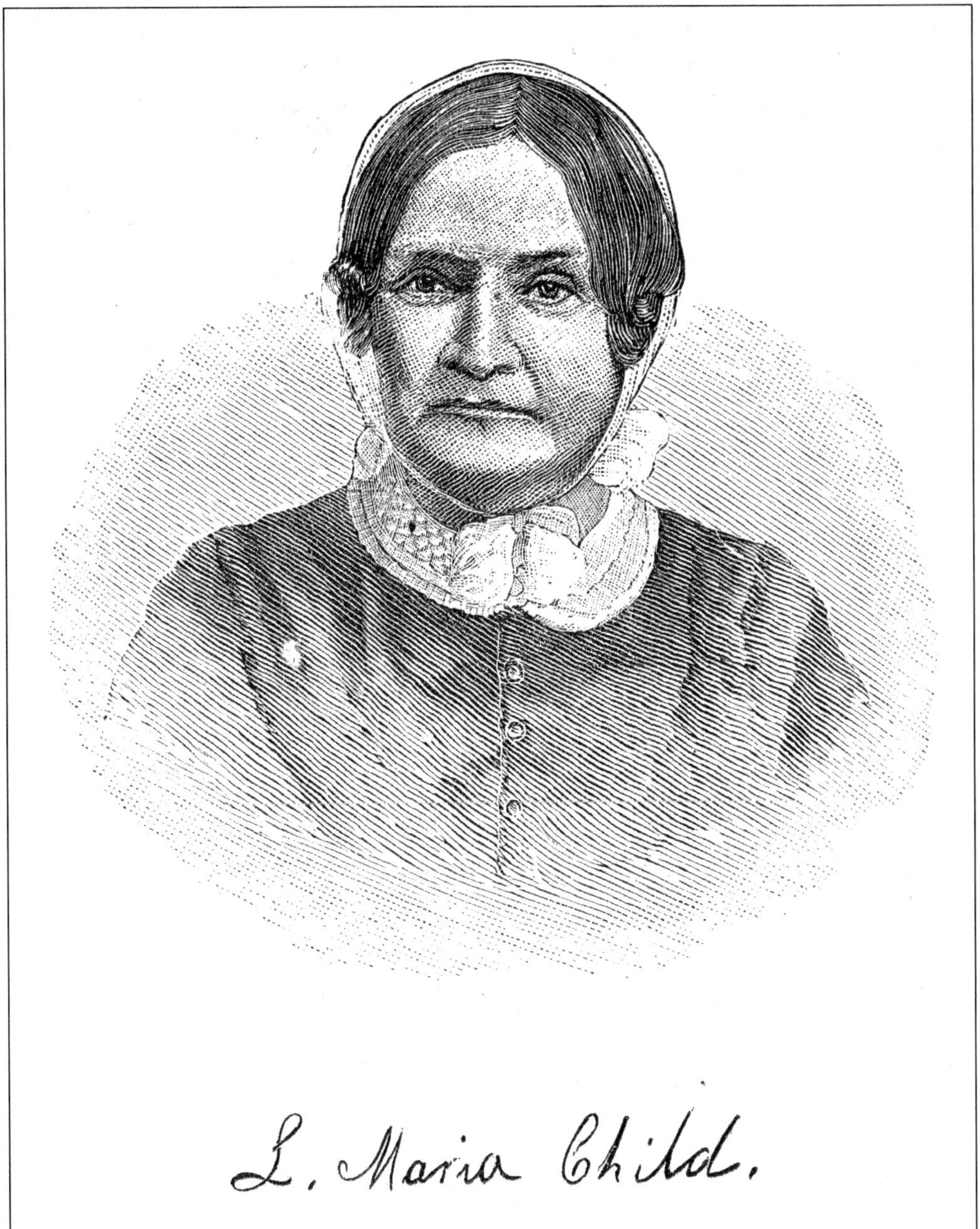

Lydia Maria Child (1802–1880) was born on Salem Street. Her father, David, a baker, was the inventor of the famous Medford Cracker. Child published her first novel, *Hobomok,* in 1824. After her 1828 marriage to David Child, she continued to write novels and articles. In the 1830s she became an abolitionist and wrote a number of influential books on the subject. In 1841 she became editor of the *National Anti-slavery Standard,* an abolitionist magazine, and she remained active in social causes until her death in 1880. Child also wrote the famous poem that begins, "Over the river and through the woods," which refers to a Thanksgiving sleigh ride in Medford. (Courtesy of the Medford Public Library.)

John Pierpont (1785–1866) became minister of the Unitarian church in 1849. Pierpont had a reputation for preaching temperance and antislavery from the pulpit, and he lived up to that reputation in Medford. True to his beliefs, he joined the Union army as a chaplain at age 73. He died in Medford in 1866. (Courtesy of the Medford Public Library.)

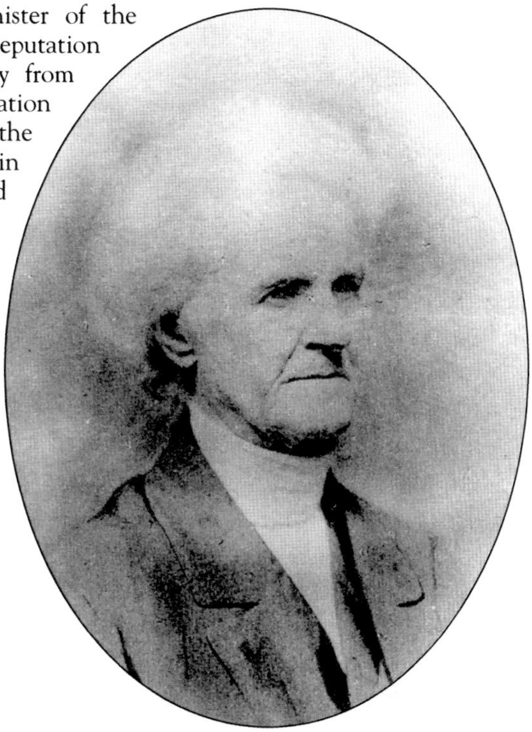

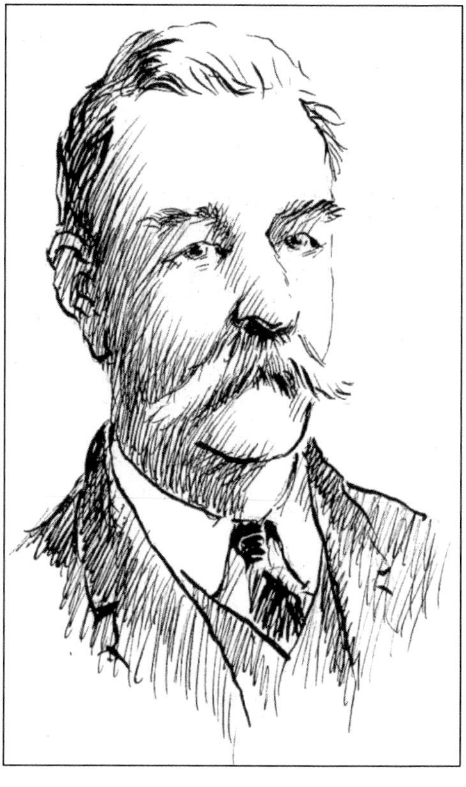

Pierpont's son James (1822–1895) became famous for less political reasons than his father. In 1852 James sat down at the piano in the family house on Mystic Street and—inspired by sleigh races on Salem Street—wrote "Jingle Bells." The song was copyrighted in 1857. James lived most of his life in the South and died in Savannah, Georgia, in 1895. (Courtesy of the Medford Public Library.)

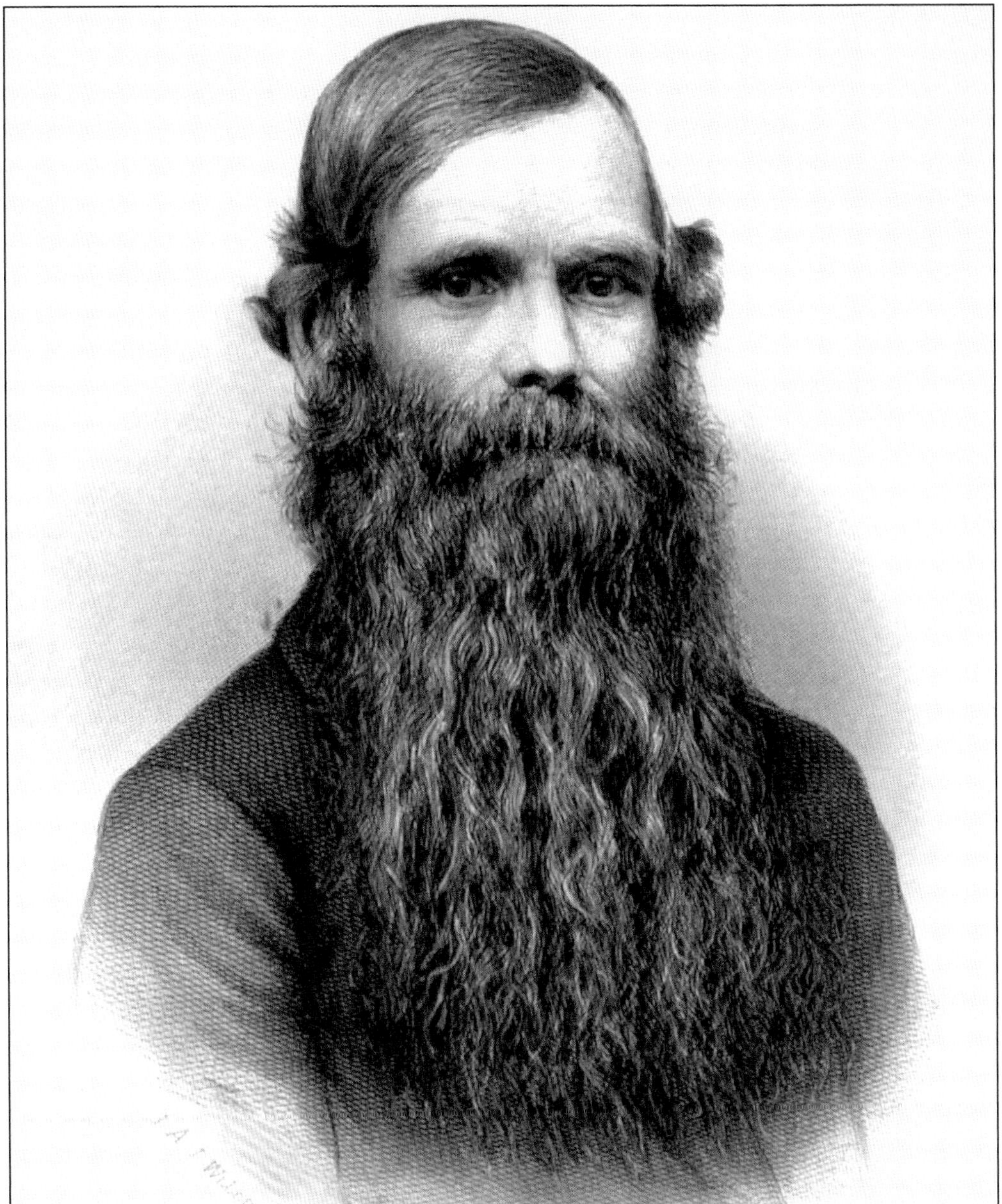

George Luther Stearns (1809–1867) was another Medford voice in the abolitionist movement. Born and educated in Medford, Stearns made a fortune in linseed oil and lead pipes. His extensive estate near Tufts College was a stop on the Underground Railroad. In the 1850s Stearns became involved with the abolitionist movement; he was one of the "Secret Six" who supported abolitionist John Brown in his raid on Harpers Ferry. Stearns poured money into the abolitionist movement and was also one of the organizers of the Massachusetts 54th Regiment of African American soldiers. After the war, Stearns was involved in the reconstruction of the South. He died in 1867 from pneumonia contracted during a fund-raising tour of New York. (Courtesy of the Medford Public Library.)

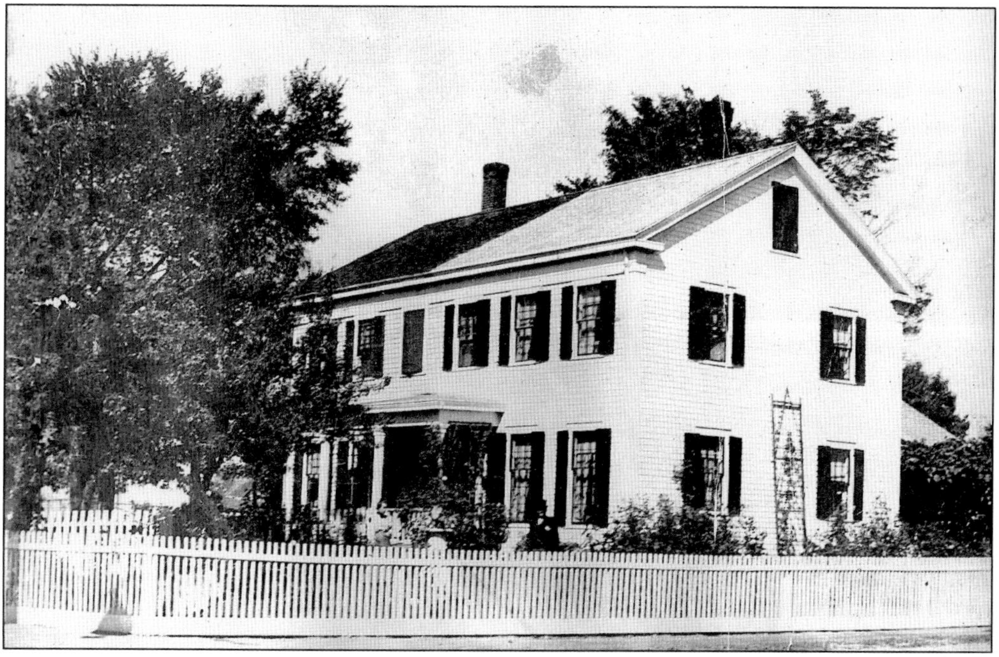

Fannie Merritt Farmer (1857–1915) came to Medford as a child and was educated in the Medford schools. Her family lived in this house on the corner of Salem and Paris Streets. Farmer attended the Boston Cooking School, graduated in 1889, and returned as a teacher. She started Miss Farmer's School of Cookery in 1902. (Courtesy of the Medford Historical Society.)

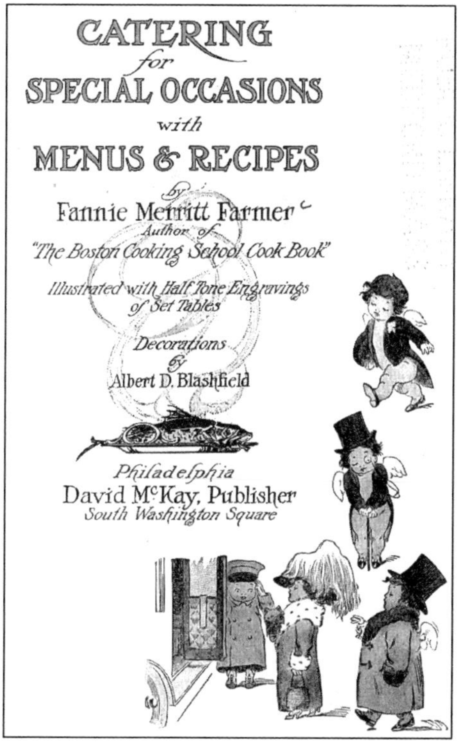

Farmer's school pioneered the use of standard weights and measurements in recipes, and her cookbooks were very popular. This one, published in 1911, features cupids helping out with every aspect of the meal. (Courtesy of the Medford Public Library.)

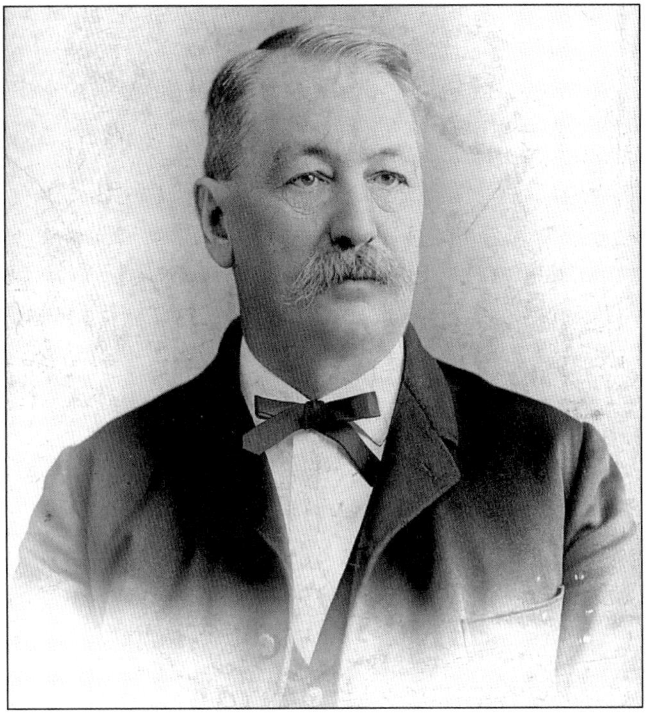

Lorin L. Dame (1838–1903) was one of Victorian Medford's major educators. Dame, a graduate of Tufts College, served in the 15th Massachusetts Light Battery during the Civil War. In 1876 he succeeded Charles Cummings as principal of Medford High School, a position he held until his death in 1903. Dame was also a poet, essayist, and amateur naturalist. (Courtesy of the Medford Historical Society.)

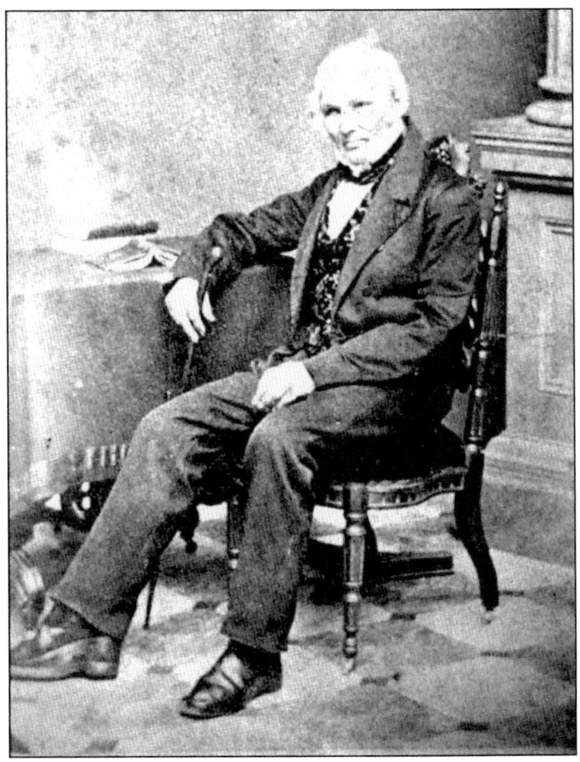

Dr. Daniel Swan (1787–1864) began his career as a teacher in Medford. He studied medicine with Dr. John Brooks and succeeded Brooks as the resident physician of Medford in 1816. He served as town physician for many years and was known for his charitable works. (Courtesy of the Medford Historical Society.)

James Swan (1818–1900) was one of Medford's Victorian adventurers. In 1849 he left his ship chandler's business for the California gold rush. Swan became an expert on Pacific Northwest American Indian culture and wrote many books and articles on the subject. He settled in Washington State. (Courtesy of the Medford Historical Society.)

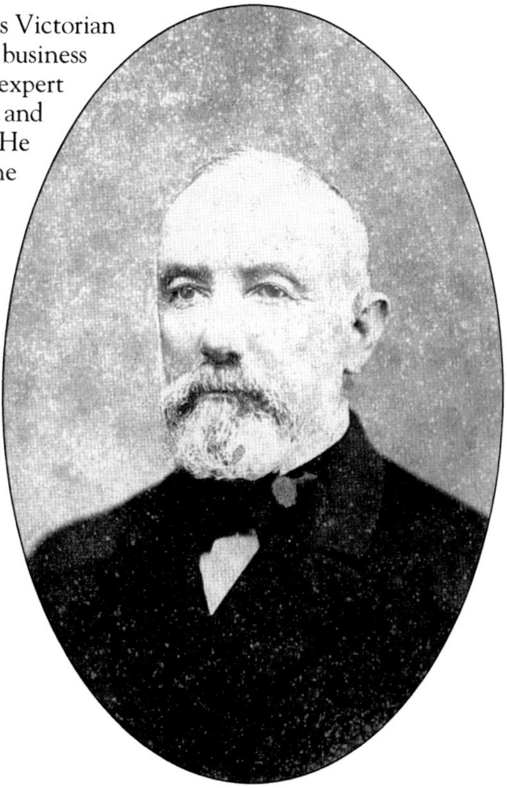

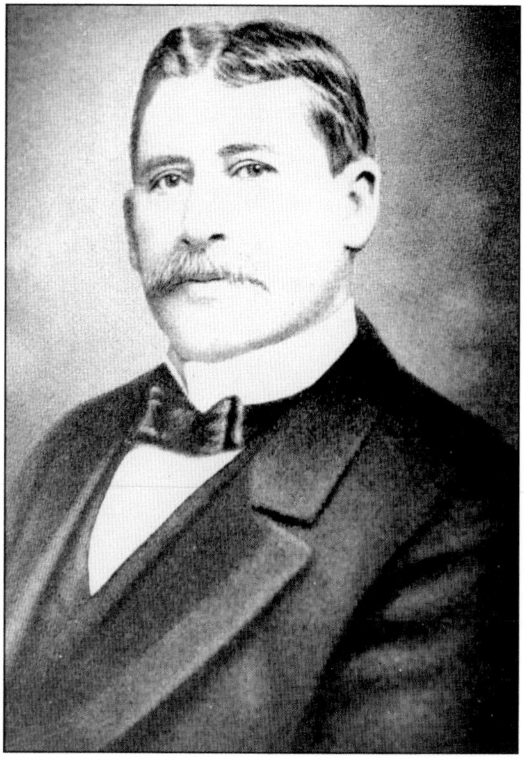

Heber N. Bishop (1840–1902) was one of two remarkable brothers who grew up on Salem Street. Heber became a multimillionaire exporting sugar from Cuba. His collection of jade, valued at more than $1 million, resides in the Metropolitan Museum of Art. His brother Nathaniel (1837–1902) was a popular travel writer who gained notoriety by walking across South America at age 16. (Courtesy of the Medford Public Library.)

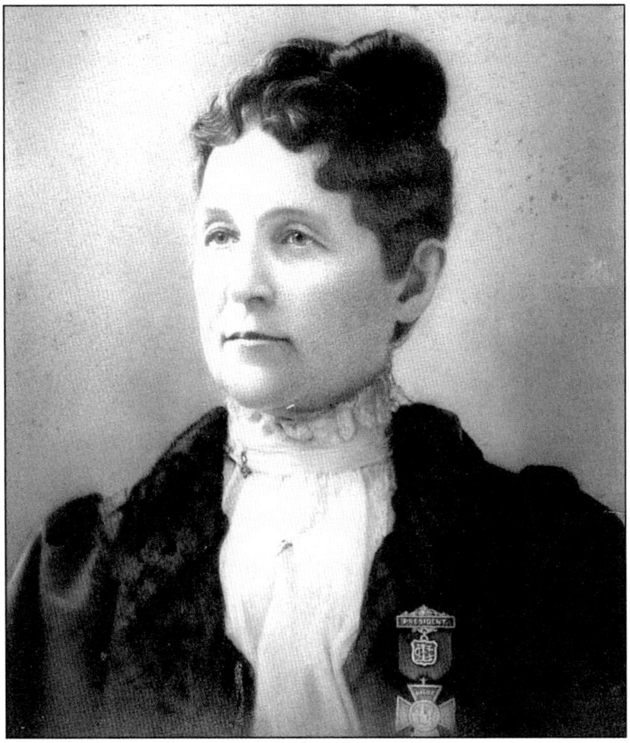

M. Susan Goodale was a leader in Medford's charitable organizations. She was the first regent of the Sara Bradlee Fulton Chapter of the Daughters of the American Revolution (DAR), which was founded in 1896. She was also president of the Samuel C. Lawrence Women's Relief Corps from 1881 to 1883. (Courtesy of the Medford Historical Society.)

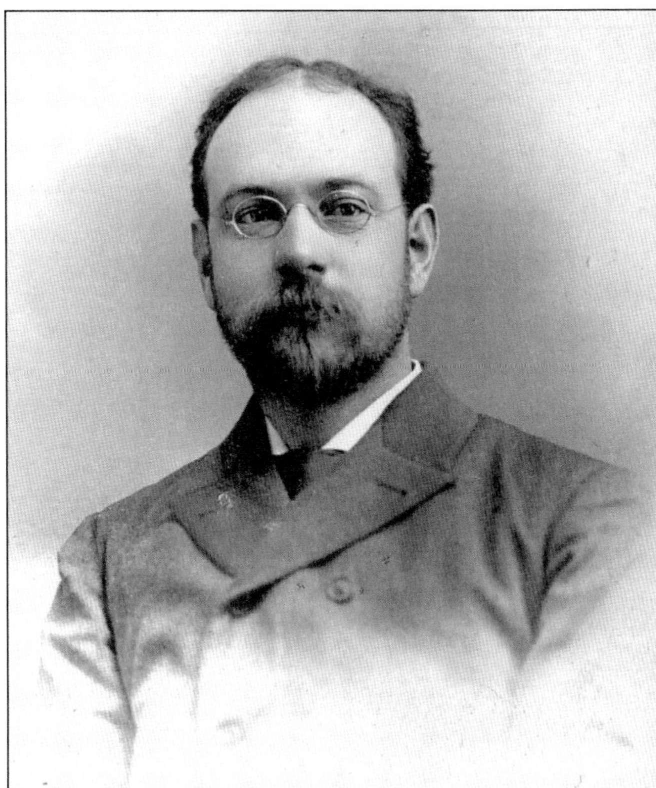

William Cushing Wait (1860–1935) was one of Medford's most distinguished jurists. He was involved in Medford politics as a member of the first board of aldermen and of the school committee. In 1889 he married Edith Wright, the granddaughter of Elizur Wright. Wait was appointed to the Superior Court in 1902 and served as an associate justice of the Massachusetts Supreme Judicial Court from 1923 to 1934. (Courtesy of the Medford Historical Society.)

Victorian Medford had its share of colorful local characters. Noah Hathaway, seen here in 1892, was a ship's carpenter. He was notable in town for having had two wives and 22 children. (Courtesy of the Medford Historical Society.)

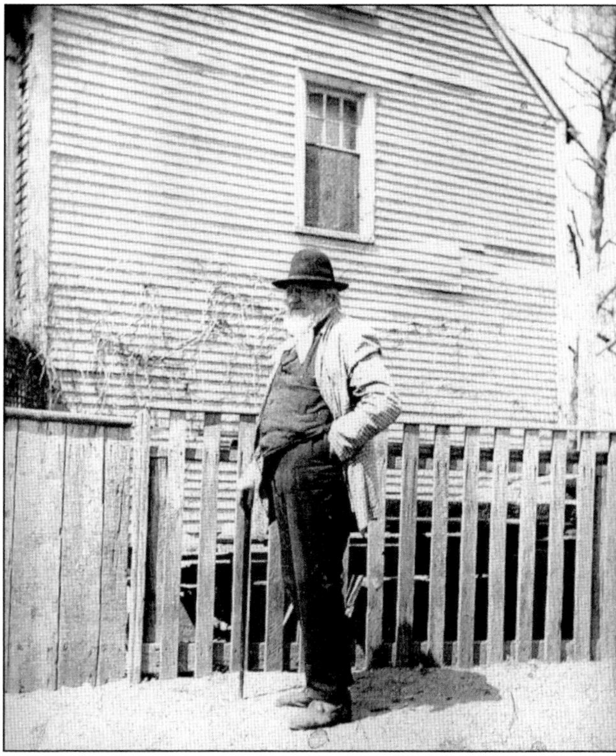

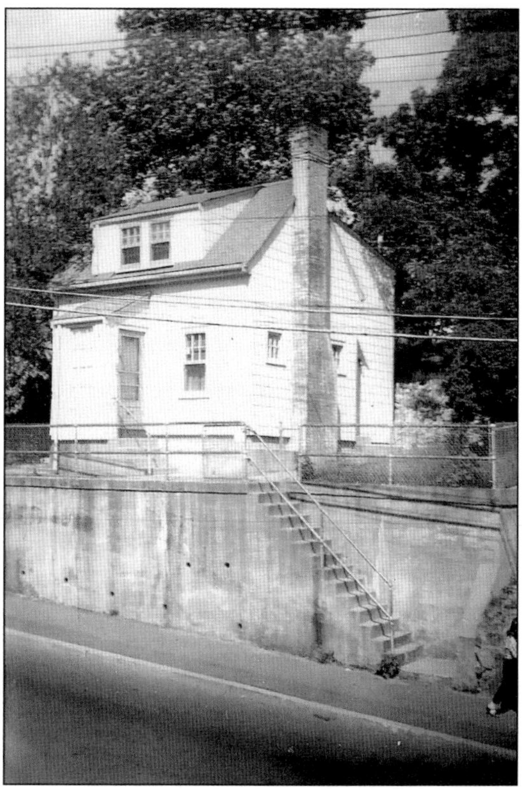

This house on Fulton Street belonged to Sarah Ann Bickers (1829–1899), known as Sailor Jack. As a teenager, Bickers, dressed as a boy, ran away to sea and sailed for a number of years. She later settled in Medford, married veteran James Bickers, and worked as the housekeeper of the town hall. She wore sailor's clothing every day except Sunday, when she wore a skirt to church. (Courtesy of the Medford Public Library.)

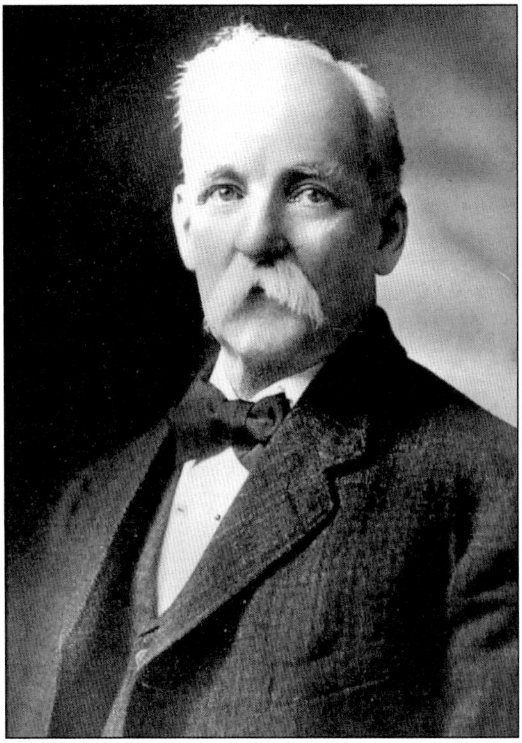

George W. Stetson was the first editor of the *Medford Mercury*, a position he held from 1880 to 1902. He was known for his peculiar attitude toward life and the news, typified by his comment, "Every man's a crook until he's proved guilty." (Courtesy of the Medford Public Library.)

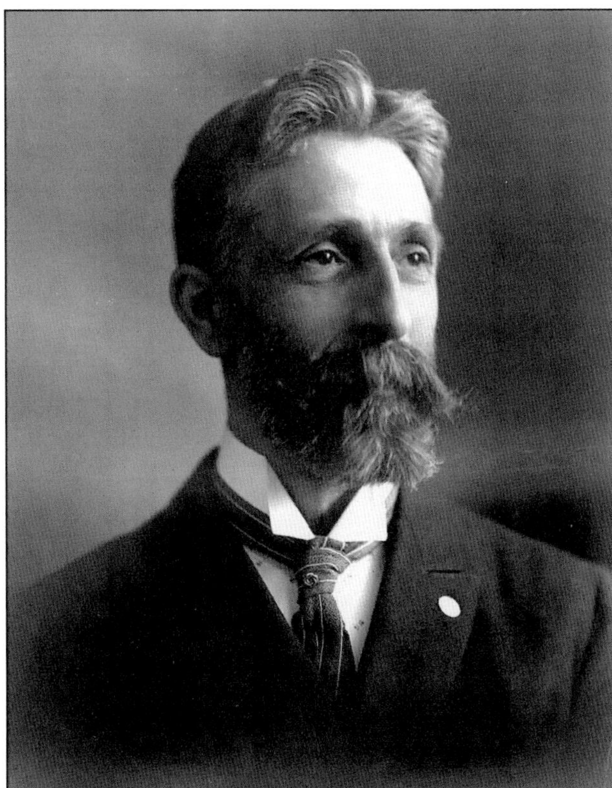

Will Eddy was a printer and publisher who became an ardent amateur photographer. Eddy, who founded the Mystic Camera Club, recorded many of the scenes of Victorian Medford that are included in this book. He was also involved with city politics, Masonry, and the Medford Historical Society. (Courtesy of the Medford Historical Society.)

Three

Business and Industry

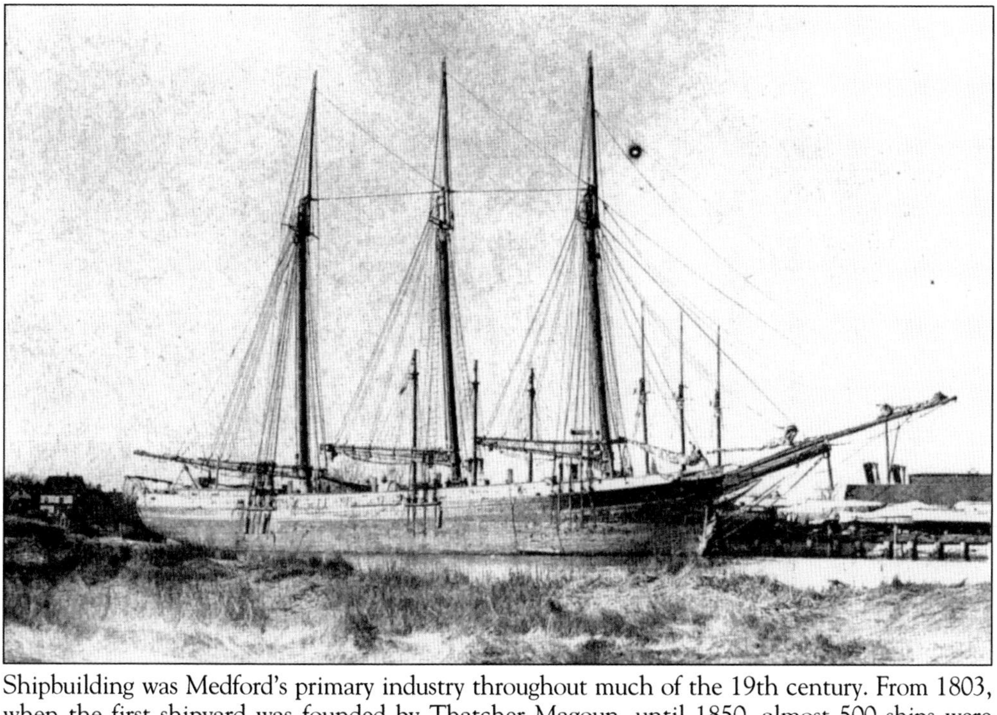

Shipbuilding was Medford's primary industry throughout much of the 19th century. From 1803, when the first shipyard was founded by Thatcher Magoun, until 1850, almost 500 ships were launched from Medford shipyards. This three-masted schooner, photographed at Foster's Wharf in the 1880s, has been identified as the *James Slater*. (Courtesy of the Medford Historical Society.)

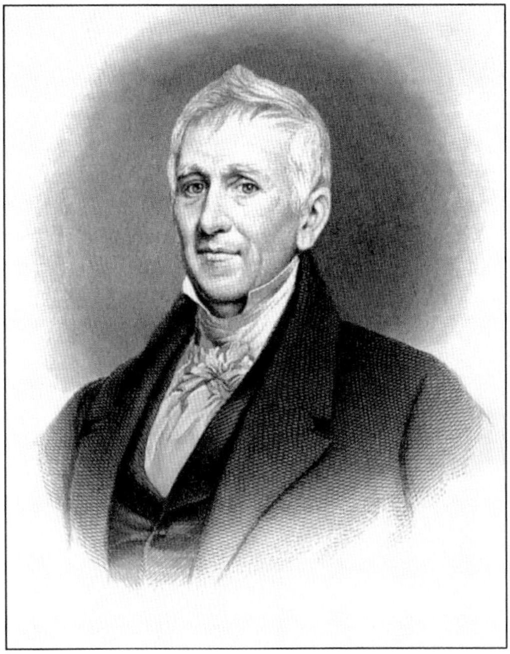

Thatcher Magoun (1775–1856) was the first Medford shipbuilder. He chose Medford as a site because of the tidal nature of the Mystic River and the ready supplies of lumber in the area. His shipyard on Riverside Avenue was opposite the end of Park Street. Under Magoun's direction, the yard produced 84 vessels between 1803 and 1836. The quality of the ships earned Magoun an international reputation. (Courtesy of the Medford Public Library.)

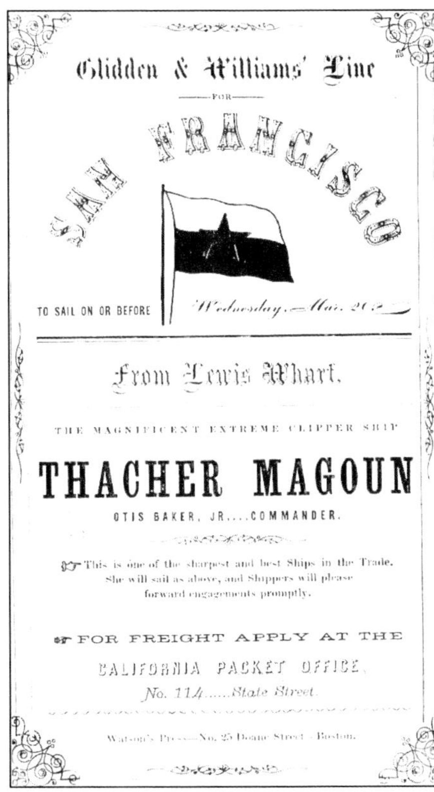

The clipper ship *Thatcher Magoun* (misspelled on this advertising card) was launched in 1856, the year that Magoun died. Its figurehead was a bronze image of the shipbuilder. The ship, which made many voyages out of Boston and New York, was reported lost off the coast of Africa in the early 1880s. (Courtesy of the American Antiquarian Society.)

The *Electric Spark*, also built in 1856, was the sister ship of the *Thatcher Magoun*. The *Spark* had an unlucky history. In 1857, on a voyage from San Francisco to Callao, the crew mutinied and locked the captain in his cabin for two weeks. In 1869, after striking a rock off the Irish coast, the *Spark* was beached and lost. (Courtesy of the American Antiquarian Society.)

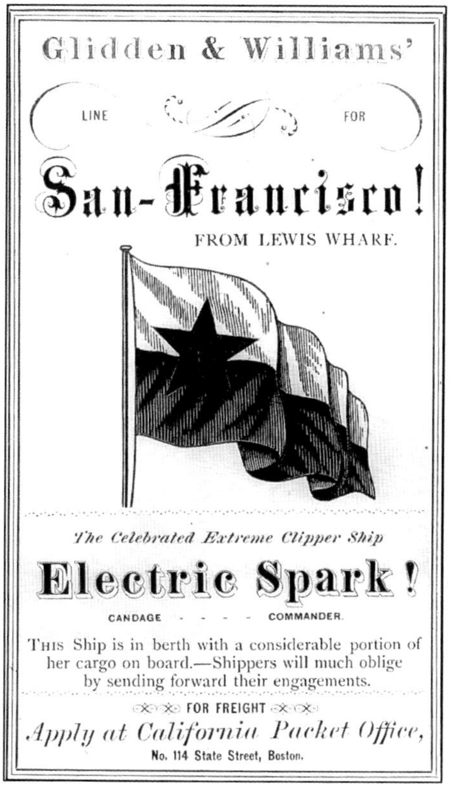

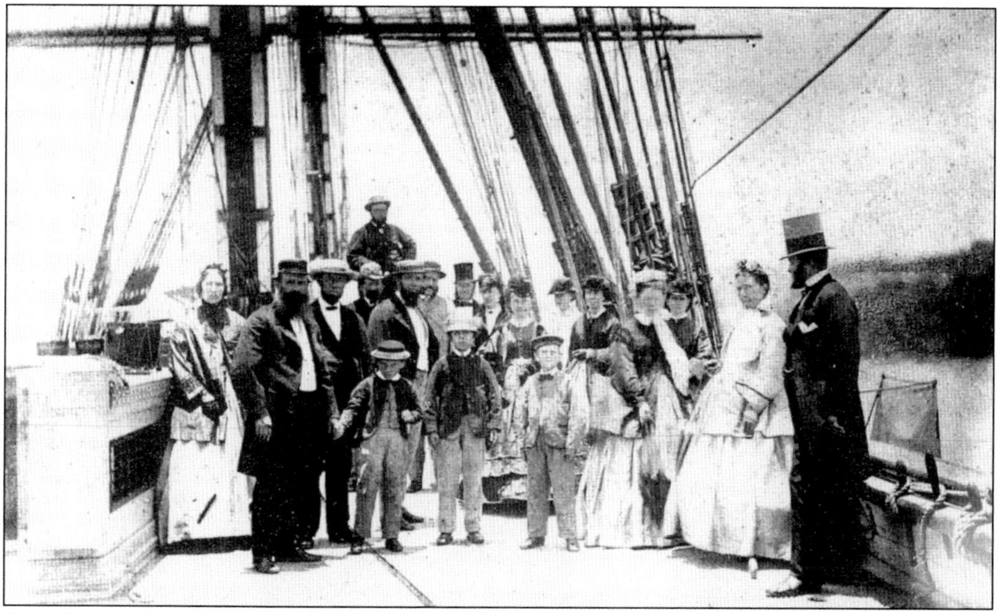

On a happier voyage in 1865, the passengers and crew of the *Electric Spark* are photographed during a party. The bearded man second from the left is Capt. R. F. D. Candage. (Courtesy of the Medford Public Library.)

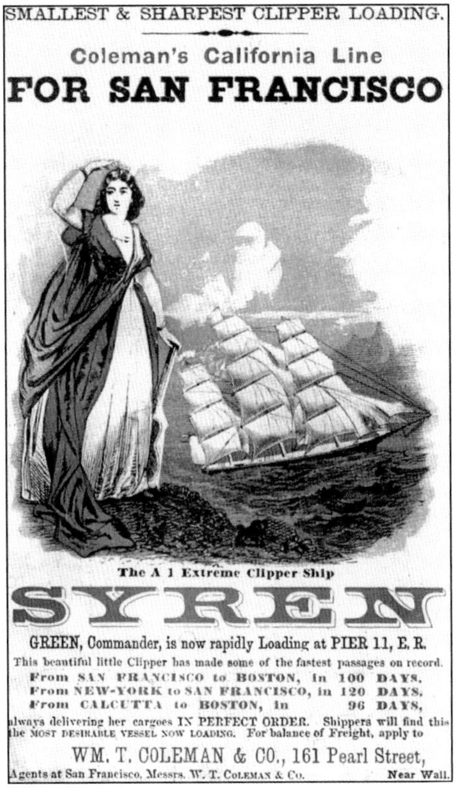

The *Syren* was launched in 1856 from John Taylor's shipyard at Labor-in-Vain Landing at the foot of Foster Court. The *Syren* suffered more accidents without sinking than any clipper ship on record. The ship also survived longer than most clipper ships, probably because it spent so much time in the shop. The *Syren* was listed with Lloyd's of London as late as 1928. (Courtesy of the Medford Historical Society.)

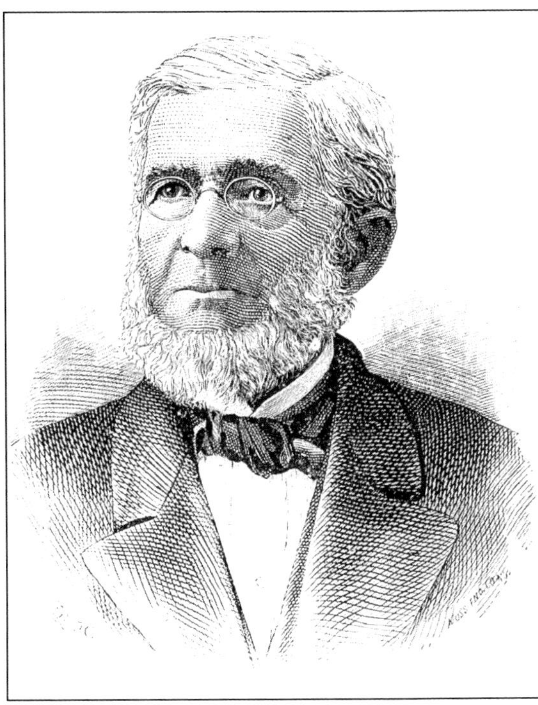

Shipbuilder Joshua T. Foster became partners with John Taylor in 1852. The Foster & Taylor yard launched 22 ships between 1838 and 1845. Foster ran the business by himself from 1846 to 1876, a period in which the yard launched 42 ships. Foster married Ellen Sprague, the daughter of shipbuilder Isaac Sprague, in 1836. (Courtesy of the Medford Public Library.)

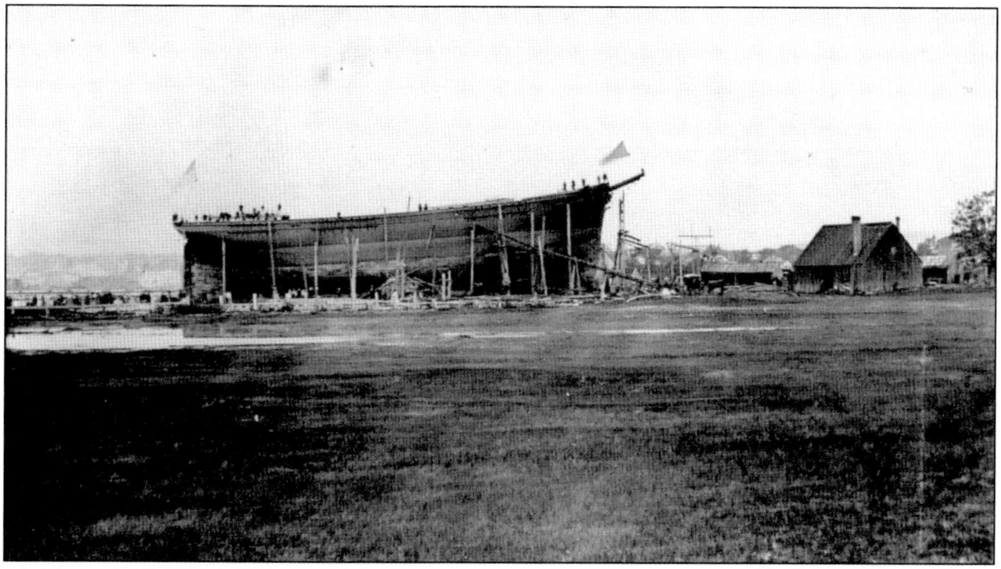

The last clipper ship built in Medford was the *Pilgrim*. After the Civil War, the shipbuilding industry gradually declined. There were 70 ships constructed between 1853 and 1862, but only 14 between 1863 and 1873. Pictured here in the last stages of construction, the *Pilgrim* was launched from Foster's yard in 1873. The ship was active until 1903, when it was wrecked on Turks Island while bound for Cuba. (Courtesy of the Medford Historical Society.)

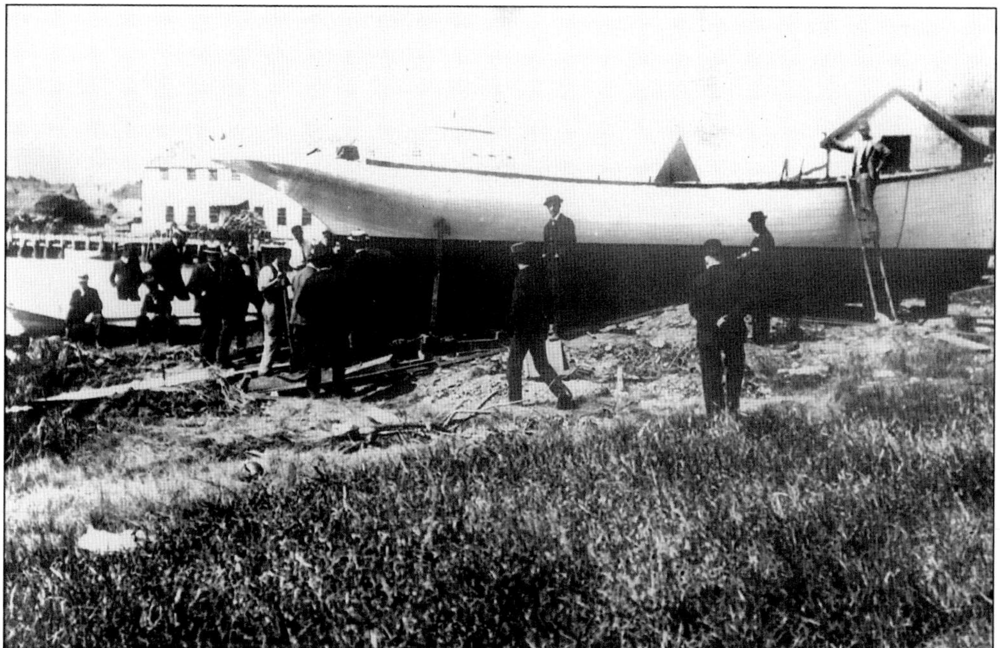

Although construction of large ships ceased in the 1870s, Medford boatyards continued to produce smaller vessels. Here, feverish activity and a lot of well-dressed gentlemen in hats attend the construction of a sloop at Foster's Wharf in the 1890s. (Courtesy of the Medford Public Library.)

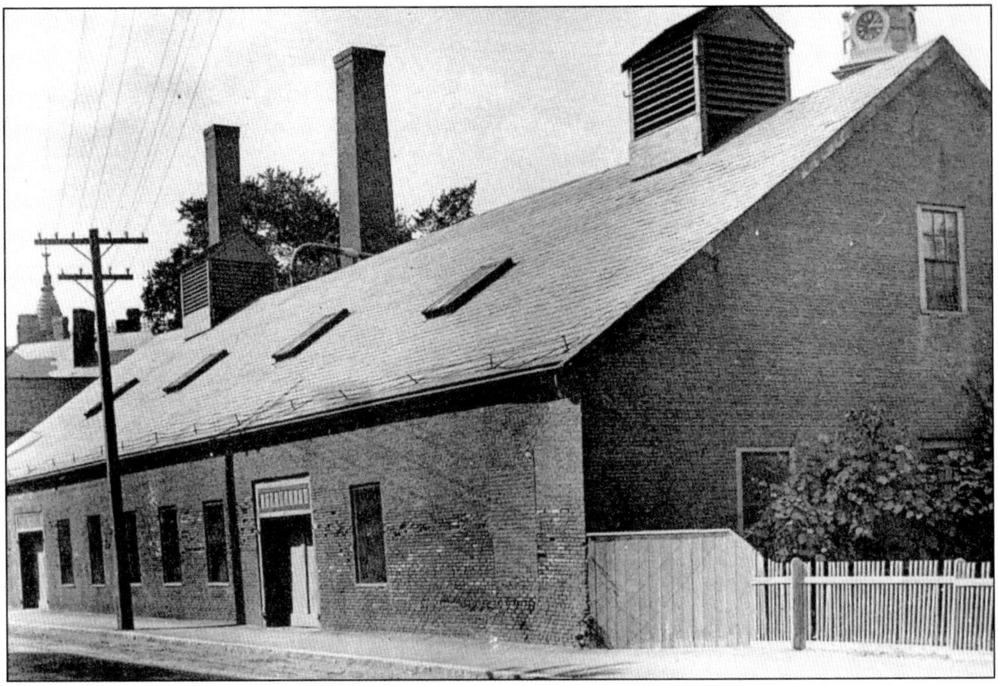

Rum was another primary industry in 19th-century Medford. Throughout the 18th century, rum had been distilled in Medford by the Hall family and others. After 1830, however, the Lawrence Rum Distillery had no competitors. Pictured here is the Lawrence distillery on Riverside Avenue. (Courtesy of the Medford Public Library.)

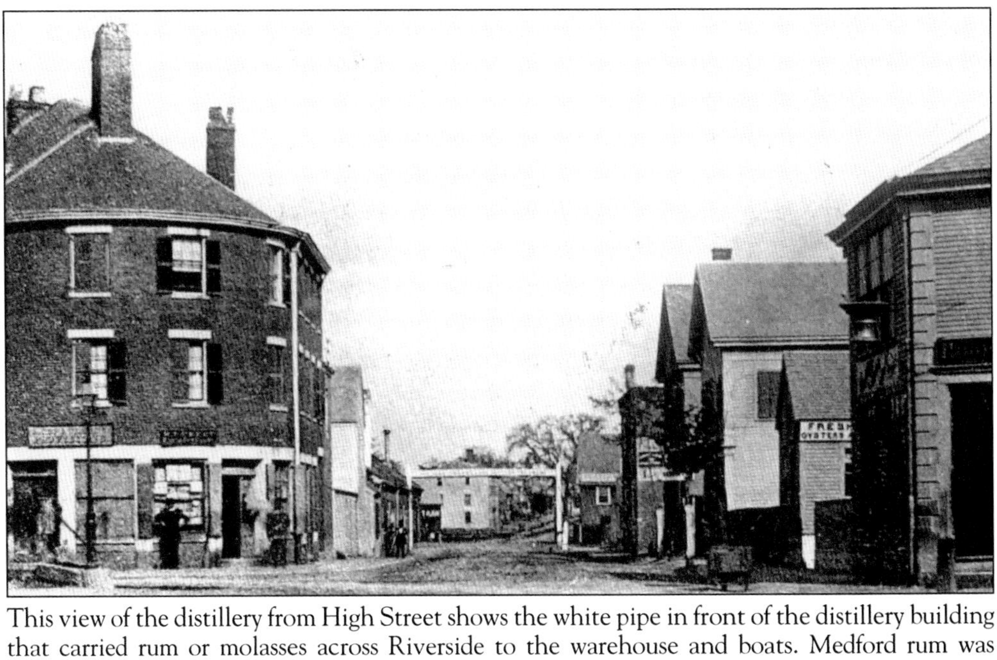

This view of the distillery from High Street shows the white pipe in front of the distillery building that carried rum or molasses across Riverside to the warehouse and boats. Medford rum was carried around the world on Medford ships, and both the rum and the shipbuilding industries were involved in the New England slave trade. (Courtesy of the Medford Public Library.)

DANIEL LAWRENCE & SONS,

THE ONLY DISTILLERS OF

Medford Rum

Still enjoy the reputation of making

THE BEST RUM IN THE STATES.

Lawrence's Medford Old Rum,

Of the Finest Grades and of All Ages.

THE LARGEST STOCK OF THE

CHOICEST OLD RUM IN THE WORLD.

THE SUPERIOR QUALITY OF

Lawrence's Medford Rum

For the past SIXTY-SIX YEARS, has made it everywhere known as the STANDARD RUM.

MEDFORD RUM received the CENTENNIAL MEDAL awarded at the INTERNATIONAL EXHIBITION in 1876, and the highest prizes, Silver Medals, awarded at the MECHANICS' FAIR in 1878 and 1881. first prize at The World's Industrial and Cotton Centennial Exposition at New Orleans in 1885, also at the North Central and South American Exposition at New Orleans, La., in 1886.

No pains are spared to maintain its purity and high reputation.

Write us for Circular. Our trade marks are patented. The public is cautioned against imitation.

Send orders direct to us, and so insure perfect satisfaction.

DANIEL LAWRENCE & SONS,

No. 127 Broad Street, BOSTON.

When Daniel Lawrence died in 1879, his will stipulated that the distillery should be closed, but his sons Samuel and William carried on the business until 1905. This glowing full-page advertisement comes from the 1890 city directory. (Courtesy of the Medford Public Library.)

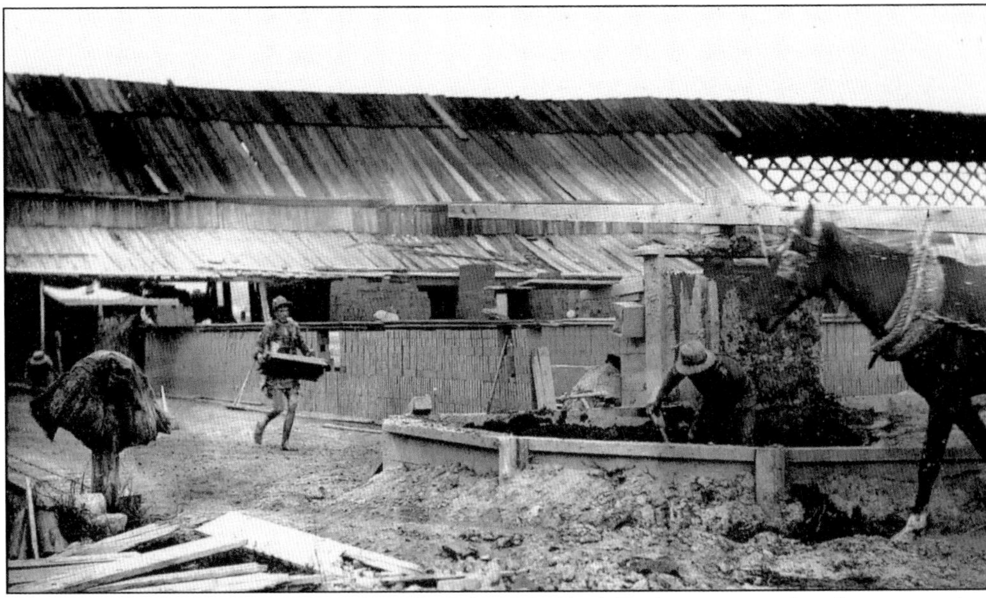

Because of the abundance of good-quality clay, Medford bricks were another famous product of the town. Brickyards were a local industry from the 17th century until the 1920s. In this photograph of the College Hill Brickyard in August 1891, one man is pouring water or clay into the horse-operated mill. Note the piles of finished bricks behind the running man. (Courtesy of the Medford Historical Society.)

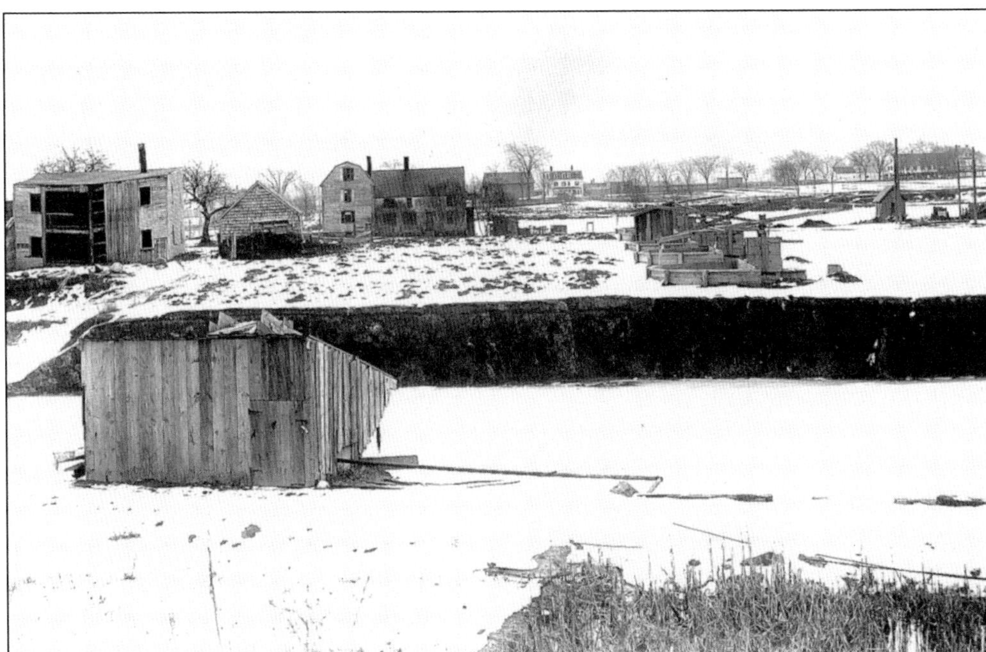

The same brickyard is seen in the winter of 1892. Medford bricks were used all over the world. In the Victorian era, they were used as ballast in ships and then sold in various countries. Toward the close of the 19th century, between 15 and 20 million bricks were made annually in Medford. The last brickyard closed in 1923. (Courtesy of the Medford Public Library.)

32 THE DRUGGISTS CIRCULAR AND CHEMICAL GAZETTE. [June, 1888

THE ARCTIC SODA WATER APPARATUS

Moderate Prices Easy Terms of Payment.

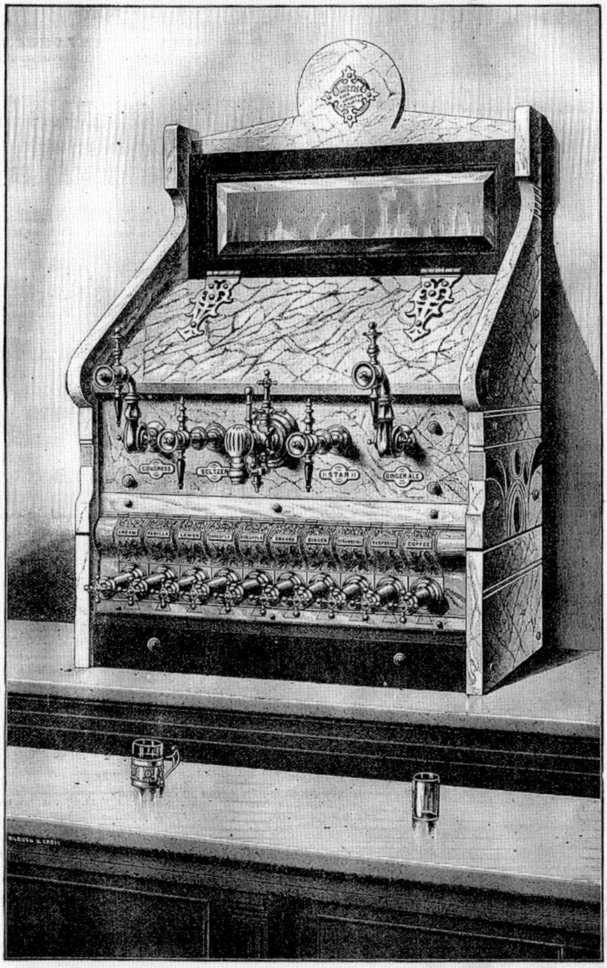

There is nothing that can be sold over a counter which is so profitable as soda water.

The materials required were never so cheap as at present.

The demand for a high grade of beverages is greater than ever before.

We can furnish formulas for a splendid line of new, delicious, and wholesome beverages.

Finer apparatus can be furnished for a given sum of money than at any previous time.

The recent improvements have revolutionized the construction of soda water apparatus.

An attractive apparatus will increase any business more than its cost invested in any other form of advertising.

It pays to exchange your old apparatus for a more attractive and convenient one.

The increased profit will frequently pay the difference in cost between an old apparatus and a new one.

Wall apparatus are cheaper and more convenient than counter apparatus.

I will sell you an elegant new apparatus and take your old one in part payment, giving ample time in which to pay the difference.

Second hand apparatus of every known make in thorough repair, at low prices and on easy terms of payment.

If thinking of buying or exchanging, send for my 1888

Illustrated Price List.

It will be sent FREE by mail.
Address all communications to

JAMES W. TUFTS, Bowker, Chardon & Portland Sts., BOSTON, MASS.

SALESROOMS:

BOSTON,	96, 98 & 100 Portland Street.	SAN FRANCISCO,	54 Second Street.
NEW YORK,	68 & 70 Park Place.	NEW ORLEANS,	456 St. Andrew Street.
CHICAGO,	84 & 86 Jackson Street.	MINNEAPOLIS,	9 Fifth Street, (South).
ST. LOUIS,	703 So. Broadway.	DETROIT,	168 Griswold Street.
BALTIMORE,	10 West Lombard Street.	OMAHA,	121 No. Fifteenth Street.

In writing for Catalogue customers will confer a favor by mentioning this Journal.

Readers, Please Mention THE DRUGGISTS CIRCULAR When Writing or Buying

One of Medford's most successful Victorian businessmen was James W. Tufts, a chemist who opened an apothecary shop in Medford Square in the 1860s. Tufts went on to invent the Arctic Soda Water Apparatus, and in 1894 he became a founder of the American Soda Fountain Company. He later became well known for the production of silver-plate servingware. (Collection of the author.)

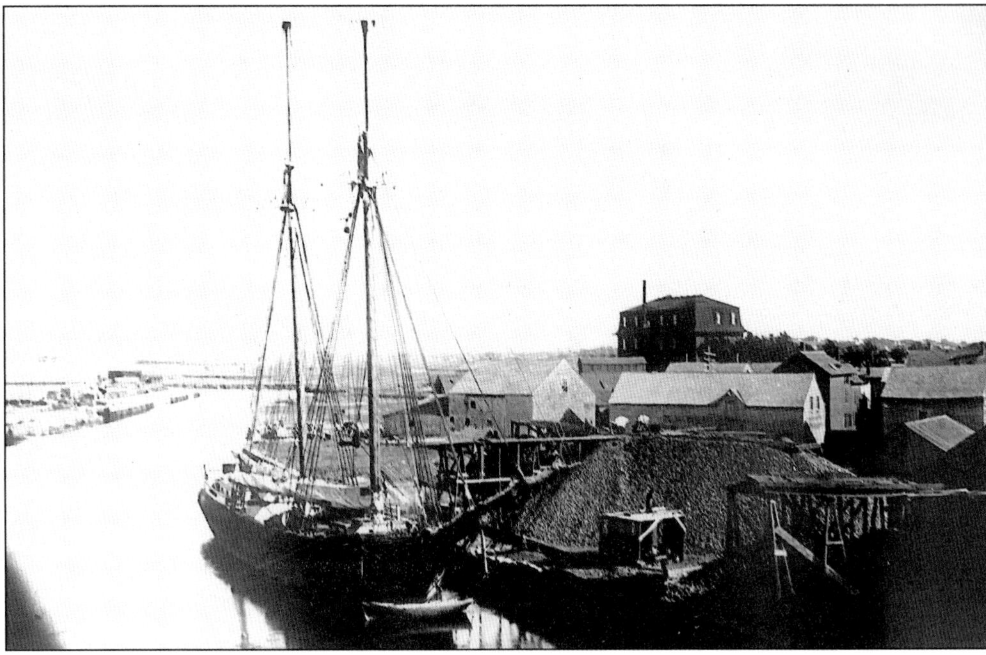

As Medford grew, businesses developed to meet the needs of all the new residents. Bean's Coal Wharf, located off Main Street, provided the town with coal, wood, hay, grain, and other staples. Supplies were transported on the river on cargo ships like this one, photographed in 1890. (Courtesy of the Medford Public Library.)

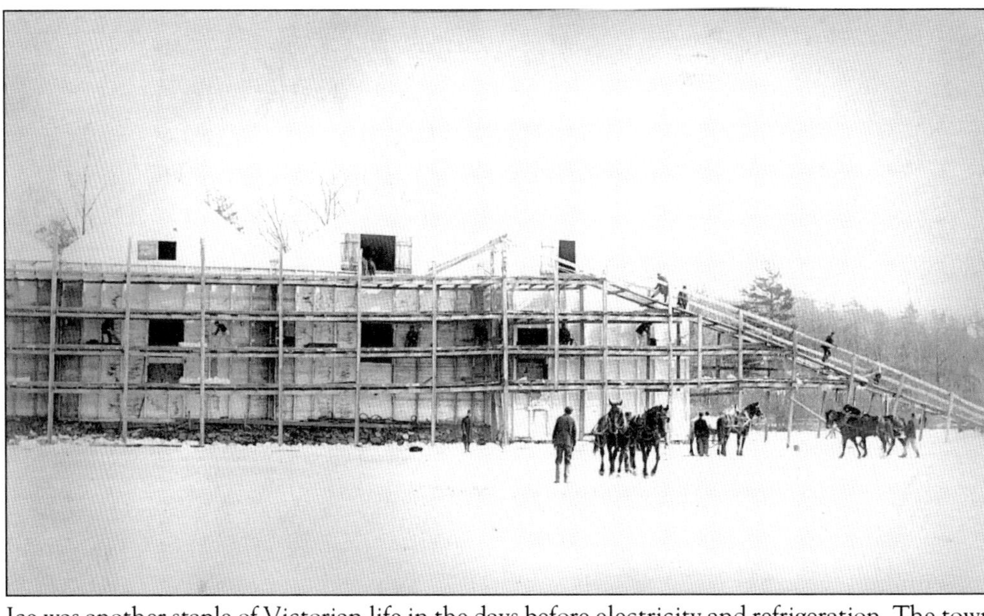

Ice was another staple of Victorian life in the days before electricity and refrigeration. The town had several ice dealers, who cut ice in the winter and saved it in icehouses for warmer seasons. This 1889 Spot Pond operation may have involved Frederic Tudor, known as the Ice King, who pioneered the idea of shipping Massachusetts ice to warmer climates. (Courtesy of the Medford Historical Society.)

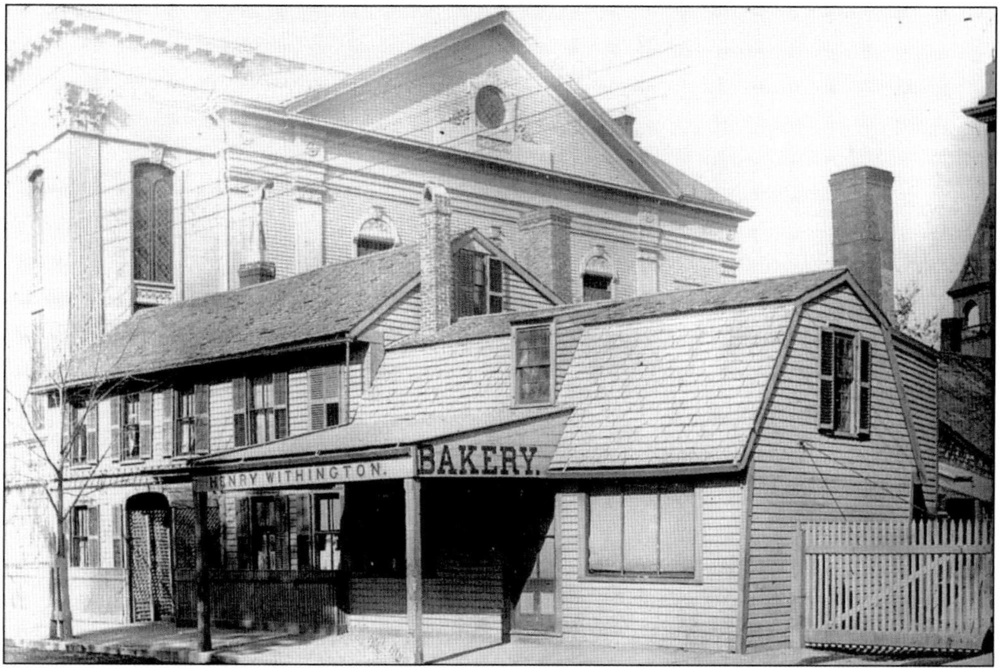

One of Medford's oldest businesses was the Withington Bakery on Salem Street. Founded in 1825 by Henry Withington, the bakery was notable for the production of Medford Crackers. Withington's son continued the business after 1870. The bakery was sold several times in later years, but new owners always retained the Withington name and reputation. It closed for good in 1915. (Courtesy of the Medford Public Library.)

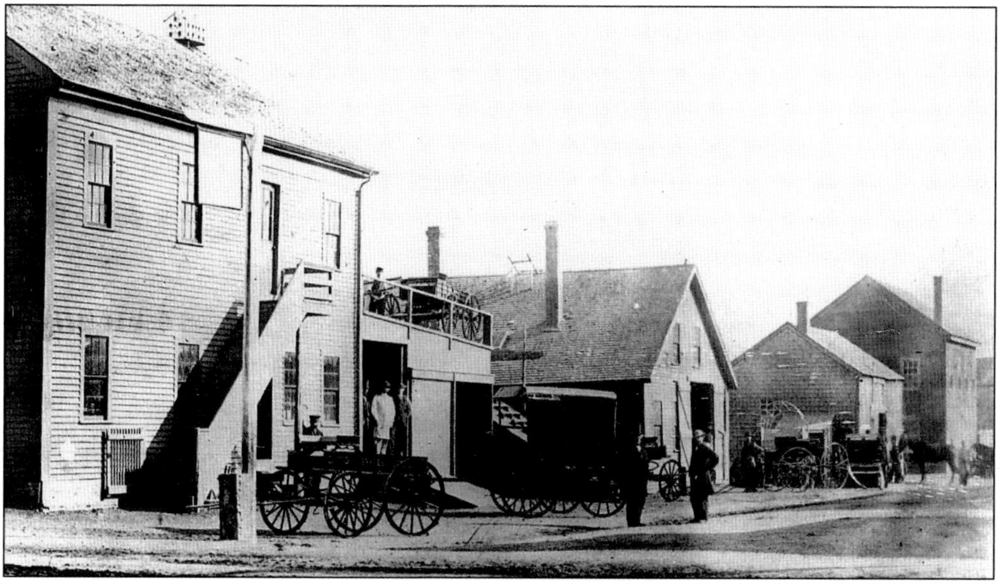

This wagon-building establishment on the corner of Mystic Avenue and Union Street was founded in 1816. After 1839 it was run by Elbridge Teel, who specialized in milk, grocer, baker, and express wagons. The blacksmith shop of Alexander Symmes was conveniently located in the rear. In the early 1900s, the Teel company became an auto dealership. (Courtesy of the Medford Public Library.)

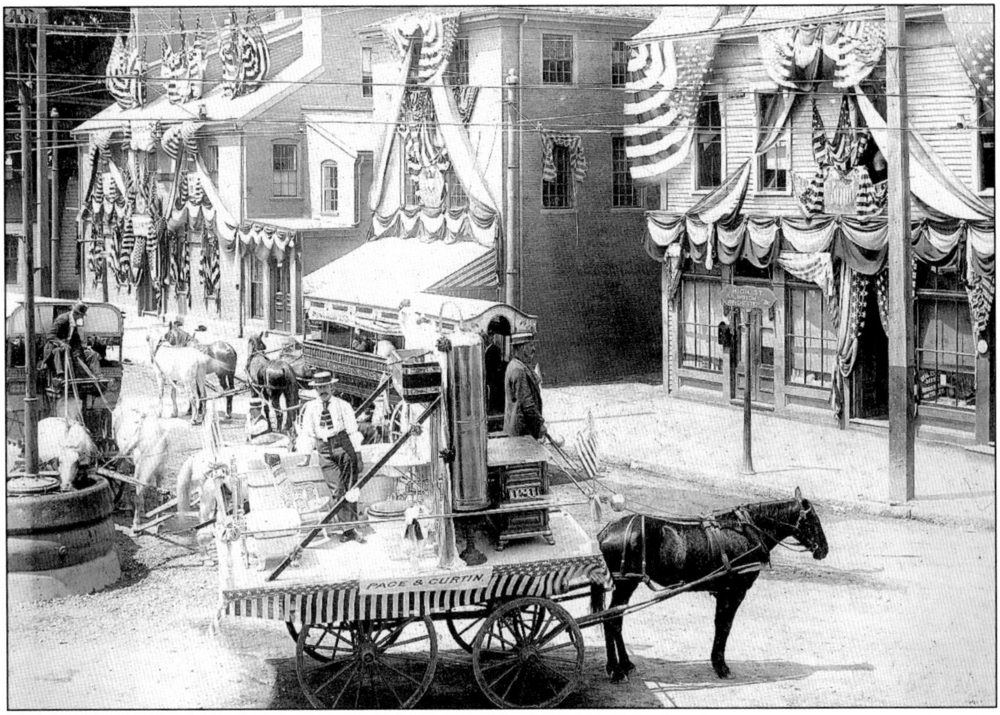

The construction of new houses in the latter half of the 19th century opened a market for domestic businesses. Page and Curtin was a supplier of household goods, including a complete line of plumbing fixtures like those displayed on this float in an 1890s Fourth of July parade. The driver was Mike O'Brien; John F. Reagan is leaning against the side of the display. (Courtesy of the Medford Historical Society.)

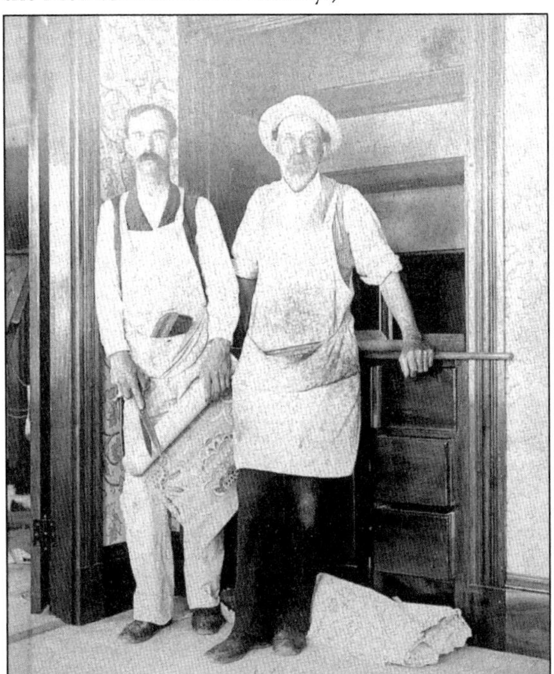

The surge in house construction provided opportunities for the building trades. One of the new firms was that of W. Swan and Son, a father-and-son paperhanging concern. This 1893 photograph shows them hard at work inside a new house. (Courtesy of the Medford Historical Society.)

Four

Civic Life

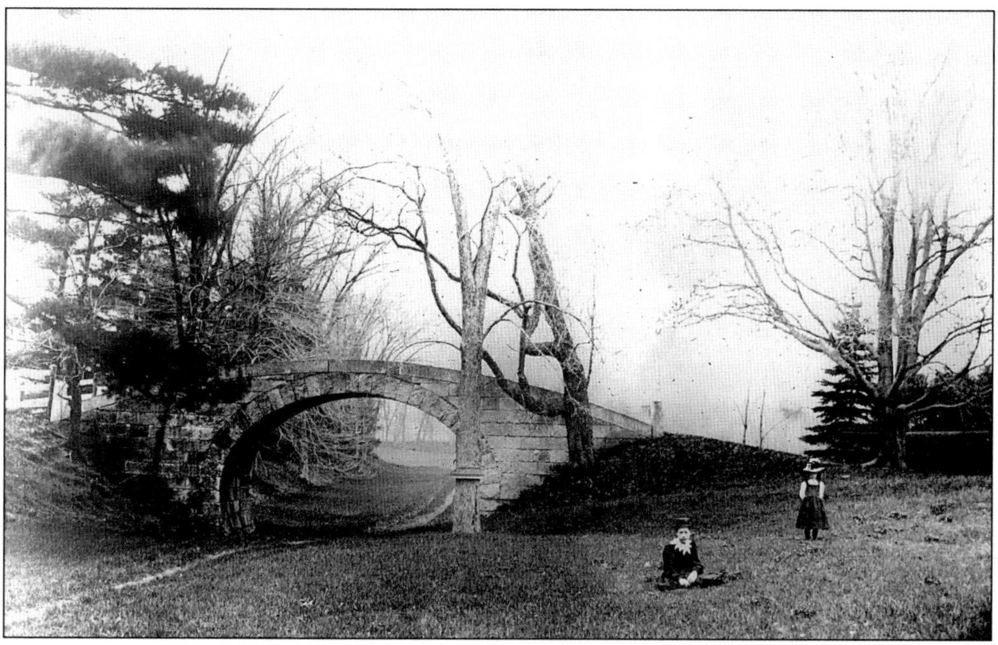

The Middlesex Canal, which opened in 1803 and passed through West Medford, was important for trade and transportation in the early 19th century. But the railroad ended the reign of the canal, and the last boat passed through in 1852. Pictured in this 1880s photograph is the Old Middlesex Canal Bridge, which was torn down to make homes on Sagamore Avenue. The girls are the grandchildren of the photographer, George Davenport. (Courtesy of the Medford Public Library.)

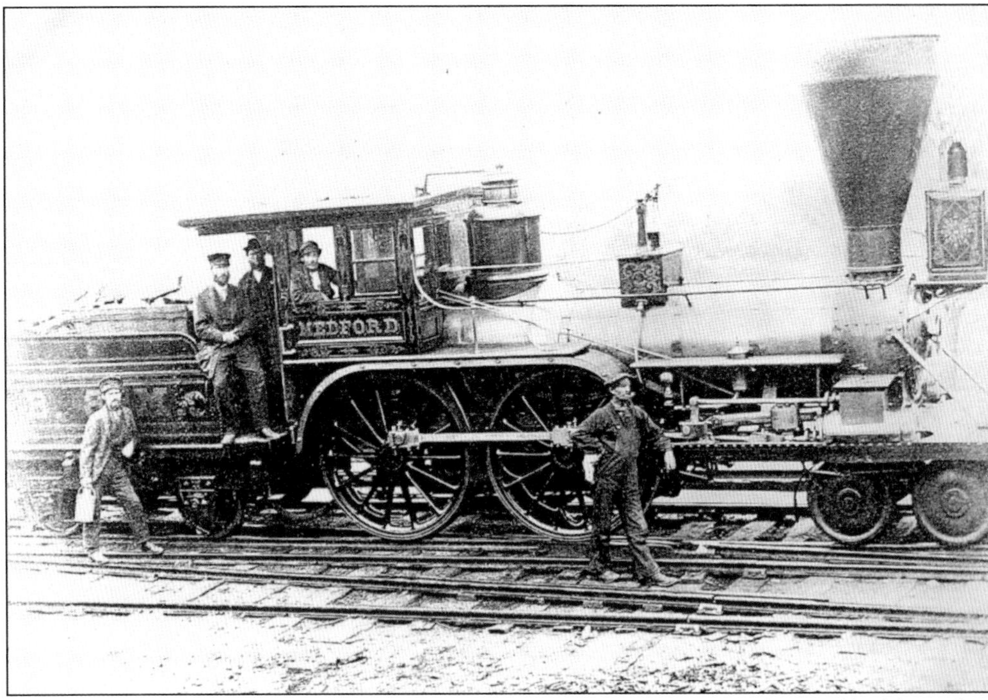

The first Boston and Lowell Railroad train came to Medford in 1835. The Medford branch of the Boston and Maine Railroad was built in 1845, with a terminal in Medford Square. This early Boston and Maine train, the *Medford*, had only one car, a combined luggage and passenger car. (Collection of the author.)

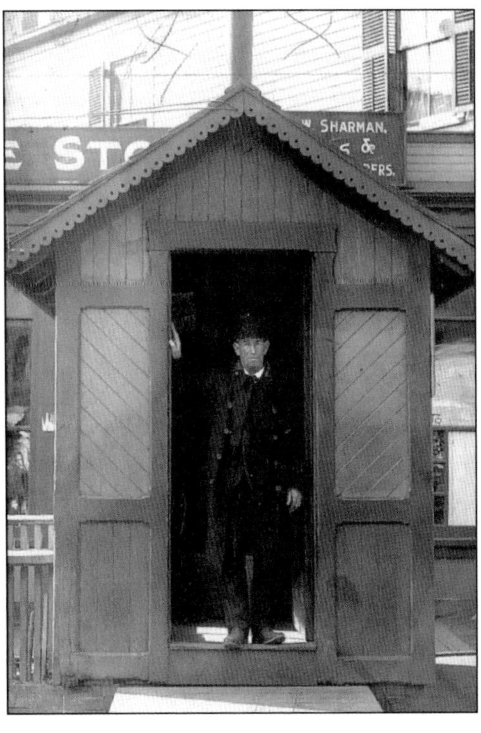

Michael Griffin served as railroad guard at the High Street crossing for 28 years, starting in 1878. Born in Ireland in 1841, Griffin began working for the Boston and Lowell Railroad in 1865. A familiar local figure, he lived in a house at 35 Canal Street that he had bought from the railroad. Griffin retired in 1906 and died in 1924. (Courtesy of the Medford Public Library.)

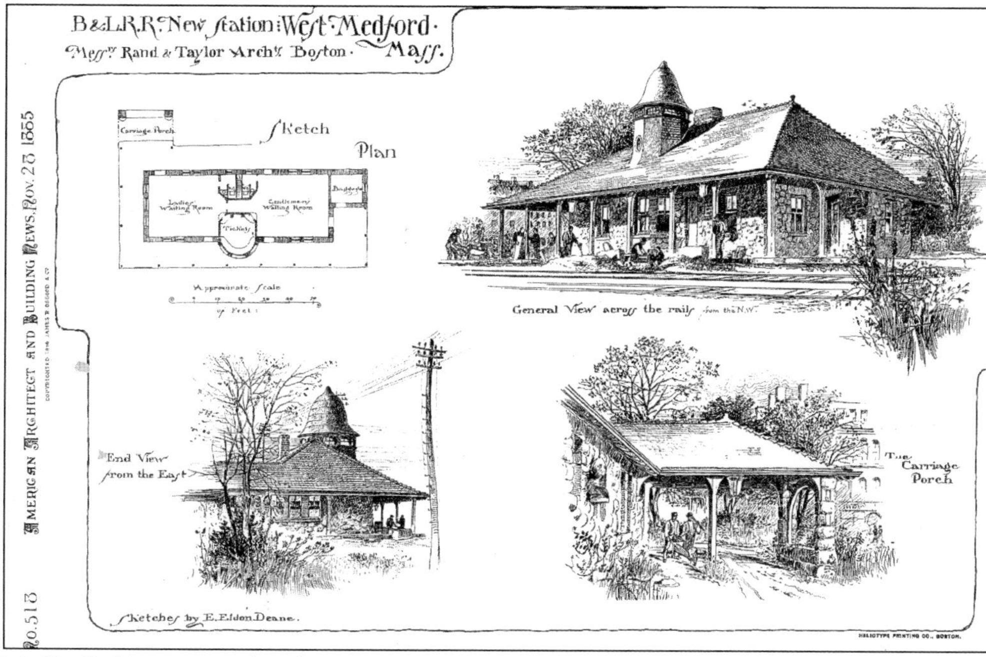

Medford's Victorian railroad stations were as ornately designed as the houses of the day. The West Medford station was built in 1885, and the plan was published in an annual of notable designs. Notice the separate ladies' and gentlemen's waiting rooms on the floor plan. (Collection of the author.)

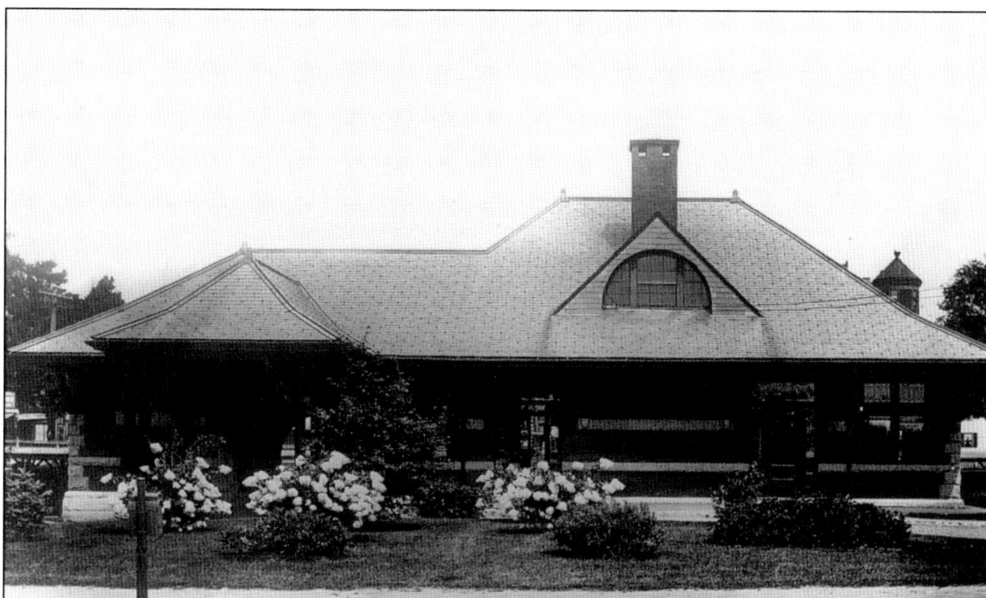

The Park Street station, shown from the Magoun Avenue side, was built in 1893. The station, designed in an eclectic style, was brick with a granite trim. Notice the dormer roof and the elaborate window decorations. (Courtesy of the Medford Public Library.)

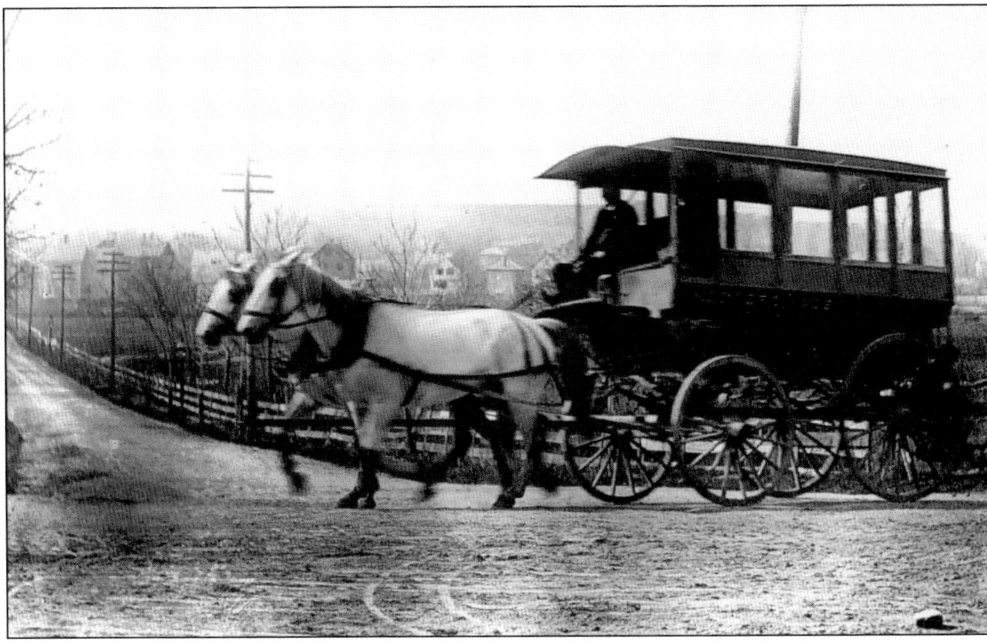

Travel around town became easier with the advent of the horse railroad, or horse streetcar, in the 1850s. The omnibus pictured here in Winthrop Circle ran between Medford Square and West Medford. College Avenue is on the left, with Tufts in the background. (Courtesy of the Medford Public Library.)

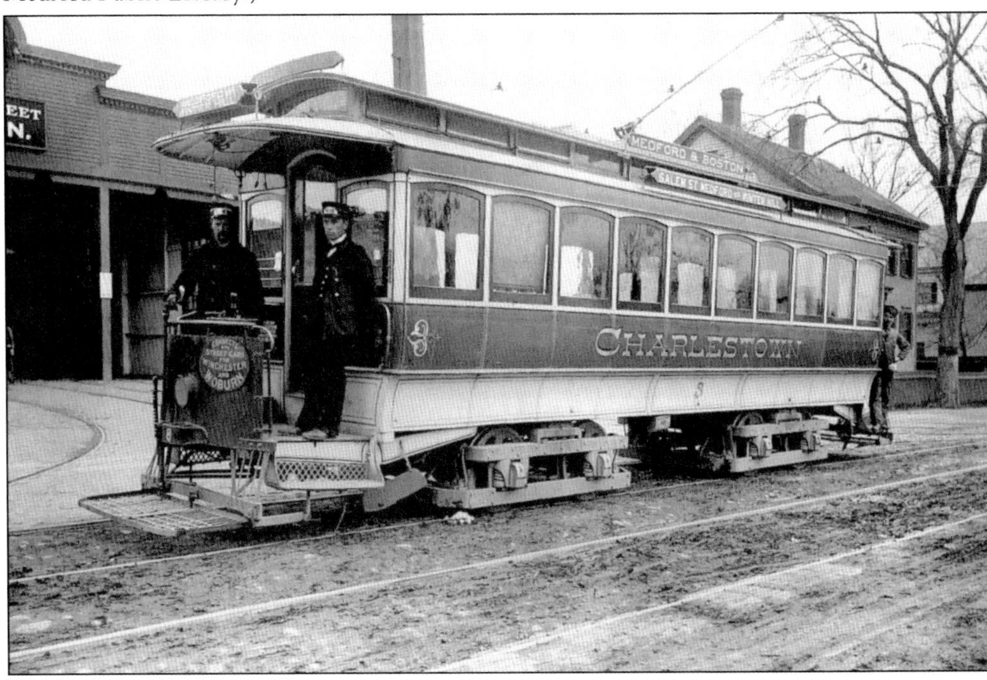

Horse-drawn streetcars ran between Medford and Charlestown from 1865 to 1873. Then service was suspended until 1883 because of objections from the Somerville selectmen about the tracks. By the late 1890s, electric streetcars like this one had replaced the horses, and tracks and wires had become a familiar sight on the city streets. (Collection of the author.)

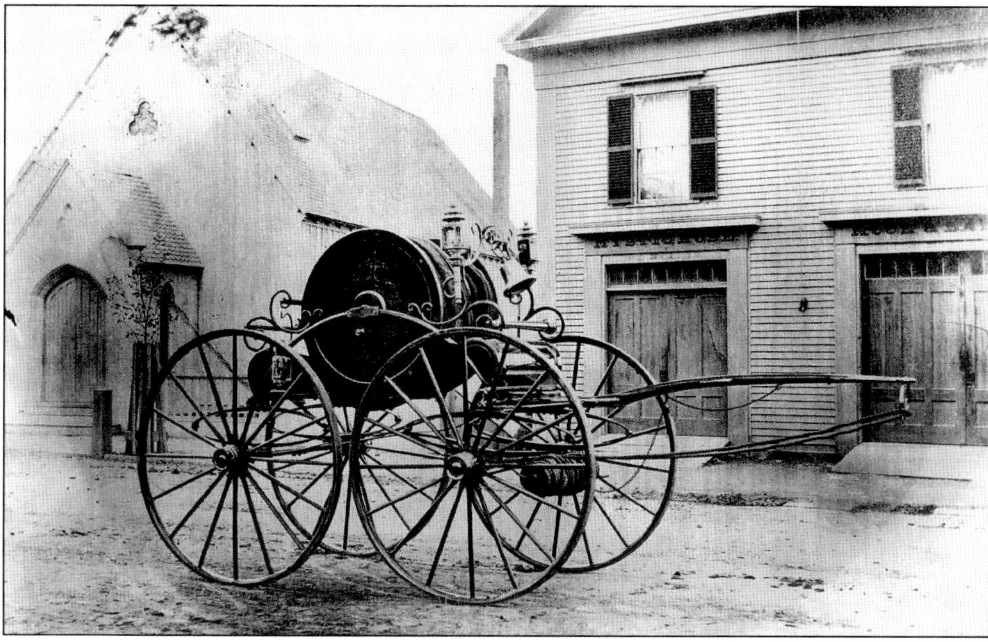

The Medford Fire Department was incorporated in 1839, and the chief engineer made his first annual report in 1842. Pictured here in 1851 is one of the department's early hand-pumped engines outside the Mystic Hose Company No. 1 on High Street. The building on the left was the Episcopal church. (Courtesy of the Medford Historical Society.)

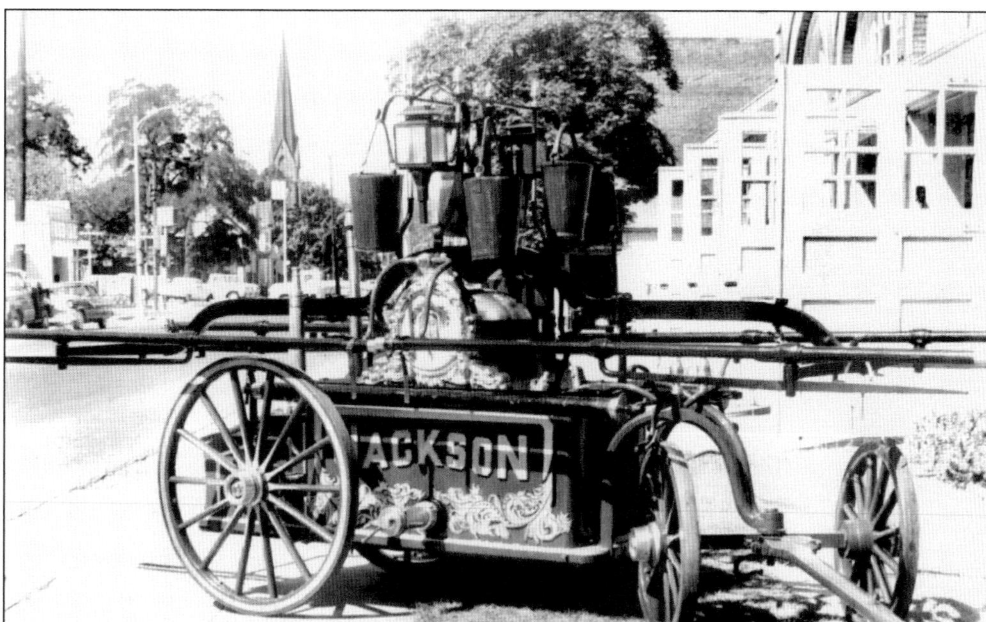

The early fire engines had their own names, and the various volunteer companies indulged in good-natured rivalry about the superiority of their engines. Shown here is the General Jackson No. 2, purchased for $800 in June 1849. The engine remained in use until 1861, when it was sold to the City of San Francisco. (Courtesy of the Medford Historical Society.)

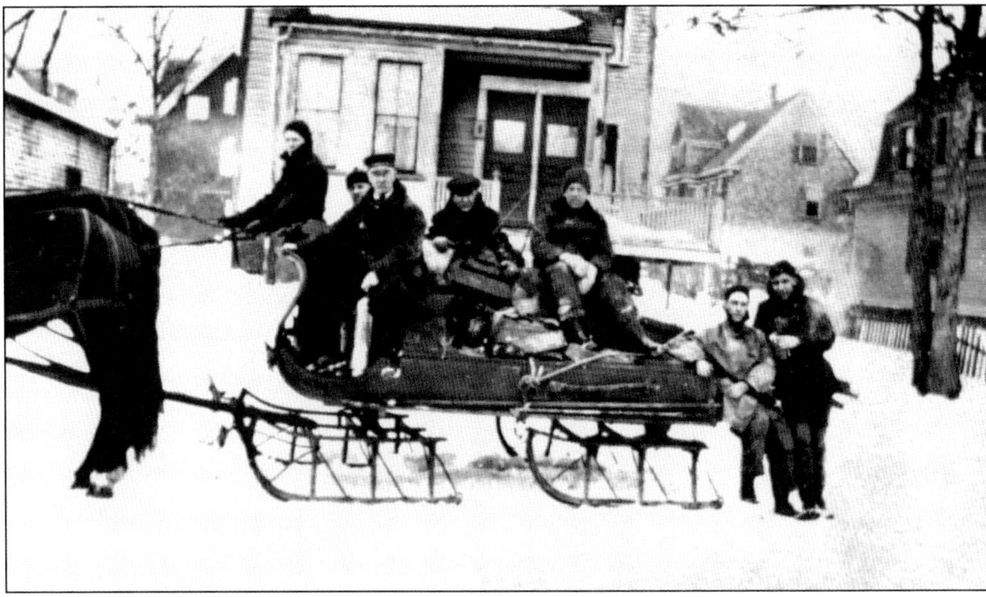

Victorian fire equipment also had to operate in snowy streets. This pung was purchased for the fire department in 1886. The pung and its riders are shown on Salem Street, which was a popular spot for sleigh rides. (Courtesy of the Medford Historical Society.)

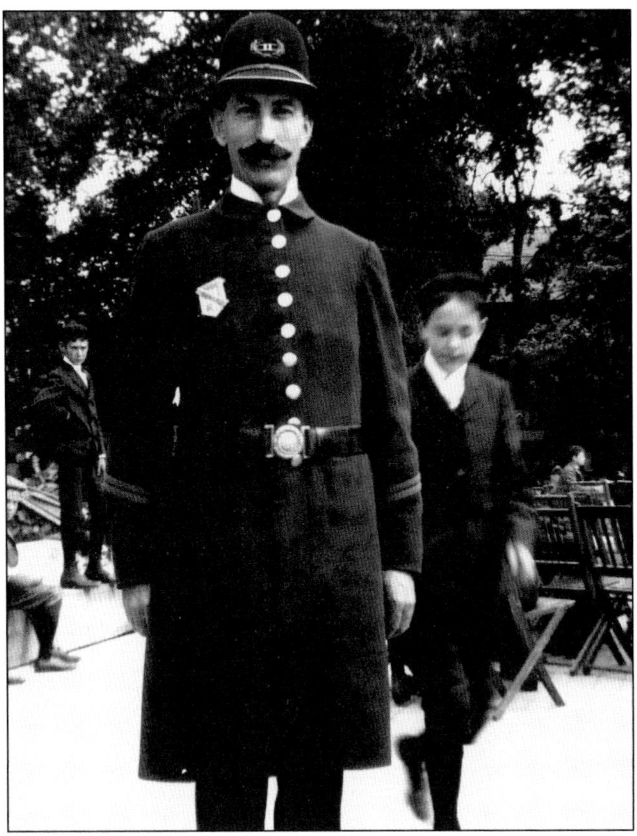

Medford's police department was founded in 1870 with a force of eight men. Patrolman William Golding (shown here) was appointed to a slightly larger force in 1894. In his first year, the police made 470 arrests, for everything from drunkenness to violations of the milk law. Police work that year also included impounding cattle and finding 29 lost children. Golding retired from the force in 1937. (Courtesy of the Medford Public Library.)

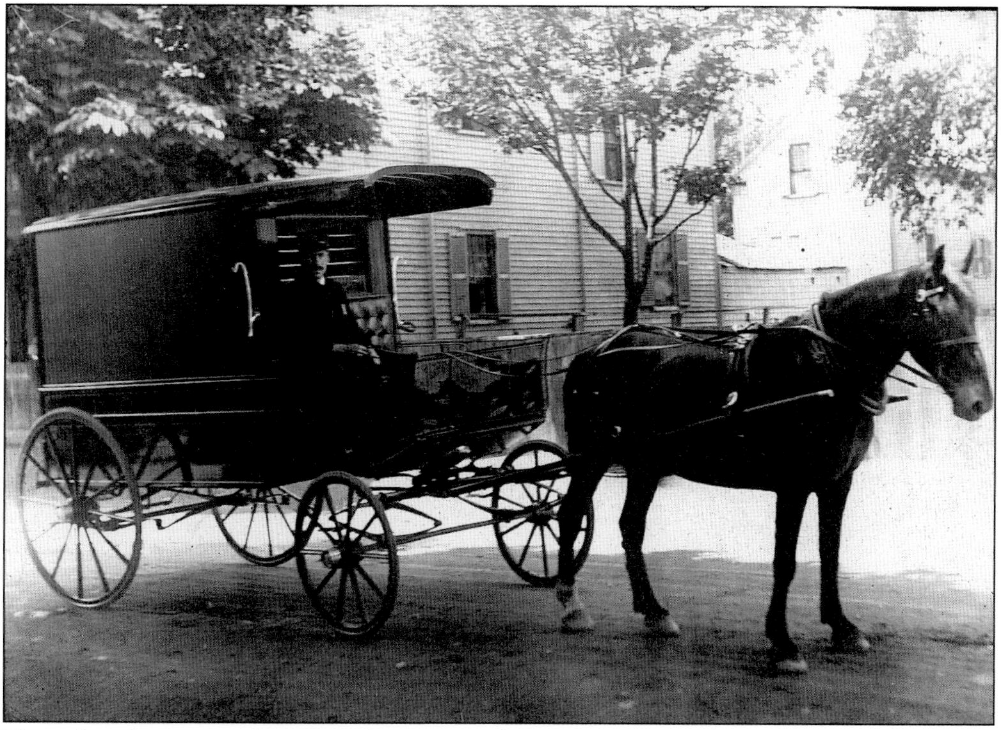

The police force grew along with the town, and equipment was added to meet the demands of a larger population. The police department purchased its first ambulance in 1904. (Courtesy of the Medford Historical Society.)

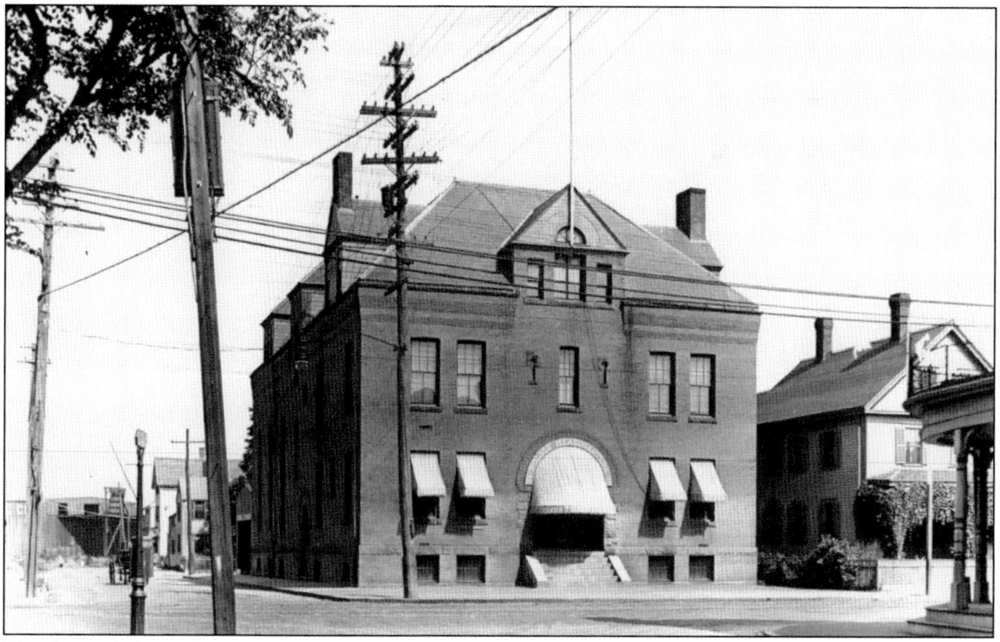

Until 1895 the police operated out of rooms in the town hall. In 1895 this brand-new red-brick police building was constructed on the corner of Swan and Main Streets. (Courtesy of the Medford Public Library.)

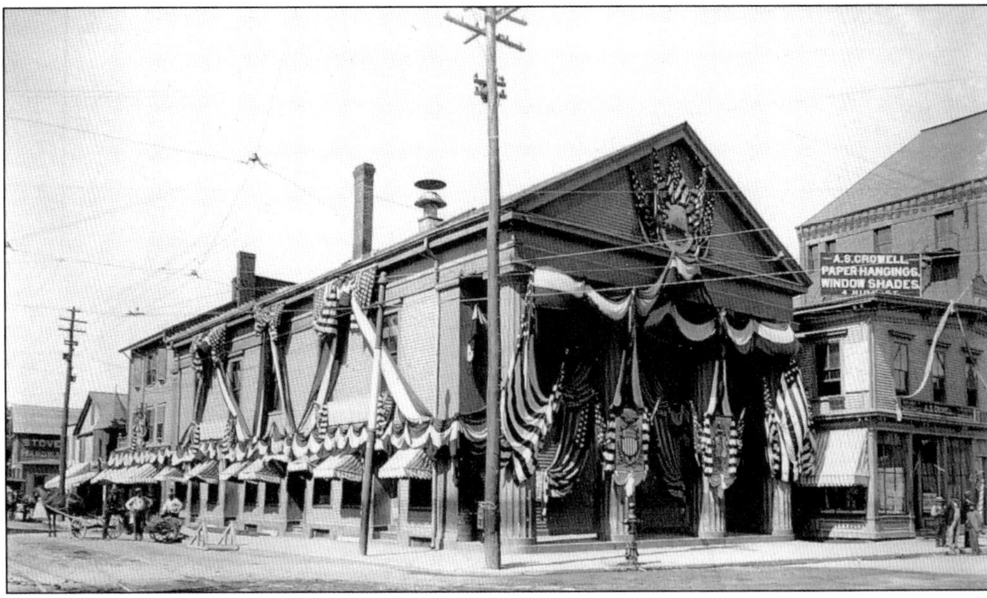

The town hall was built on the corner of Main and High Streets in the 1830s. It was damaged by fire twice (in 1839 and 1850) and was enlarged after each fire. The building stood until 1916. It is shown here on July 4, 1894, all dressed up for the Fourth of July parade. (Courtesy of the Medford Public Library.)

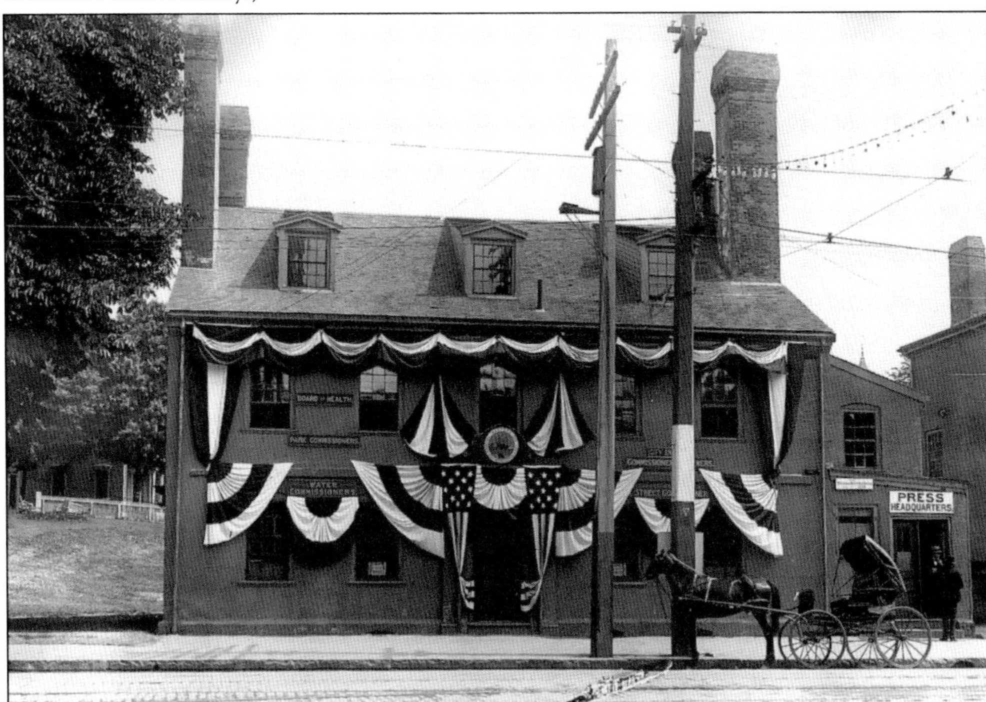

Offices that did not fit into the town hall were housed in the town hall annex on the corner of High Street near Forest Street. The annex, originally the Thomas Seccomb House, was built in 1756 and was later known as Simpson's Tavern. Here the offices are decorated for another Fourth of July celebration, this time in 1895. (Courtesy of the Medford Public Library.)

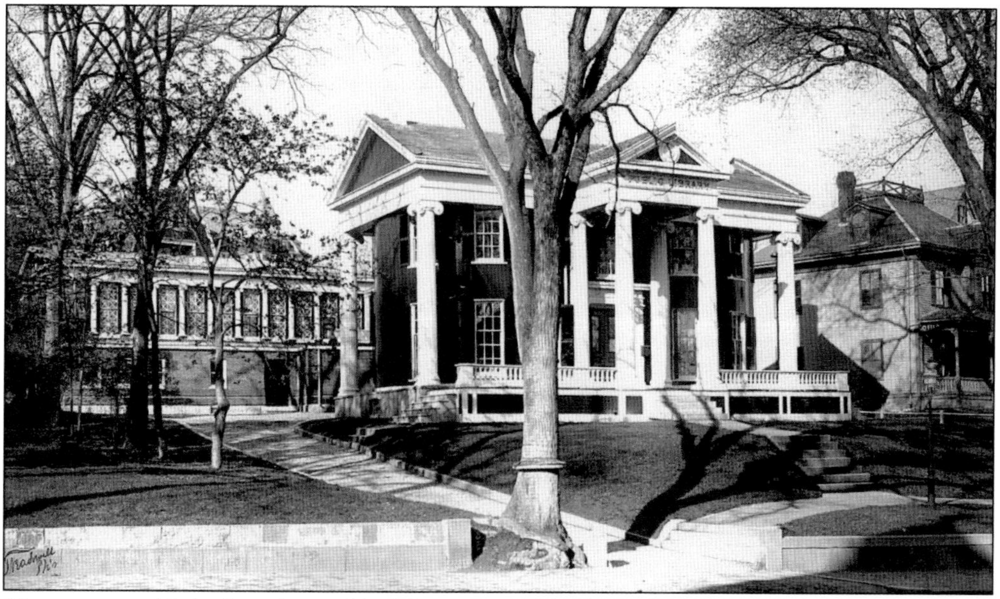

The town established its first public library in 1855. The collection moved from the railroad station in Medford Square to the Usher Block to the town hall. In 1875 Thatcher Magoun Jr. secured his place in Medford history by giving the town his father's imposing High Street mansion to use as a library. The Magoun Mansion and various additions housed the library until 1960, when the present building was constructed. (Courtesy of the Medford Public Library.)

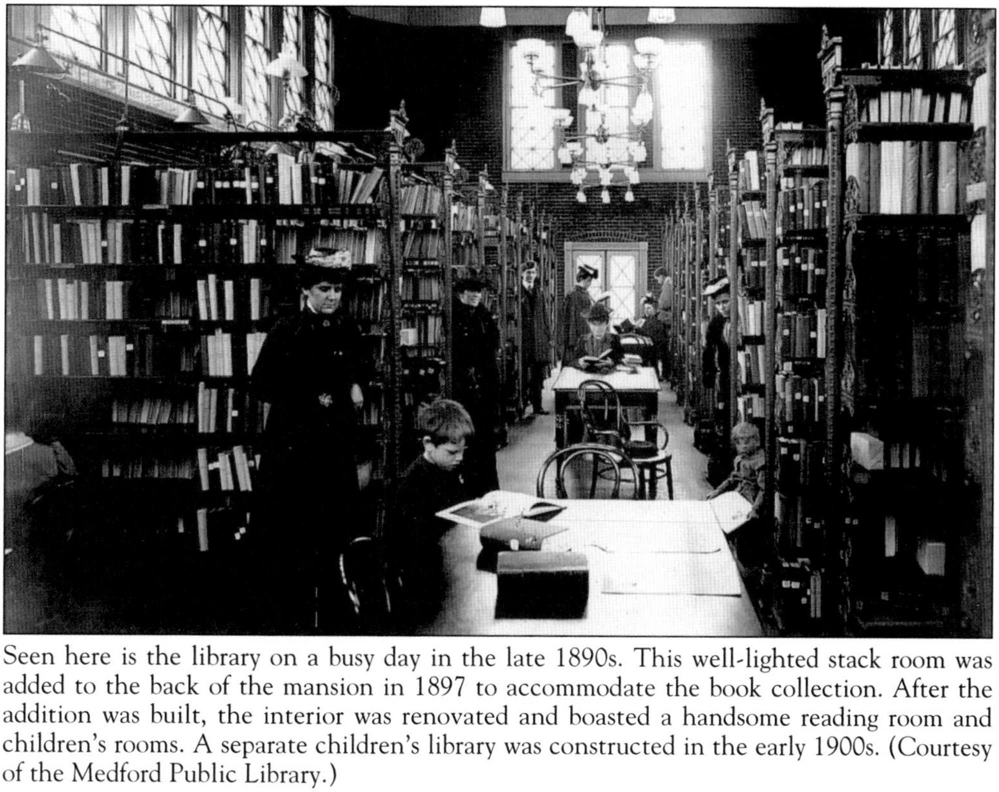

Seen here is the library on a busy day in the late 1890s. This well-lighted stack room was added to the back of the mansion in 1897 to accommodate the book collection. After the addition was built, the interior was renovated and boasted a handsome reading room and children's rooms. A separate children's library was constructed in the early 1900s. (Courtesy of the Medford Public Library.)

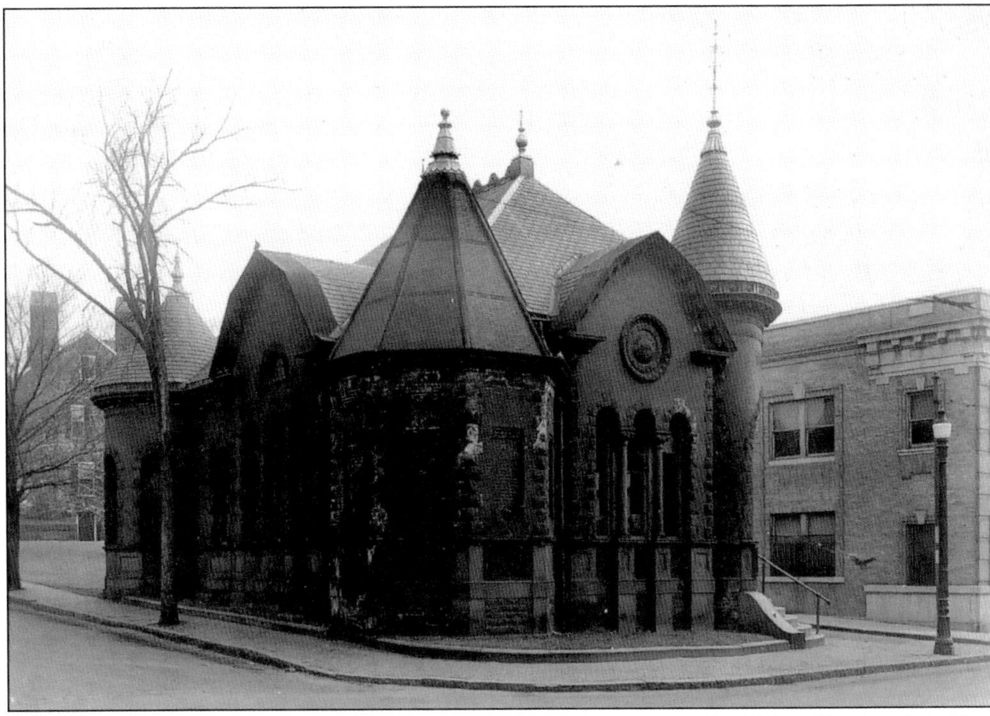

The Medford Savings Bank opened on May 5, 1869, in a room in the Usher Block in Medford Square. In 1890 the first bank building was built on the corner of High Street and Bradlee Road. The new bank building, with its towers and arches, added a delightful Gothic touch to Medford Square. (Courtesy of the Medford Public Library.)

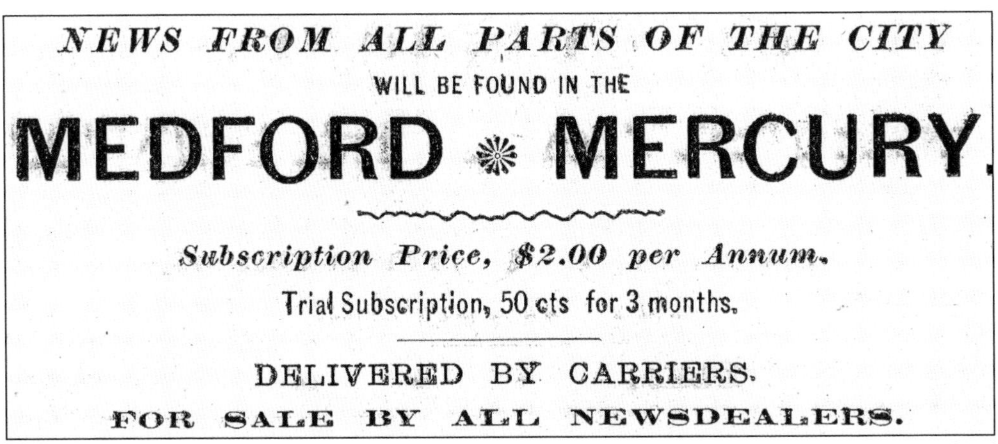

The earliest Medford newspapers were the *Medford Journal* (1870–1874) and the *Medford Chronicle*, which began publication in 1882. The first *Medford Mercury* was issued on December 18, 1880, and combined with the *Chronicle* in 1882. The paper was published by printer Samuel W. Lawrence and local editor George Stetson in offices on Riverside Avenue. (Courtesy of the Medford Historical Society.)

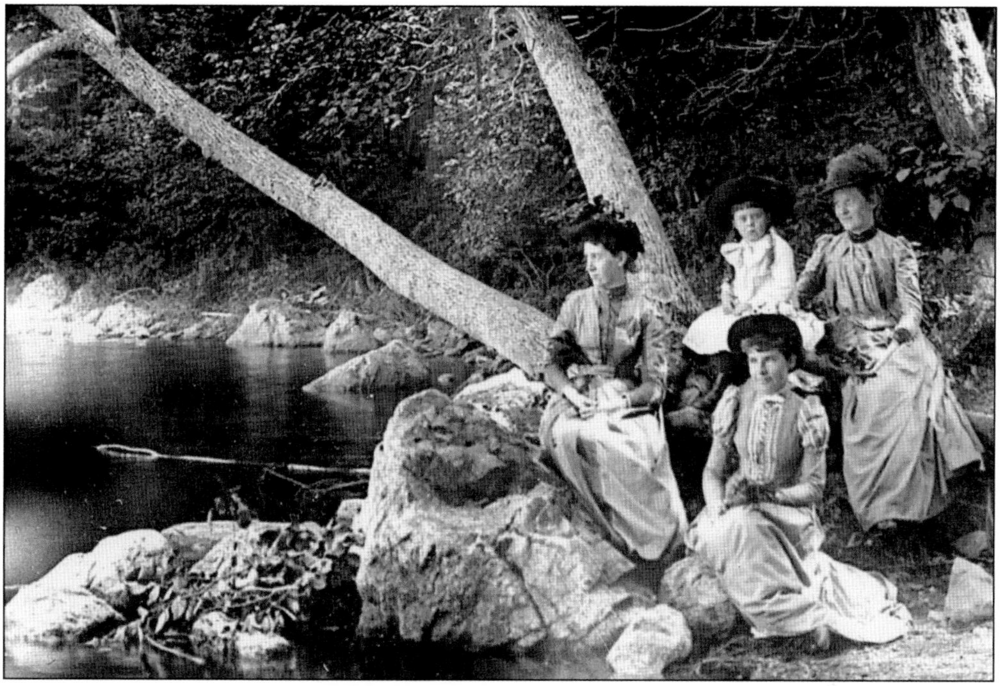

Spot Pond, a popular picnic spot, became the source of the city's water supply in the 1870s. The pond provided water to Medford, Melrose, and Malden. The first pipes were laid in 1870, and the entire town was supplied with pond water by the spring of 1871. (Courtesy of the Medford Public Library.)

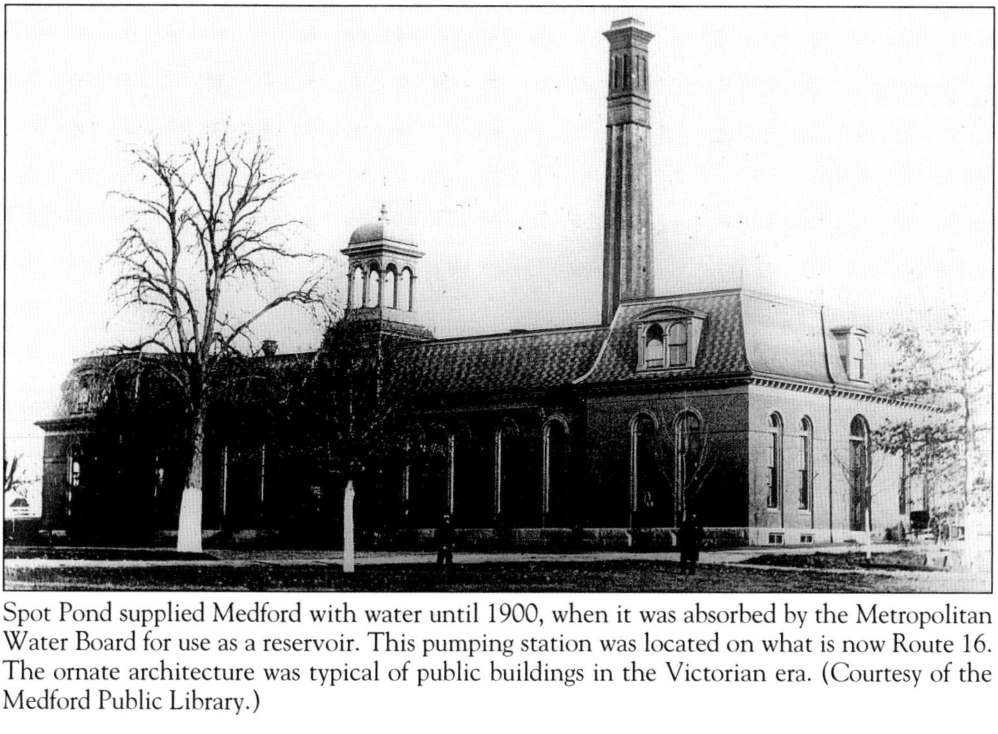

Spot Pond supplied Medford with water until 1900, when it was absorbed by the Metropolitan Water Board for use as a reservoir. This pumping station was located on what is now Route 16. The ornate architecture was typical of public buildings in the Victorian era. (Courtesy of the Medford Public Library.)

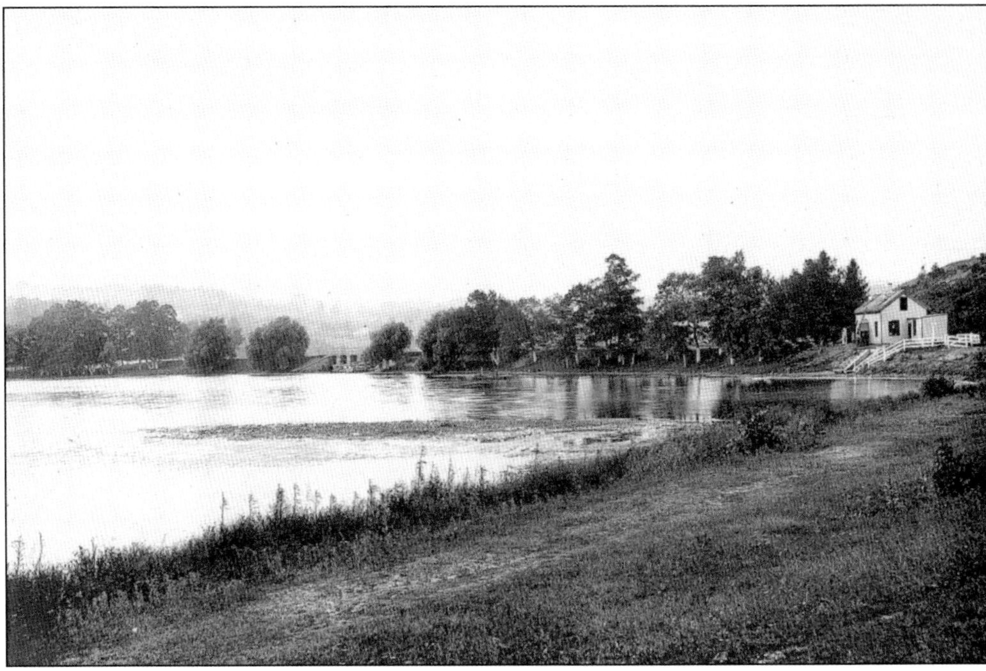

Before 1862 the upper and lower Mystic Lakes were a single body of water called Medford Pond. In 1863 a dam was built in a narrow section of the pond to create two lakes. The dam—seen in the distance in this photograph—was completed in 1863, and the upper Mystic Lake became the water supply for Charlestown. (Courtesy of the Medford Public Library.)

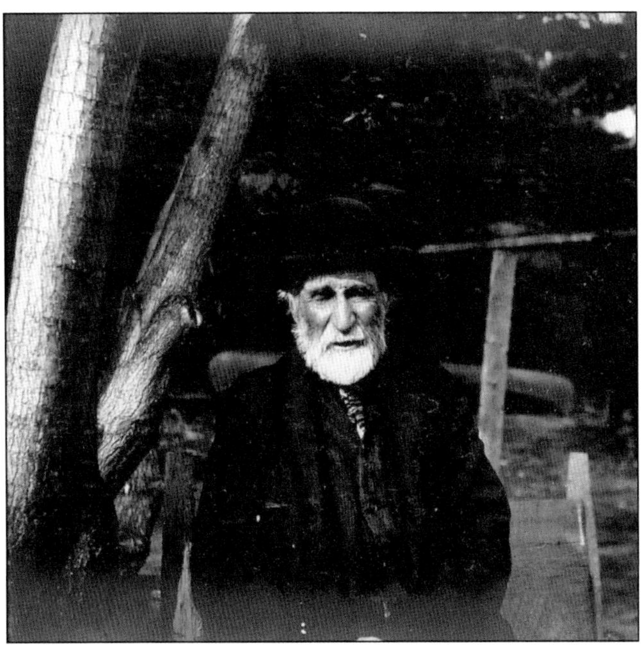

Gatekeeper Thomas Daly, who lived on the edge of the lower Mystic Lake, monitored the water levels and controlled the overflow mechanisms for the upper lake. Born in Ireland in 1838 to a family of 16 children, Daly became gatekeeper in 1872 and remained at his post until his death in 1905. (Courtesy of the Medford Public Library.)

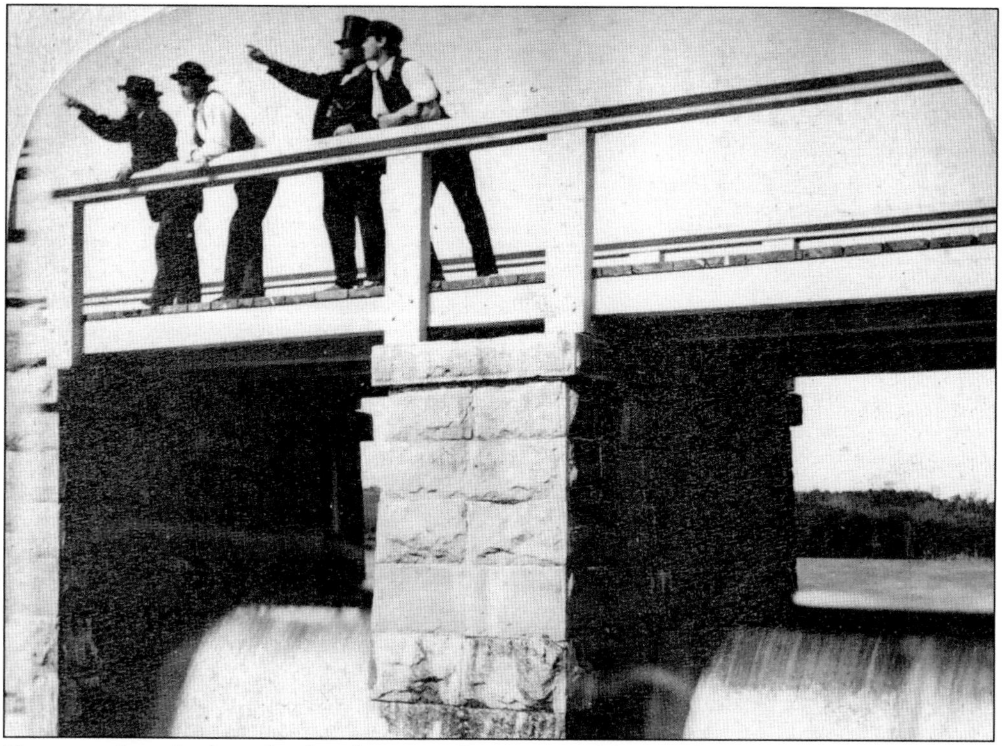

Here is a closer look at the dam between the upper and lower lakes. Enjoying the view from the bridge are, from left to right, Elijah Smith, unidentified, George Nichols, and Cyrus Gibbs. (Courtesy of the Medford Historical Society.)

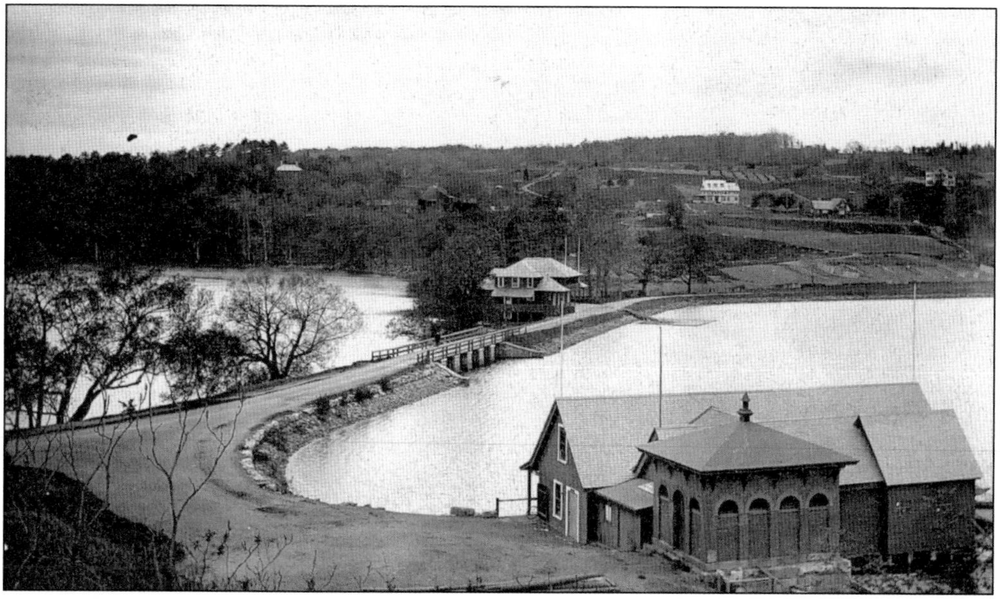

The Medford Boat Club was formed in 1898 to take advantage of the boating opportunities on the Mystic Lakes. The clubhouse seen in the rear of the picture was built in 1899. In the foreground is the pumping station for the Mystic Water Works, which supplied water to Charlestown. (Courtesy of the Medford Historical Society.)

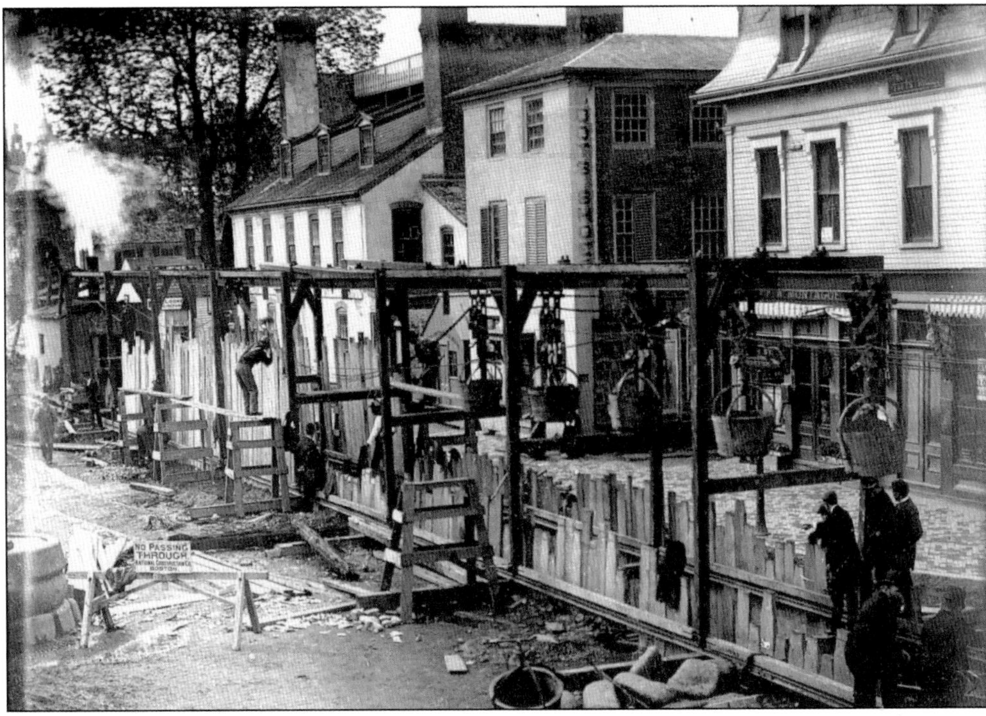

Discussion of a town sewerage system began in the 1870s, but no action was taken until the Metropolitan Sewer Commission was created. The Medford Sewer Commission started work in the 1890s. This 1891 photograph captures the National Construction Company of Boston installing the sewer system in the middle of High Street. (Courtesy of the Medford Public Library.)

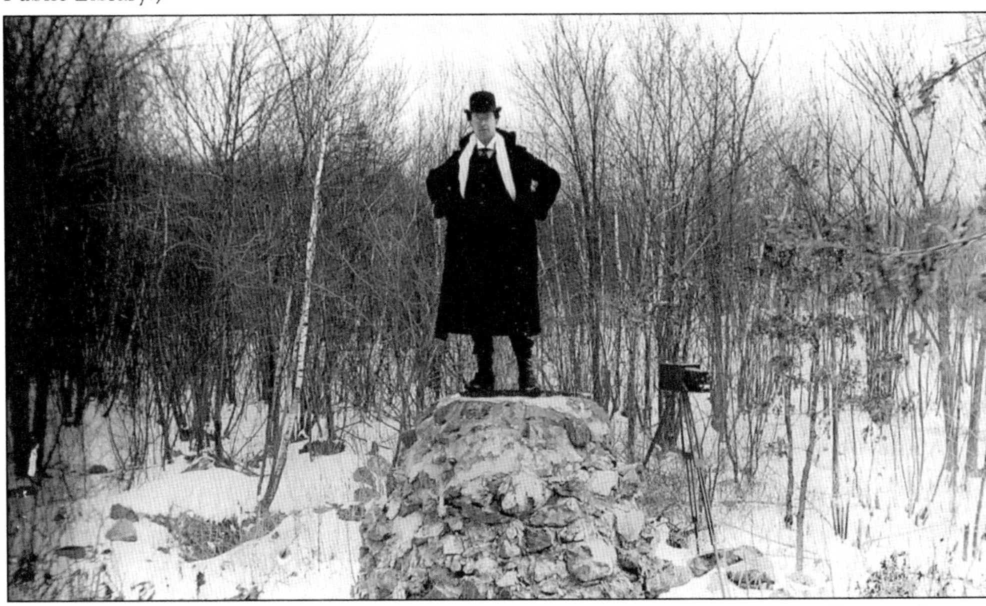

Victorian manholes were more substantial than the modern variety. Seen standing on this one is Arthur Peabody Pratt of Hillside Road, who later became minister of the Congregational church in Greenfield, Massachusetts. (Courtesy of the Medford Historical Society.)

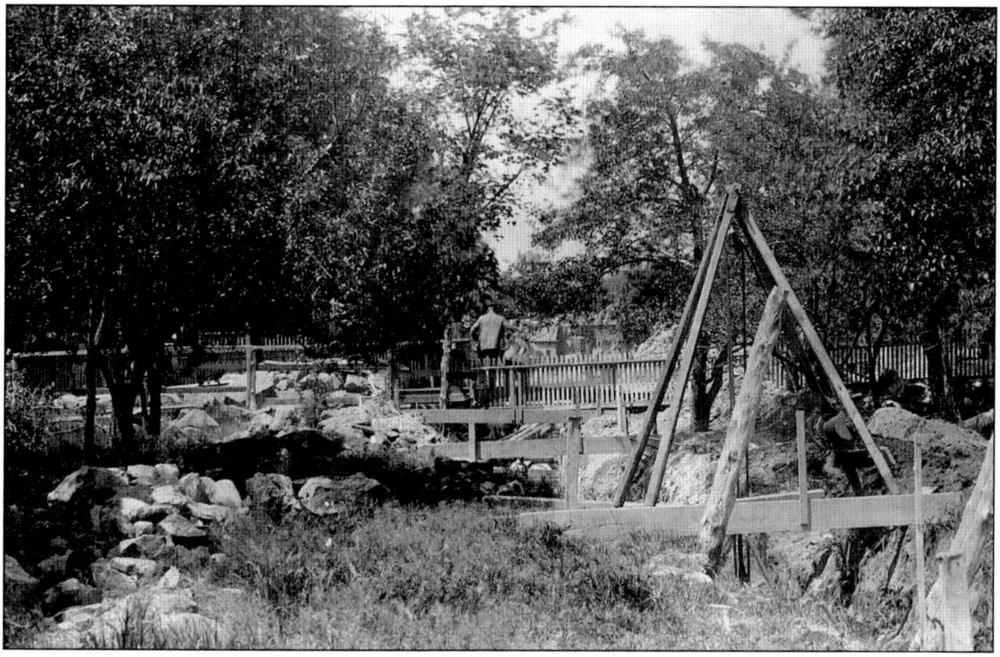

In the last decades of the 19th century, the city was busy with improvements of all kinds. The improvement of Gravelly Creek has gone down in town history as an engineering nightmare. The creek frequently overflowed and leaked into houses, and the town was constantly filling it in, building retaining walls, and rerouting the flow. This 1890s photograph shows one of the town's many attempts to conquer nature. (Courtesy of the Medford Historical Society.)

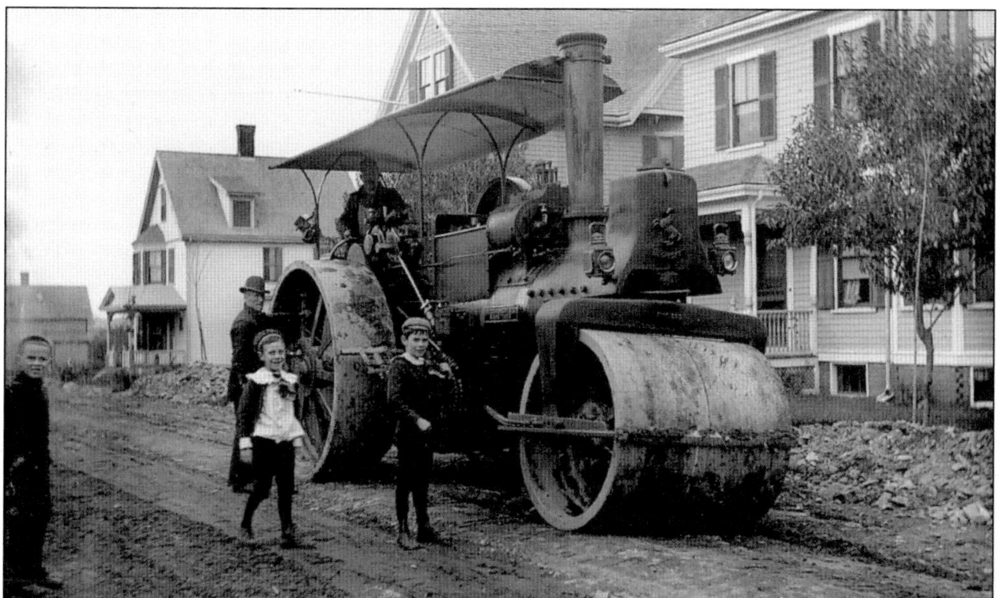

A crowd of children and a very big steamroller attend the paving of Emery Street on October 8, 1896. The steamroller was a sign of the times; the city purchased it for $4,200 in order to put new streets in front of all of the new houses. The steamroller used a ton of coal every four days. (Courtesy of the Medford Public Library.)

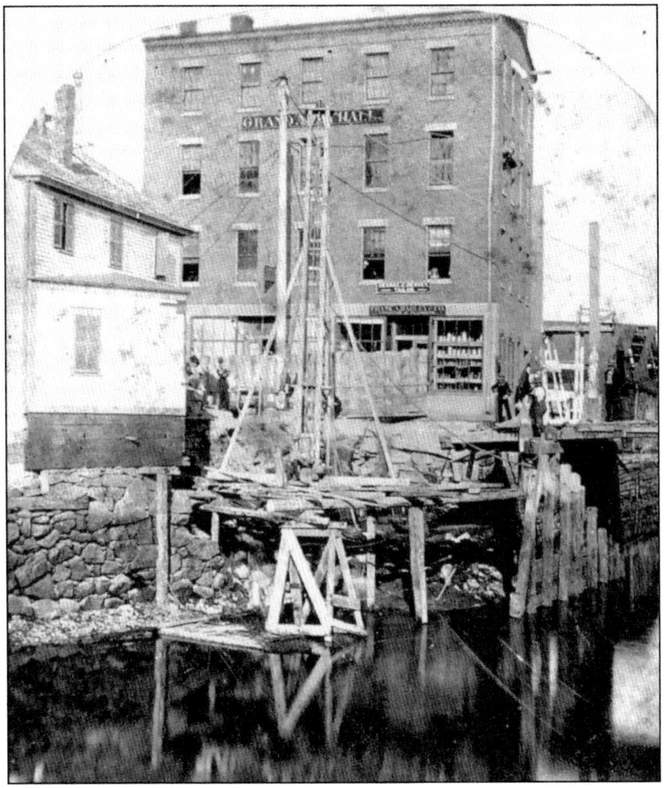

Until 1879 Cradock Bridge was a wooden drawbridge that allowed passage of large ships. In 1879, however, the shipyards along the upper part of the river had closed, and the town voted to built a permanent stone bridge. Here, the wooden bridge is being demolished. In the background is the Grand Army Hall. (Courtesy of the Medford Historical Society.)

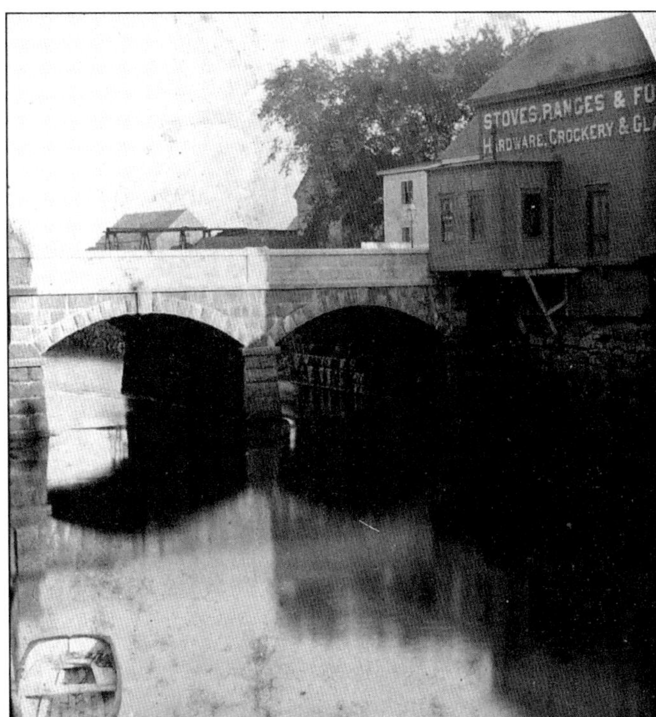

The new granite bridge is photographed on its completion in 1880. The town was pleased with the design of the new bridge, but its construction also served as a sad reminder that Medford's shipbuilding days were past. (Courtesy of the Medford Historical Society.)

Five

THE CIVIL WAR

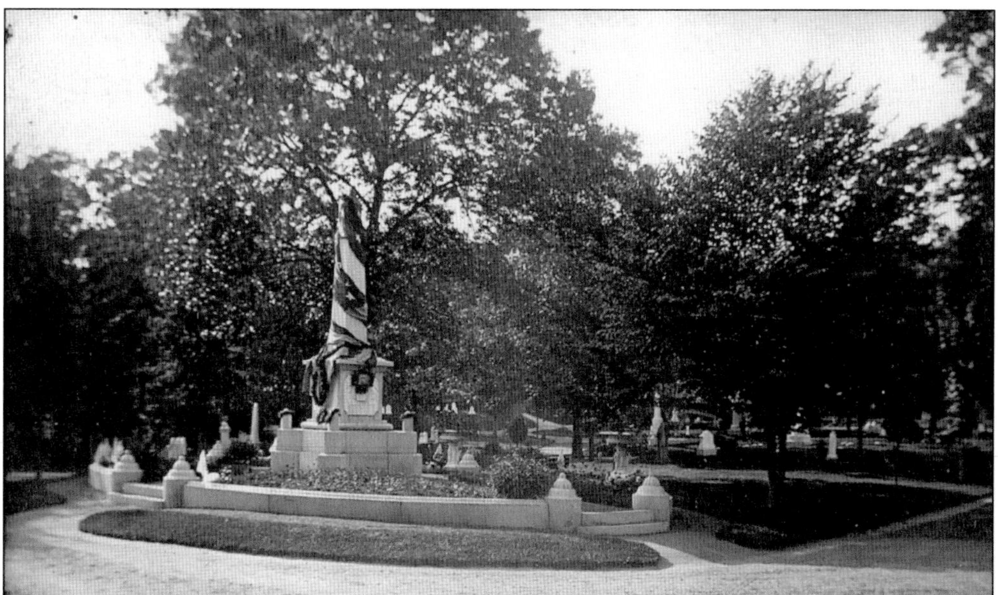

The monument to Medford's Civil War dead was dedicated in Oak Grove Cemetery in 1866. Of the 769 Medford men who fought in the war, 43 died in the conflict. (Courtesy of the Medford Historical Society.)

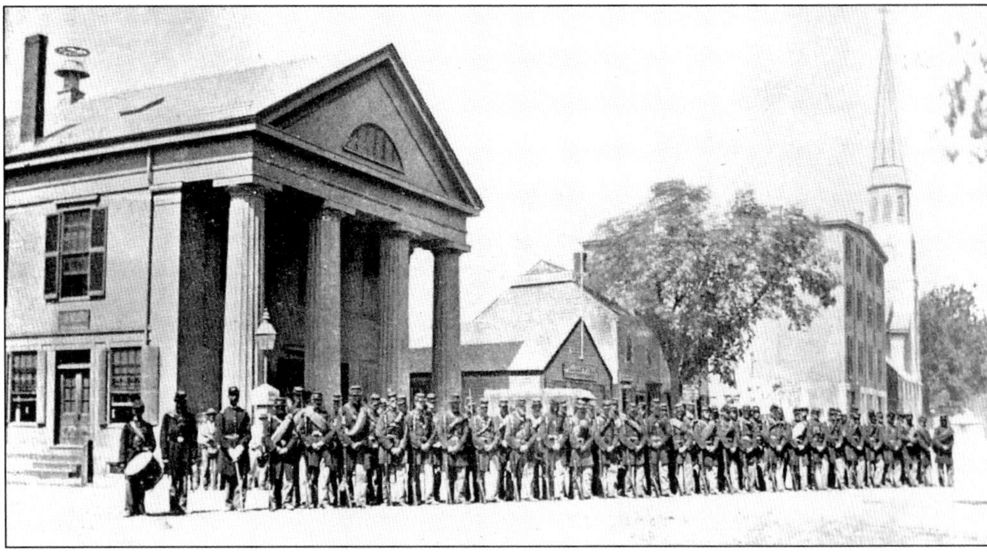

The Lawrence Light Guard, Company E of the Massachusetts Militia, was formed in 1854. In 1861 the regiment went into service for three months and fought at the First Battle of Bull Run. In 1862 the company responded a second time and mustered in for three years. This rare photograph of the Medford Company shows the Lawrence Light Guard ready for departure under Capt. Charles Currier on September 23, 1862. (Courtesy of the Medford Historical Society.)

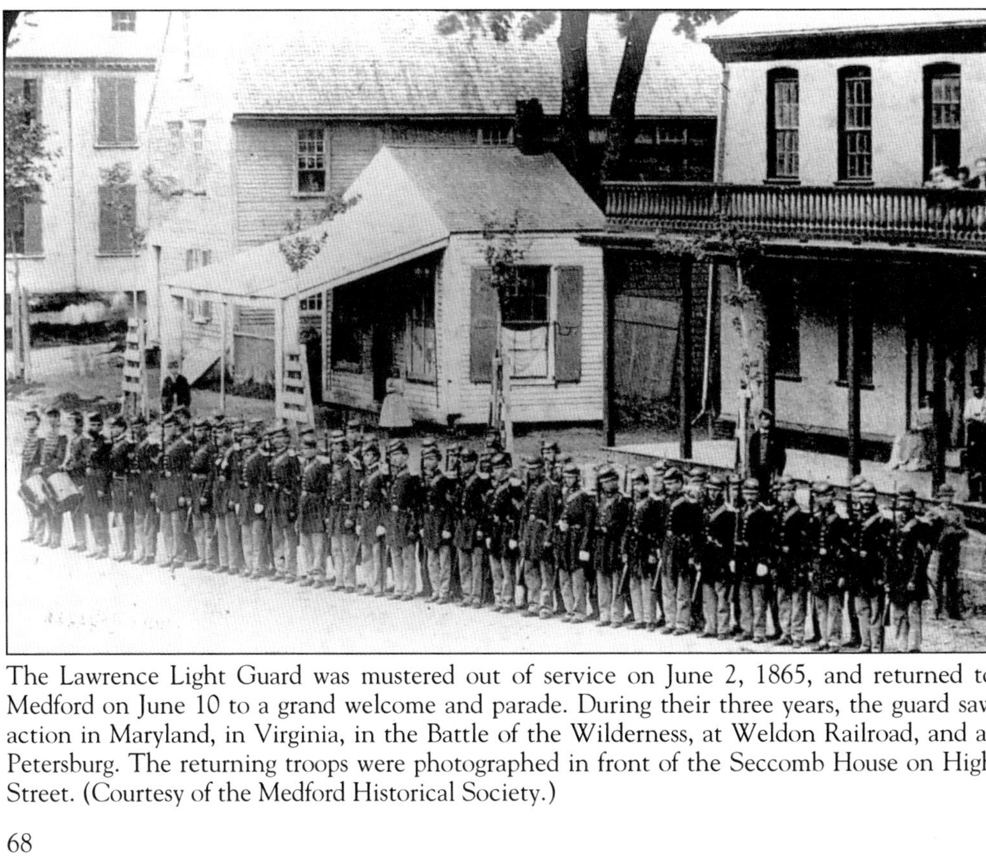

The Lawrence Light Guard was mustered out of service on June 2, 1865, and returned to Medford on June 10 to a grand welcome and parade. During their three years, the guard saw action in Maryland, in Virginia, in the Battle of the Wilderness, at Weldon Railroad, and at Petersburg. The returning troops were photographed in front of the Seccomb House on High Street. (Courtesy of the Medford Historical Society.)

Samuel Crocker Lawrence joined the Massachusetts Militia in 1854. The Medford Company adopted the name of Lawrence Light Guard in honor of his father, Daniel, and Samuel held the rank of colonel when the regiment mustered into service in 1861. He was wounded at the First Battle of Bull Run but recovered and led the guard in their other engagements. He mustered out at the rank of brigadier general. (Courtesy of the Medford Historical Society.)

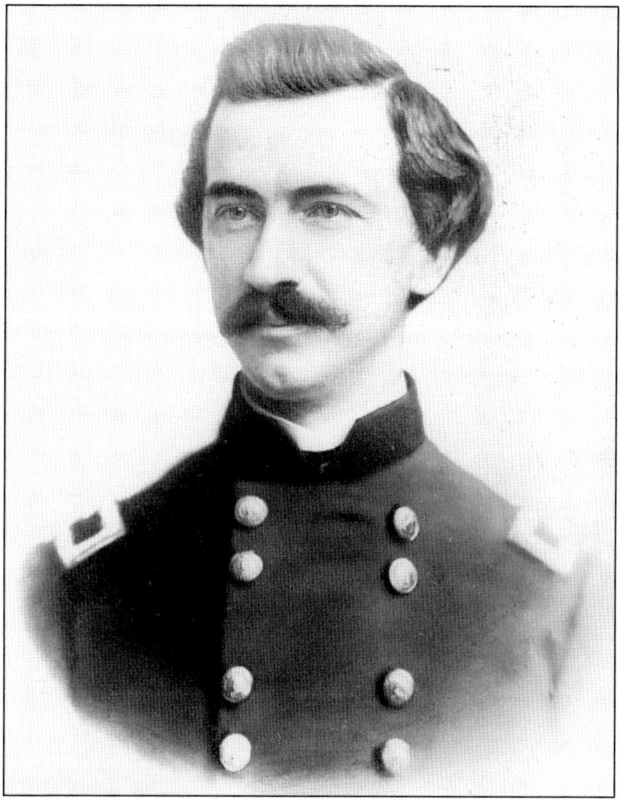

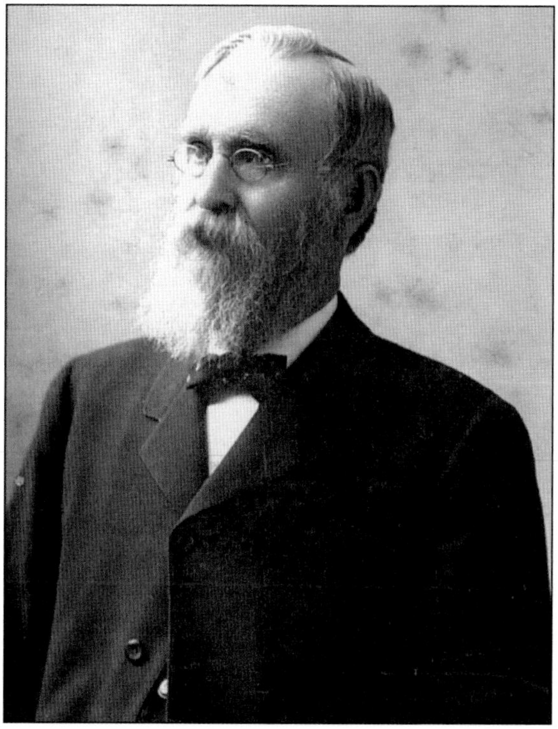

Capt. John Hutchins was a ship's carpenter in civilian life. During the war, in 1863, Hutchins and nine other Medford soldiers were captured at Weldon Railroad. They were imprisoned at Libby Prison and Belle Isle prison, where they suffered great hardships, and several of them died. After the war, Hutchins worked as a carpenter in the Charlestown Naval Yard. (Courtesy of the Medford Historical Society.)

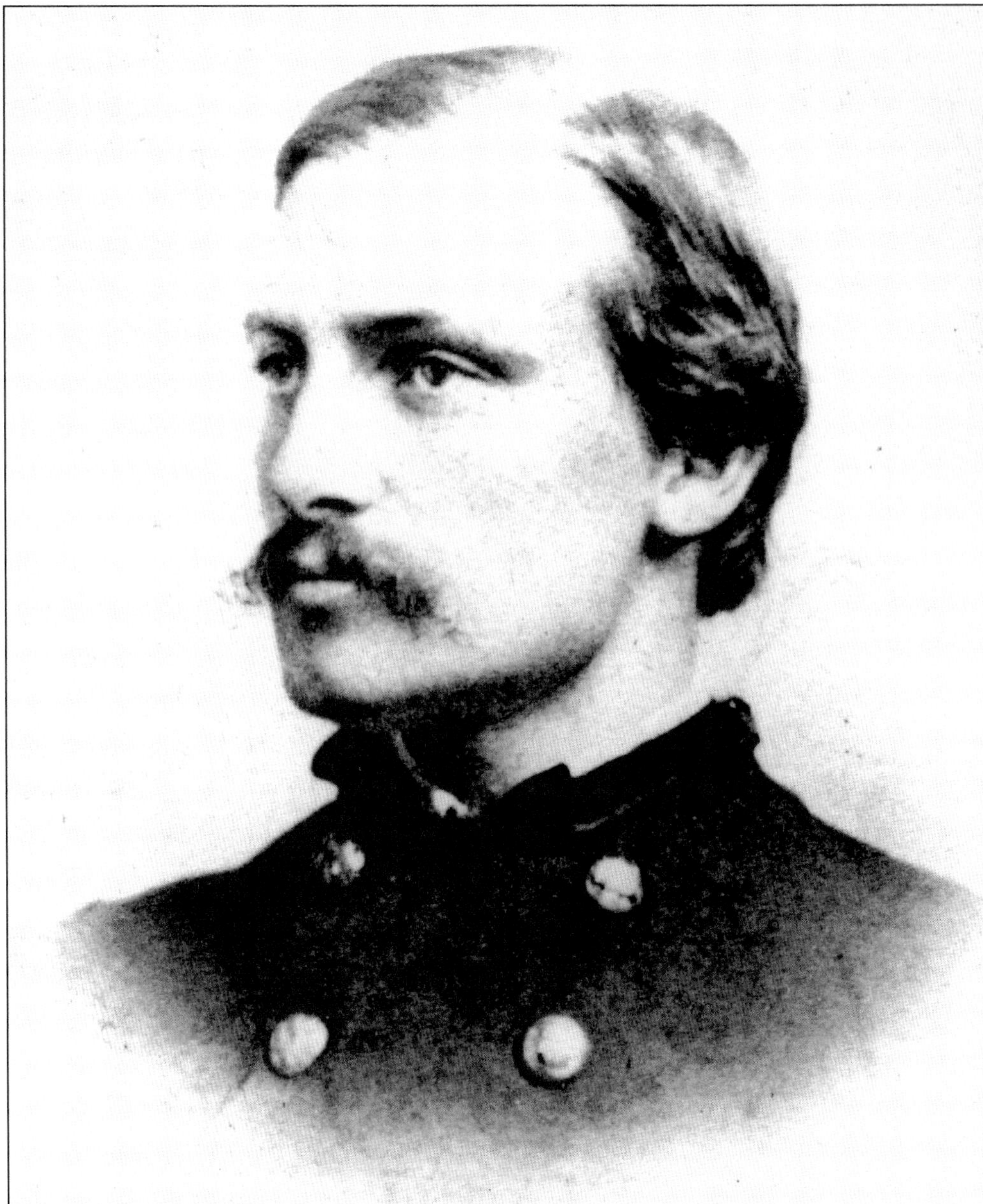

Medford men served in many regiments other than the Lawrence Light Guard. Edward and Norwood Hallowell were officers in the Massachusetts 54th and 55th Regiments of African American soldiers. The Hallowells were Quakers who set aside their pacifism because of their abolitionist beliefs. The dashing Edward joined the 20th Massachusetts in January 1862 and was commissioned captain of the 54th in March 1863, after the death of Robert Gould Shaw. (Courtesy of the Massachusetts Historical Society.)

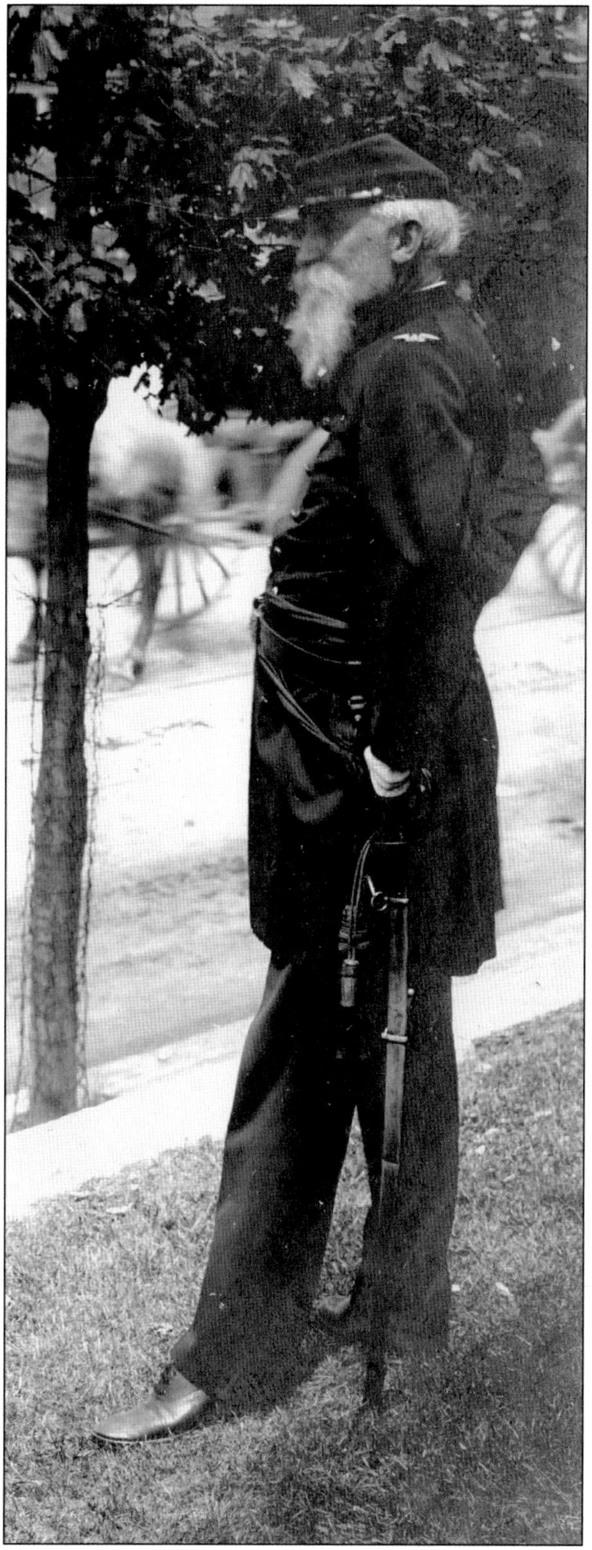

Norwood Hallowell joined the 20th Massachusetts in 1861 and was wounded at Antietam. In April 1862 he was appointed lieutenant of the 55th Massachusetts, the second African American regiment. He was discharged in November 1863 for disability resulting from battle wounds. The Hallowells settled in Medford and worked in the wool trade. Edward died in 1871 from an illness that he had contracted while in military service. Norwood lived in Medford until his death on April 11, 1914. This splendid photograph shows him in his uniform at a Memorial Day parade in the early 1900s. (Courtesy of the Massachusetts Historical Society.)

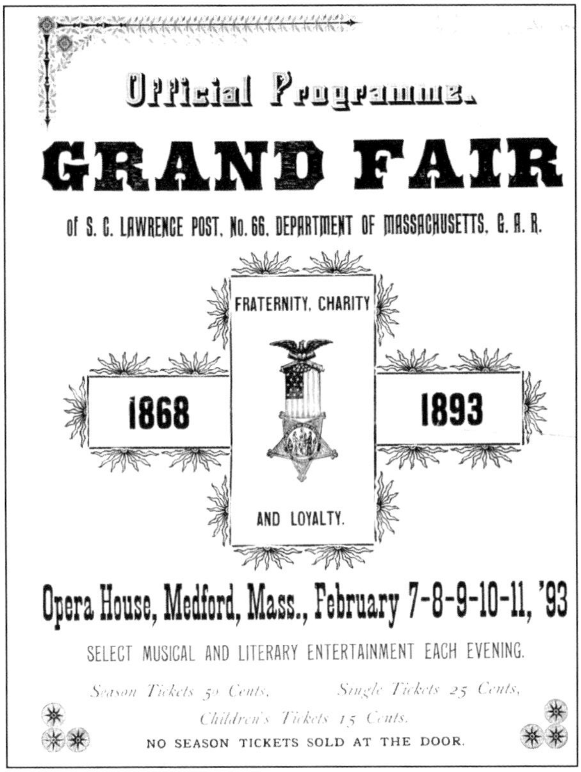
Official Programme.

GRAND FAIR

of S. C. LAWRENCE POST, No. 66, DEPARTMENT OF MASSACHUSETTS, G. A. R.

FRATERNITY, CHARITY

1868

1893

AND LOYALTY.

Opera House, Medford, Mass., February 7-8-9-10-11, '93

SELECT MUSICAL AND LITERARY ENTERTAINMENT EACH EVENING.

Season Tickets 50 Cents, Single Tickets 25 Cents,

Children's Tickets 15 Cents.

NO SEASON TICKETS SOLD AT THE DOOR.

The Samuel Crocker Lawrence Post, No. 66, Grand Army of the Republic (GAR), was organized in 1868. The organization raised funds for the relief of veterans and their families through social events like this grand fair in 1893. (Courtesy of the Medford Public Library.)

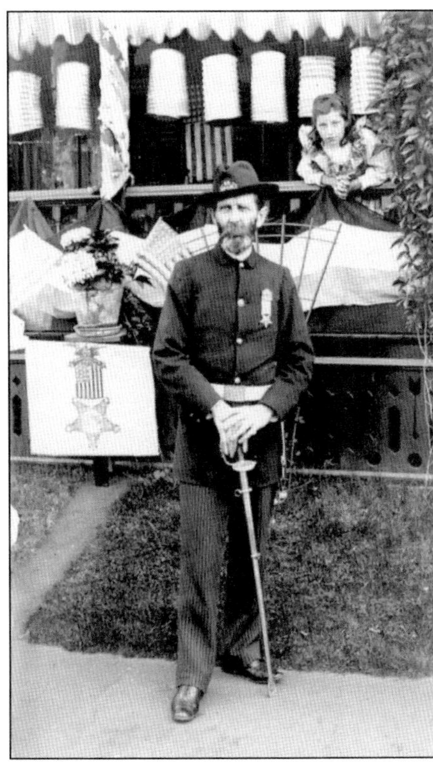

Oscar Allen is seen here on July 4, 1891, with his granddaughter Grace in the background. Allen, a resident of Boston at the time of the war, saw action with the 44th Massachusetts. He settled in Medford in the 1880s and was very active in the GAR. The banner hanging beside him bears the GAR insignia. (Courtesy of the Medford Public Library.)

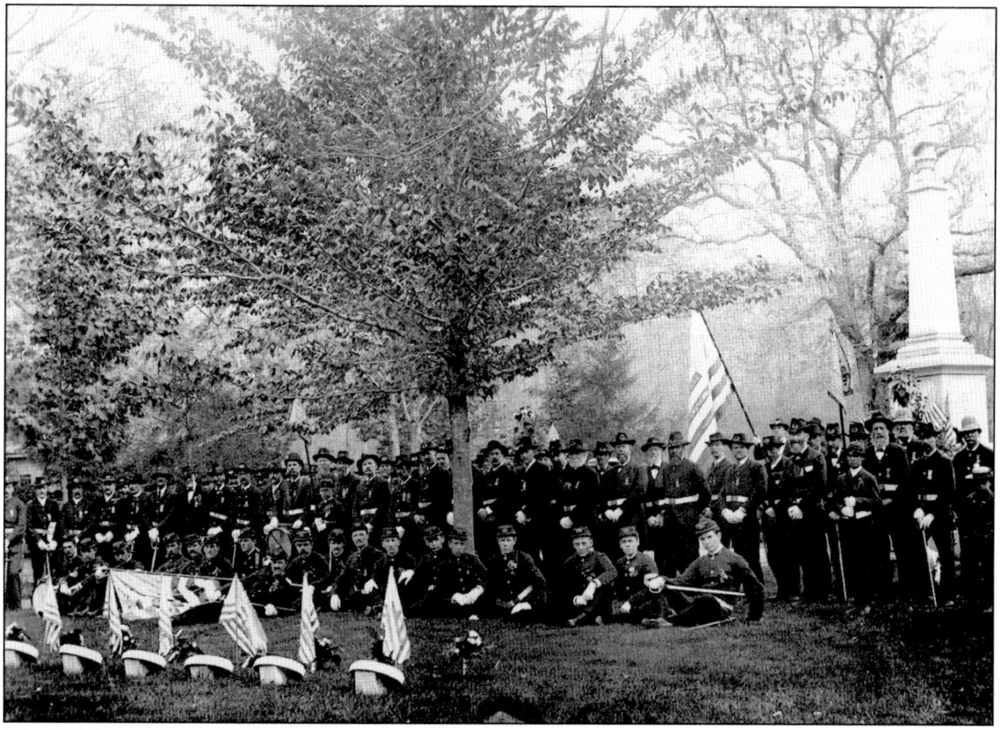

The GAR was particularly involved with the town's Memorial Day celebrations. The membership is seen here in 1888 at Oak Grove Cemetery. (Courtesy of the Medford Historical Society.)

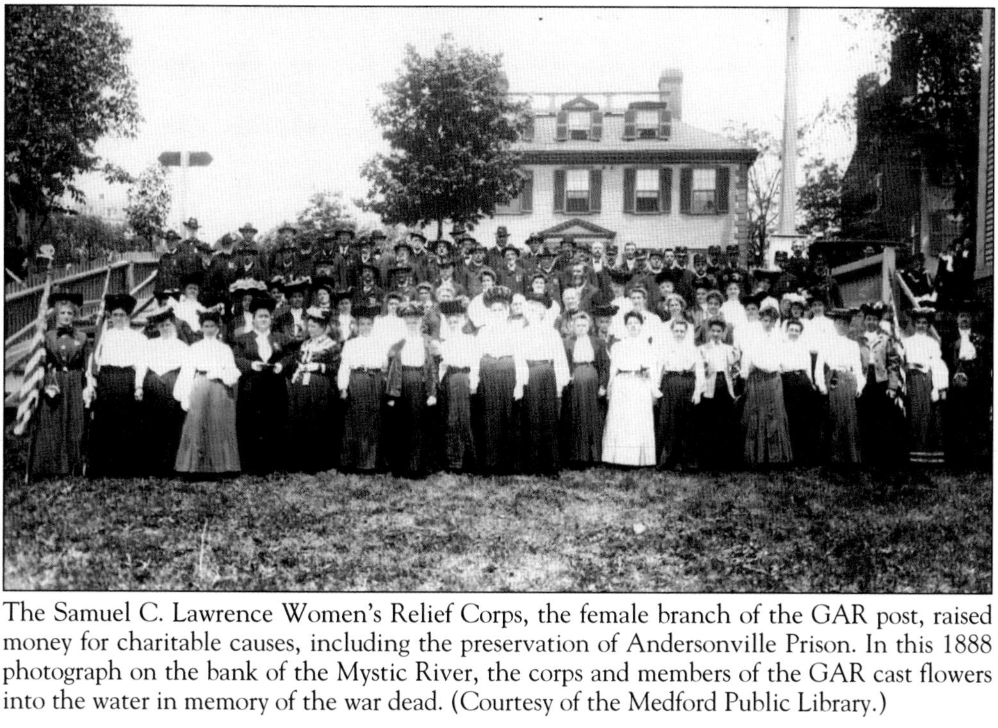

The Samuel C. Lawrence Women's Relief Corps, the female branch of the GAR post, raised money for charitable causes, including the preservation of Andersonville Prison. In this 1888 photograph on the bank of the Mystic River, the corps and members of the GAR cast flowers into the water in memory of the war dead. (Courtesy of the Medford Public Library.)

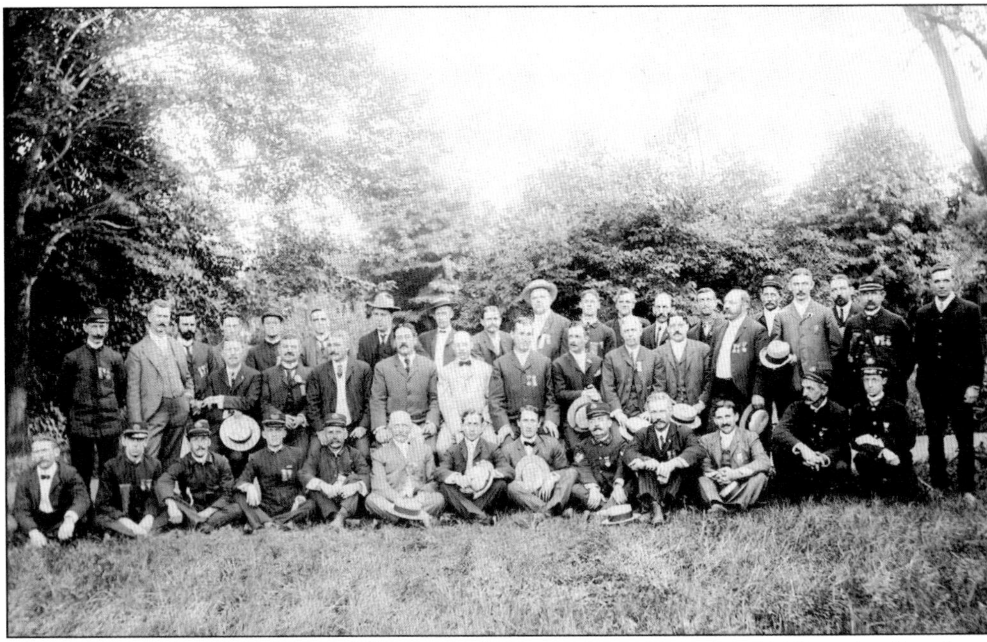

The S. C. Lawrence Corps 54 of the Sons of Veterans was formed in 1888, and a Daughters of Veterans organization in 1898. The members of the Sons of Veterans are seen here in 1904 posing on the lawn of the Royall House after a Grand Army of the Republic encampment in Boston. (Courtesy of the Medford Historical Society.)

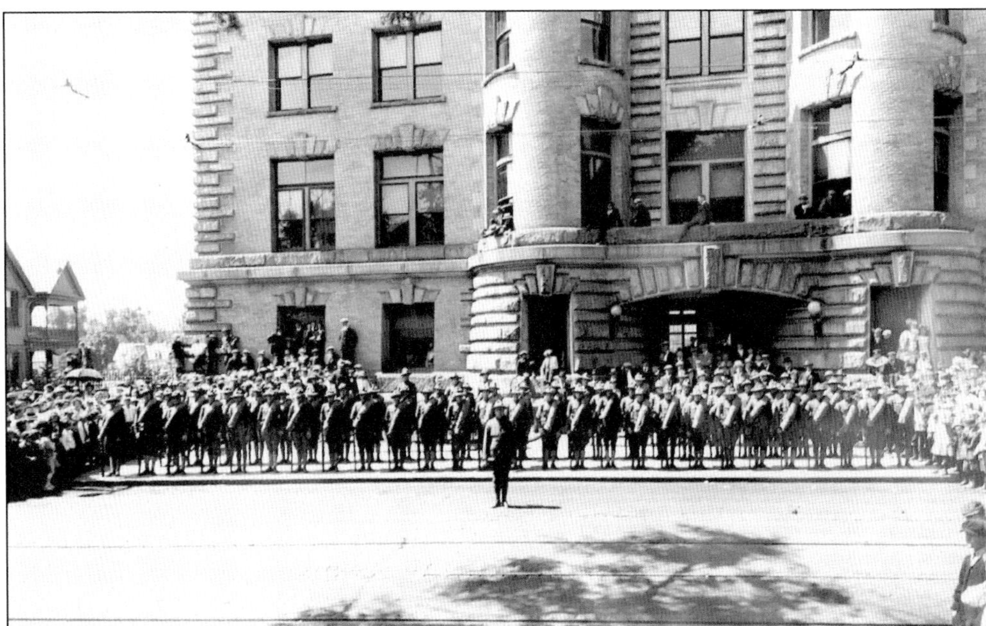

In 1902 Samuel Crocker Lawrence built the armory on High Street as quarters for the Grand Army of the Republic and the Lawrence Light Guard. The building was a substantial tribute to Medford's veterans and housed the guard until the 1980s. Members of the Lawrence Light Guard are shown here prior to their departure for service in World War I. (Courtesy of Joseph McGonagle.)

Six

SCHOOLS

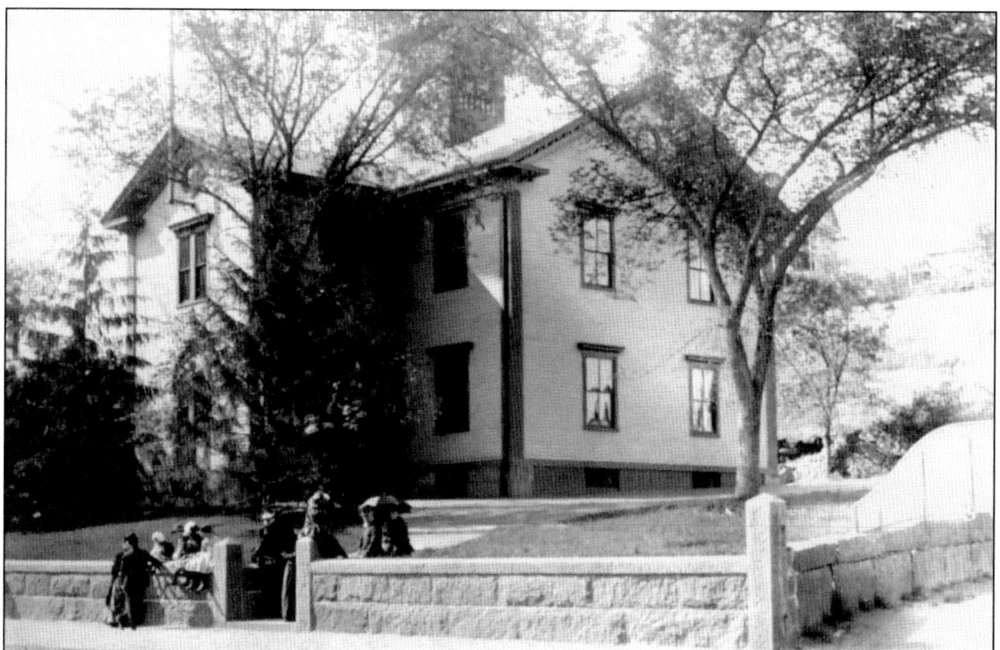

The first Medford High School was established in 1835 in the rear of the Unitarian church. In 1843 a new high school was built to accommodate the growing population. The wooden building on High Street was enlarged in 1866 and again in 1890. (Courtesy of the Medford Historical Society.)

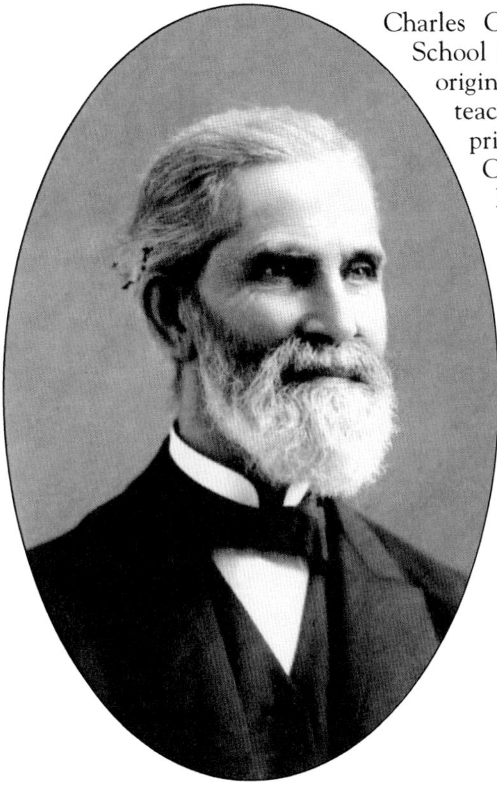

Charles Cummings was principal of Medford High School for 30 years, from 1846 to 1876. Cummings originally studied for the ministry but became a teacher instead. It is calculated that in his years as principal he was in charge of over 1,100 students. Cummings was also an active member of the Mystic Congregational Church. (Courtesy of the Medford Public Library.)

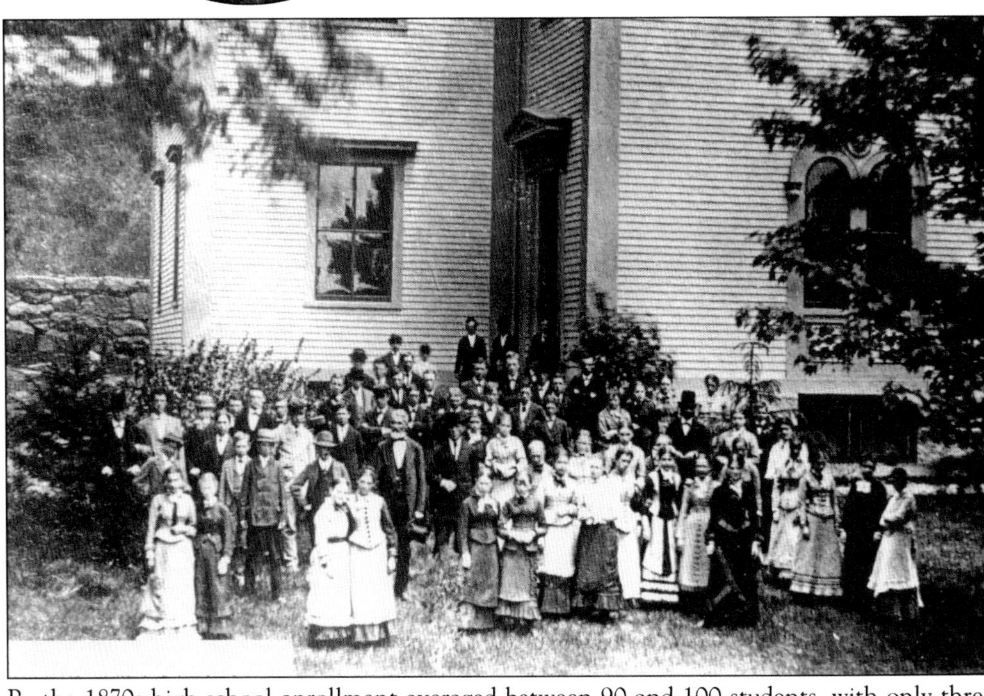

By the 1870s high school enrollment averaged between 90 and 100 students, with only three teachers. Seen here are the classes of 1876, 1877, and 1878. Principal Cummings is fifth from the left in the second row. (Courtesy of the Medford Public Library.)

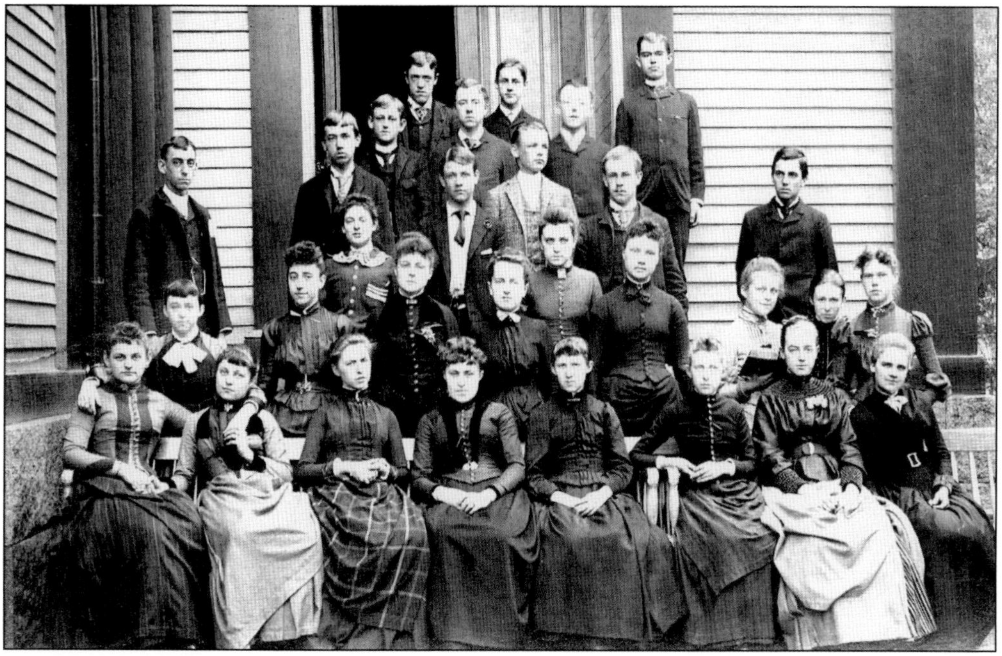

The class of 1889 poses in front of the high school. The size of the student body put a strain on the resources of the building, and in 1890 the school was remodeled and doubled in size. (Courtesy of the Medford Public Library.)

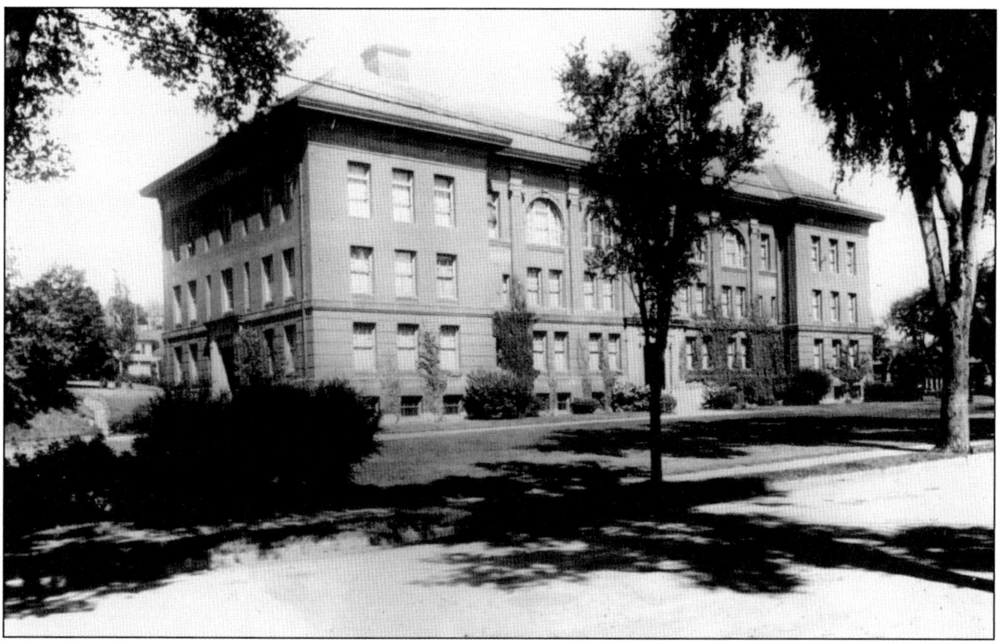

By the 1890s the high school held close to 300 students. To handle the growing population, a new building, which could hold up to 600 students, was constructed on Forest Street. It was designed in a Renaissance style, with Greek details, by the architectural firm of Hartwell, Richardson, and Driver. The building was dedicated with great ceremony in May 1896. (Courtesy of the Medford Public Library.)

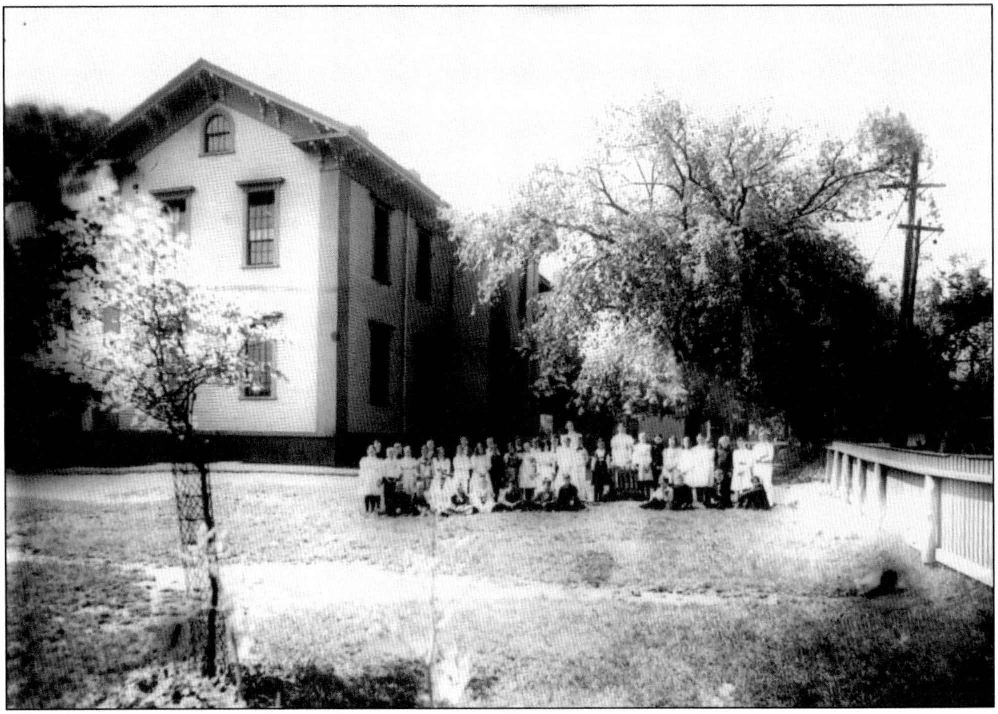

The Swan Primary School, named for Dr. Daniel Swan, was built on the corner of Park and Washington Streets in 1837. The original building was destroyed by fire in 1855 and was replaced by the structure seen in this 1880s photograph. The building stood until 1916, when it was torn down to make room for the Swan Junior High School. (Courtesy of the Medford Public Library.)

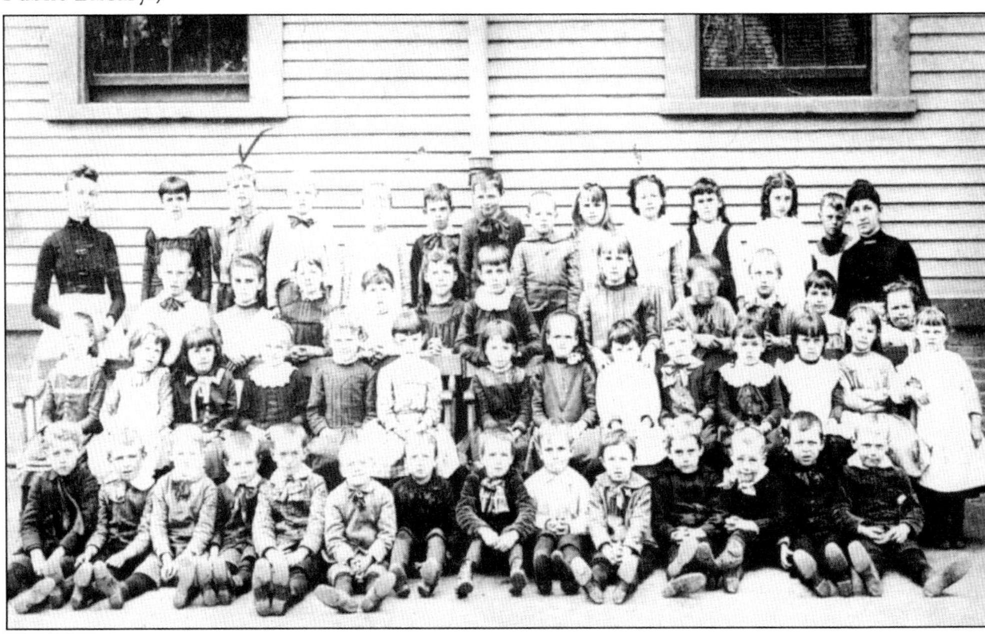

The unsmiling students of the Swan School pose in 1888. Teacher Anna Plunkett is at the left of the back row, and Carrie Hollis is on the right. (Courtesy of the Medford Historical Society.)

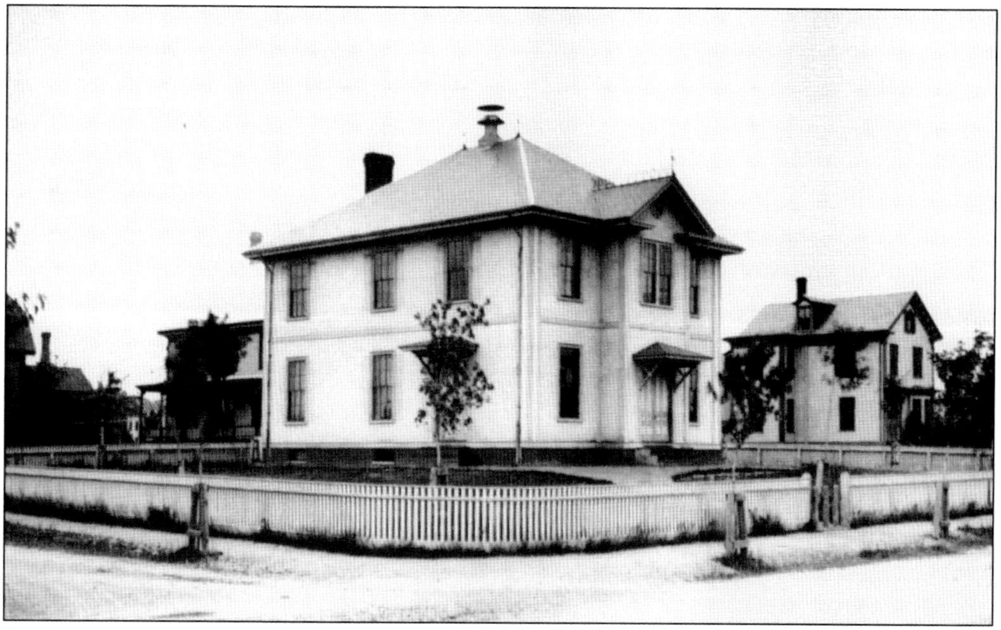

As the town grew, new schools were built to meet the demand in developing areas. The Hall School was built in 1879 to accommodate the students of West Medford. The building, located on the corner of Harvard Avenue and Sharon Street, remained in use until 1908. (Courtesy of the Medford Historical Society.)

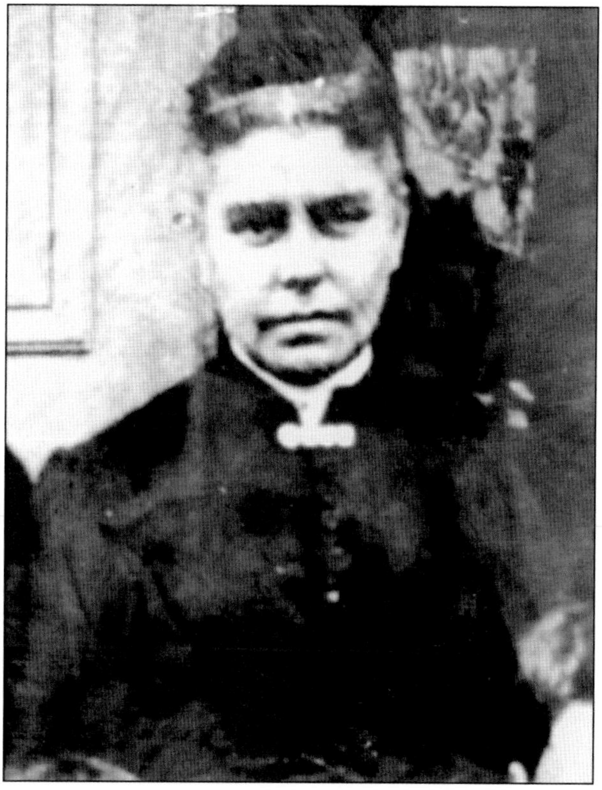

Ellen Lane was born in 1845 and was educated in the Medford schools. She began teaching in Medford in 1865. Lane was teacher and principal of the Hall School from its opening in 1879 until it closed—and she retired—in 1908. (Courtesy of the Medford Public Library.)

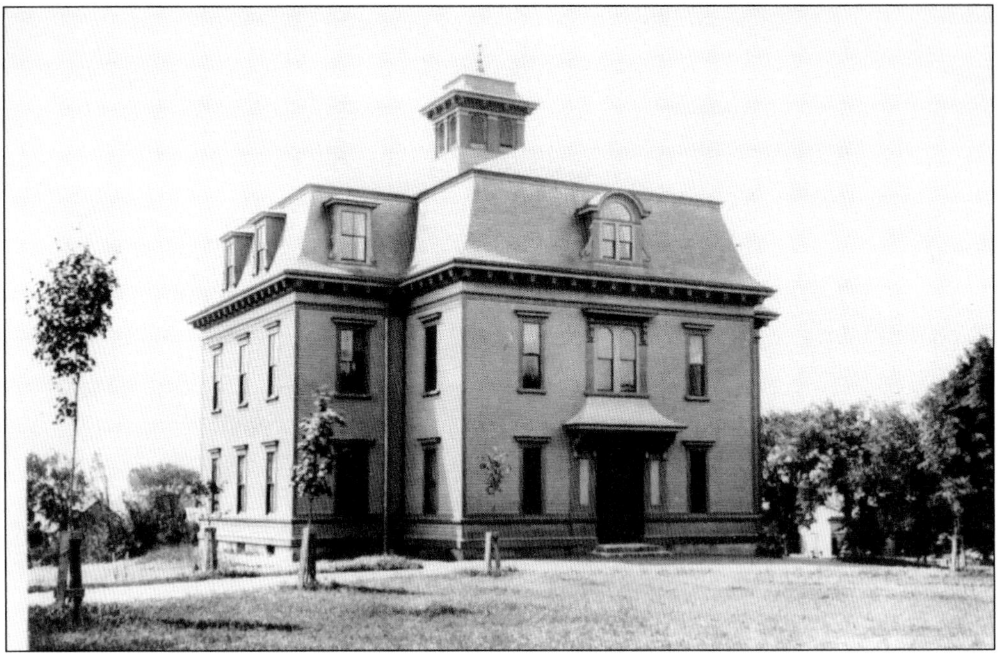

The Brooks School was erected in 1851 on the corner of Brooks and Irving Streets. The building had a distinctive architectural style, with a mansard roof and a cupola. It was used as a school until 1867, when it was sold to Edward Kakas, a furrier, as a residence. (Courtesy of the Medford Historical Society.)

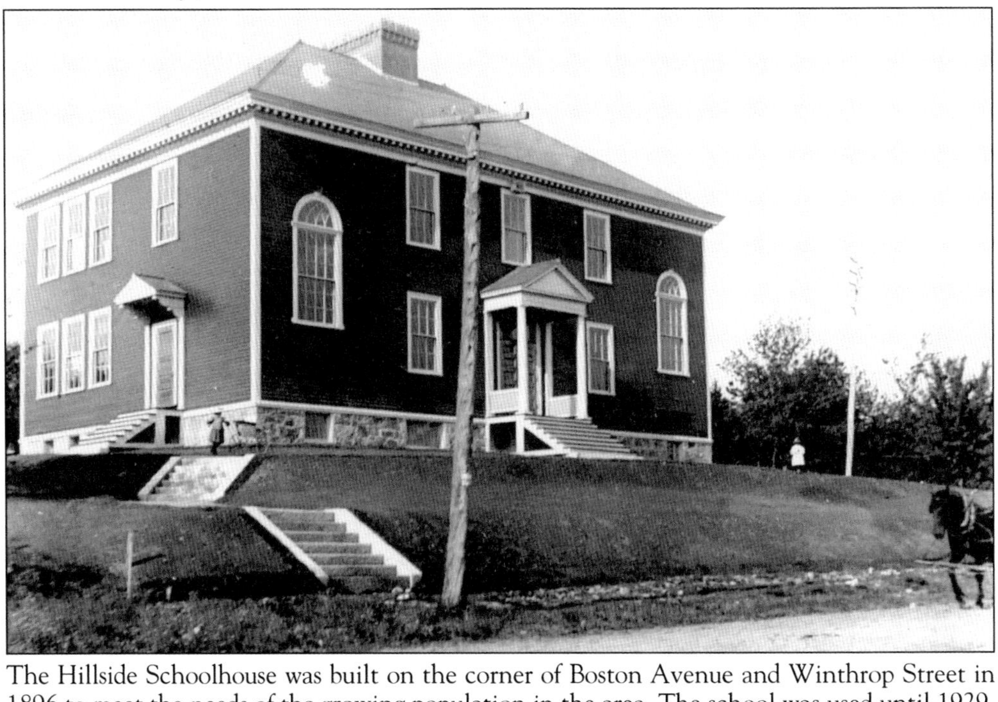

The Hillside Schoolhouse was built on the corner of Boston Avenue and Winthrop Street in 1896 to meet the needs of the growing population in the area. The school was used until 1929, when a new structure was built between Capen and Emery Streets. Notice the child on the left posing with her doll carriage. (Courtesy of the Medford Public Library.)

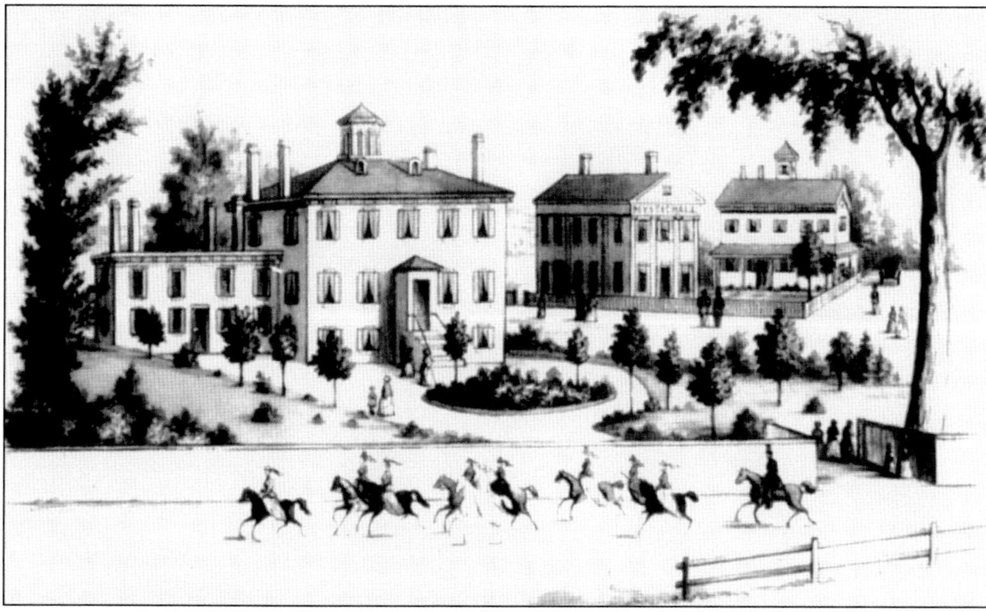

Private schools also flourished in Victorian Medford. The Mystic Hall Seminary for Young Ladies opened its doors in February 1855. The seminary had about 60 students, who were tutored in "the physical, the moral, the mental and the graceful." Henry Wadsworth Longfellow was a member of the board. In 1859 the seminary was moved to Washington, D.C., where its visitors included the Prince of Wales. (Courtesy of the Medford Public Library.)

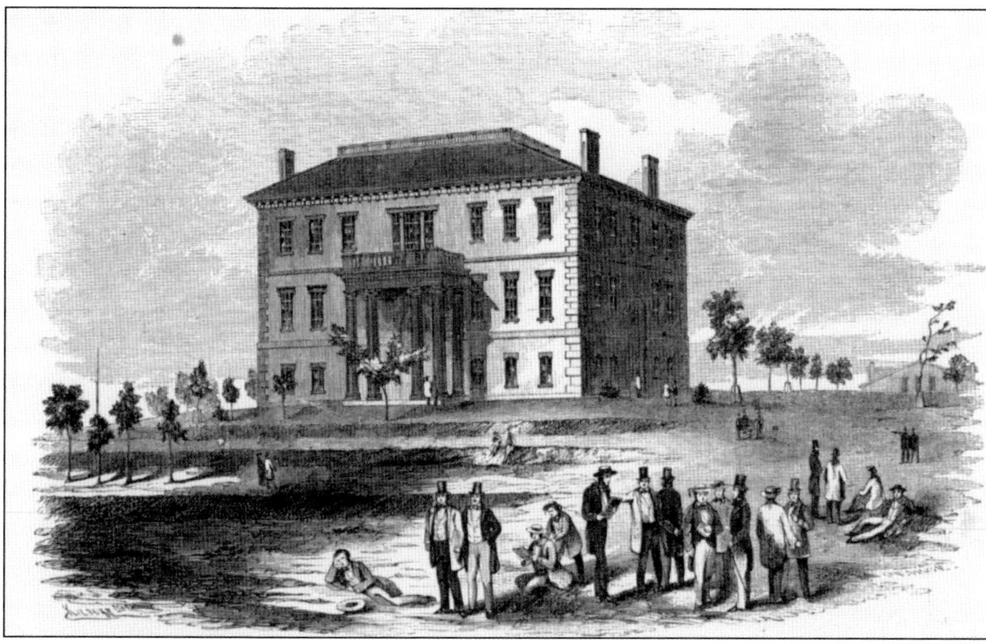

The most influential private school in Medford was Tufts College, which was founded in 1852. The college was built on land inherited by Universalist Charles Tufts, who offered the site to the Universalist church for a college. The first president was Hosea Ballou, a widely respected scholar and Universalist minister. This 1856 etching shows Ballou Hall, the first building of the college. (Collection of the author.)

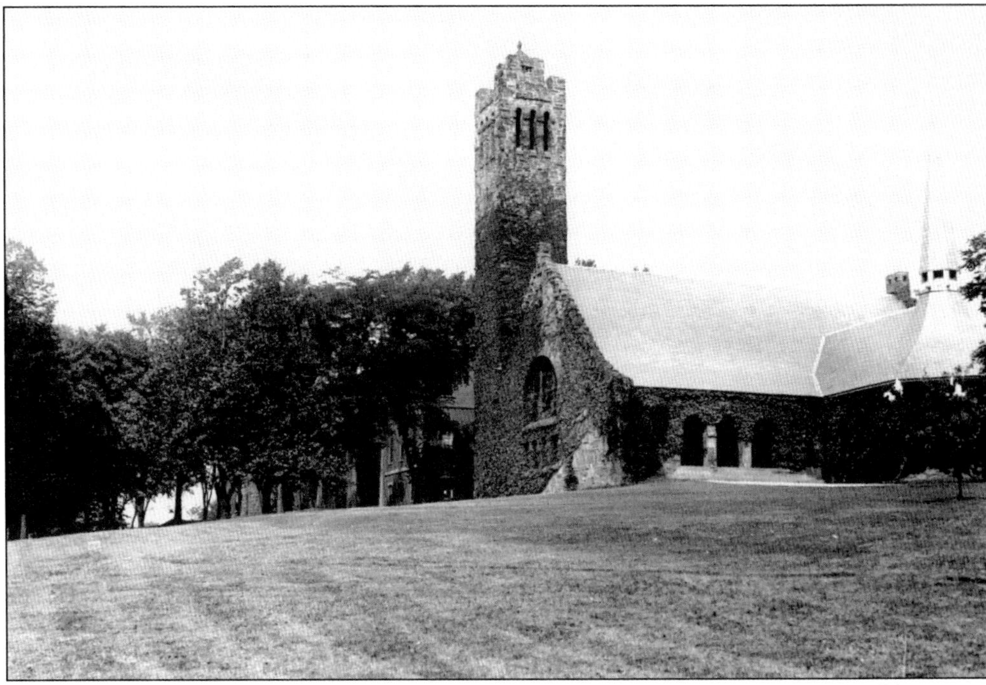

The college expanded gradually throughout the latter half of the century. The library was built in 1856, East Hall in 1860, and West Hall in 1872. The Goddard Chapel, seen here, was built in 1882 in memory of Thomas Goddard, a trustee and benefactor of the college. (Courtesy of the Medford Public Library.)

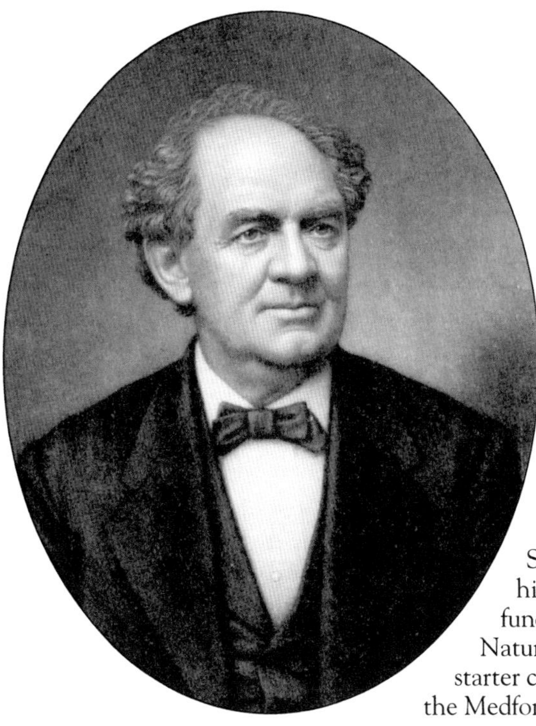

Showman P. T. Barnum entered into the history of Tufts in 1882, when he donated funds for the construction of the Barnum Natural History Museum, and also donated a starter collection of preserved animals. (Courtesy of the Medford Public Library.)

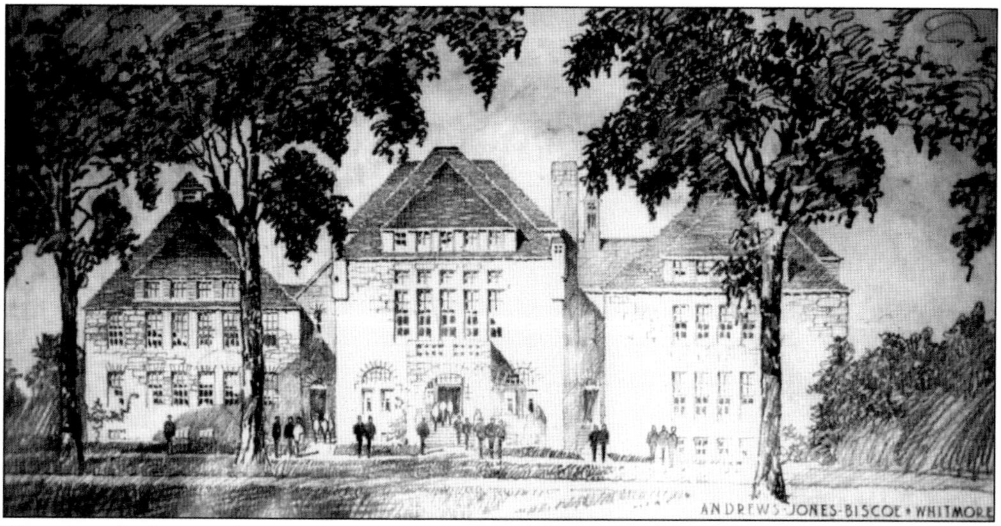

The plans for Barnum's museum were impressive. The center portion was built first, and wings were added later with money left to the college in Barnum's will. The museum, built of gray slate, contained classrooms and laboratories as well as exhibit space. (Courtesy of the Medford Public Library.)

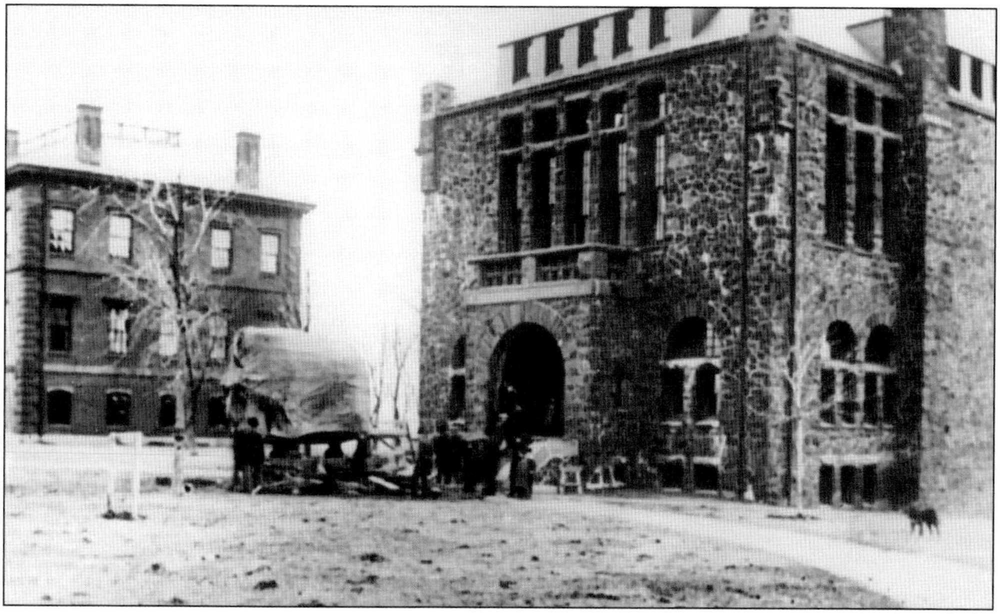

One of the biggest attractions in the Barnum Museum was Jumbo the Elephant. The elephant, a featured performer in the Barnum and Bailey Circus, was killed by a railroad train in 1885. This photograph shows the shrouded figure of the elephant being wheeled into the museum in 1889. (Courtesy of the Medford Public Library.)

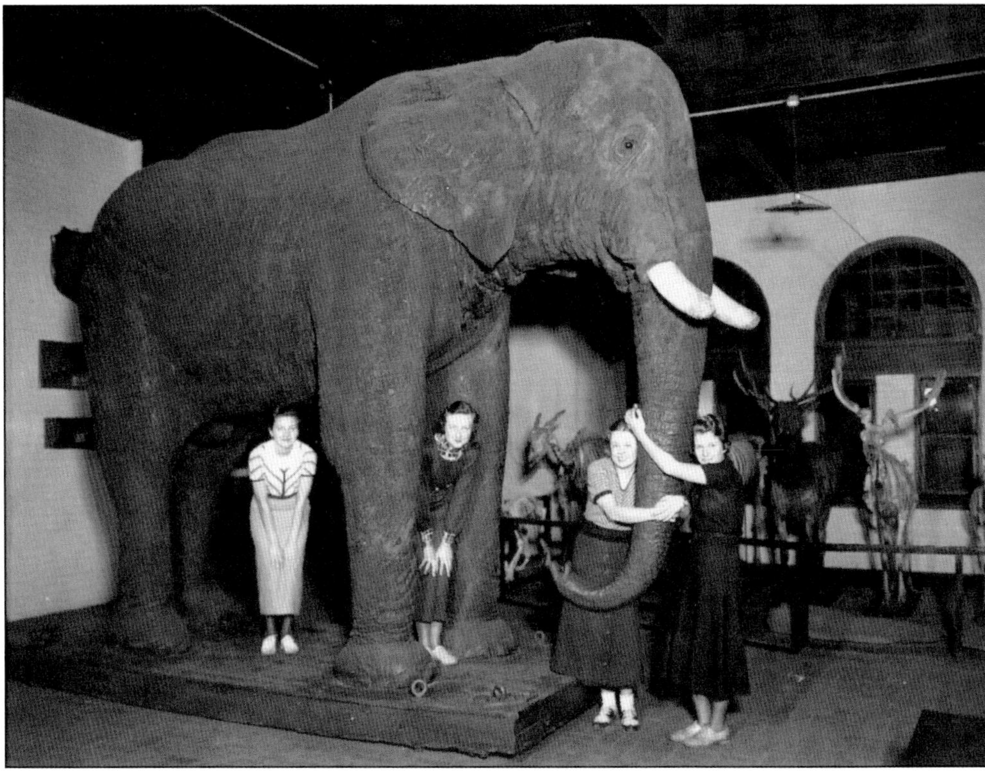

Jumbo became the mascot of the college and remained the museum's most popular exhibit until he was destroyed in a fire in 1975. He is seen here (with a twinkle in his eye), surrounded by coeds, sometime in the 1930s. (Courtesy of the Medford Public Library.)

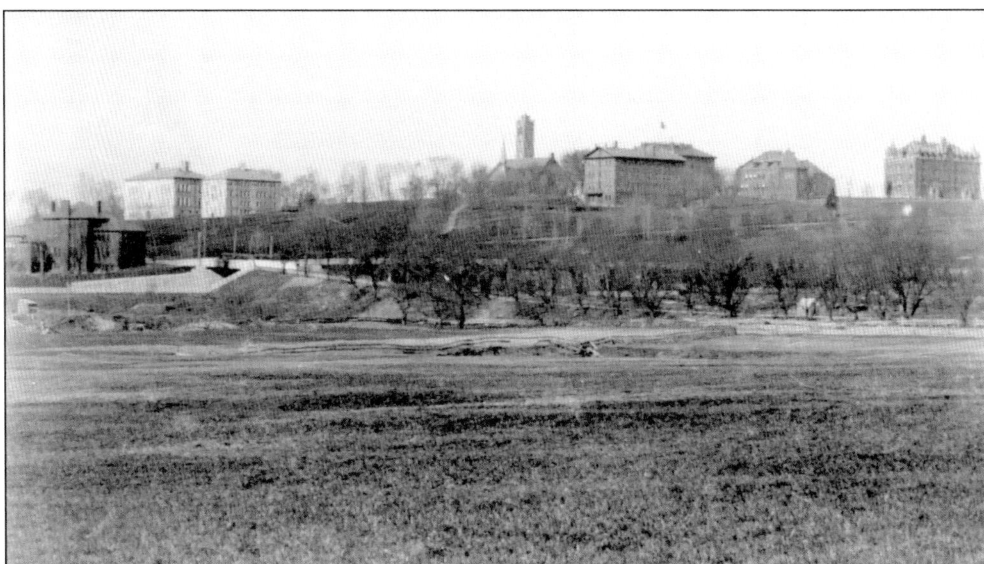

By the 1890s the college included a divinity school and a medical school, and female students had been admitted to the student body. The 1890s campus is seen here, high on the hill over Medford. (Courtesy of the Medford Public Library.)

Seven

CHURCHES

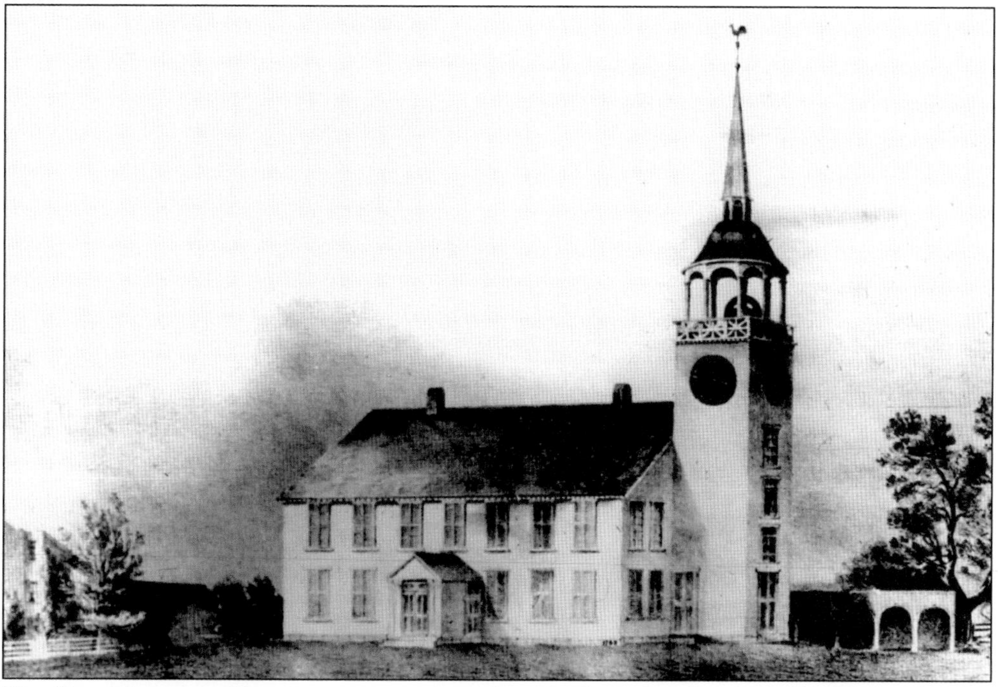

The First Unitarian Church was incorporated as the First Parish of Medford in 1824. This meetinghouse on High Street, built in 1770, was torn down in 1839. The number of churches in Medford grew along with the population throughout the 19th century. Until 1823 the Unitarian church was the only church in town, but by 1880 there were almost a dozen churches. (Courtesy of the Medford Public Library.)

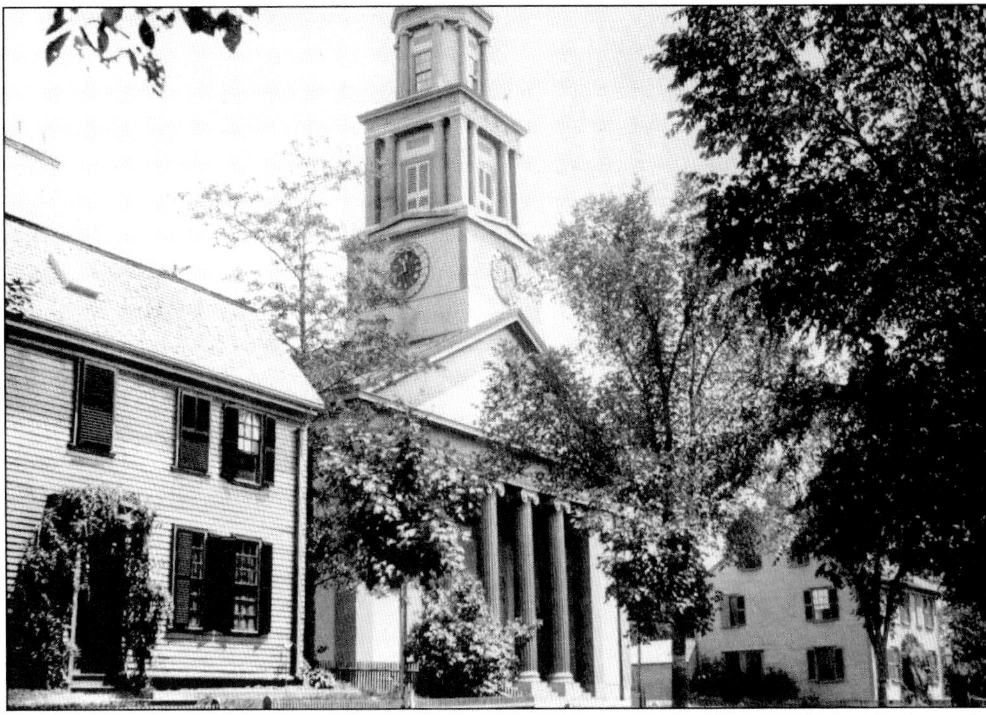

The new Unitarian church was dedicated on December 4, 1839. The church was built in the Greek Revival style popular in the 1830s. Notice the Greek columns and Doric pediments on the entrance. (Courtesy of the Medford Historical Society.)

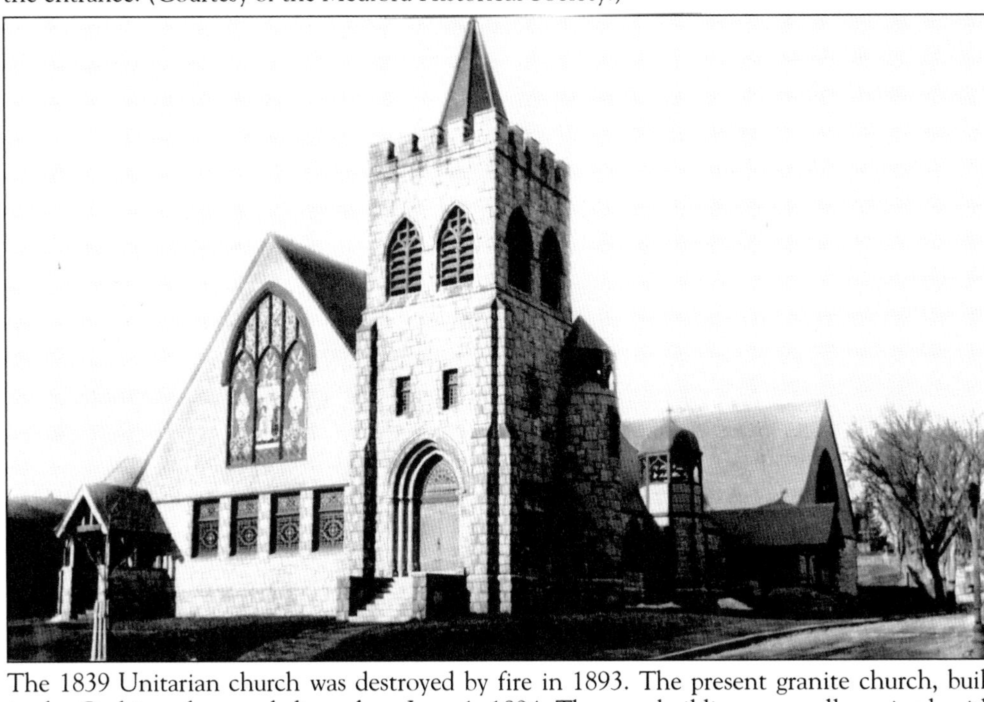

The 1839 Unitarian church was destroyed by fire in 1893. The present granite church, built in the Gothic style, was dedicated on June 1, 1894. The new building was well received, with special praise for the electric and gas chandeliers. (Courtesy of the Medford Historical Society.)

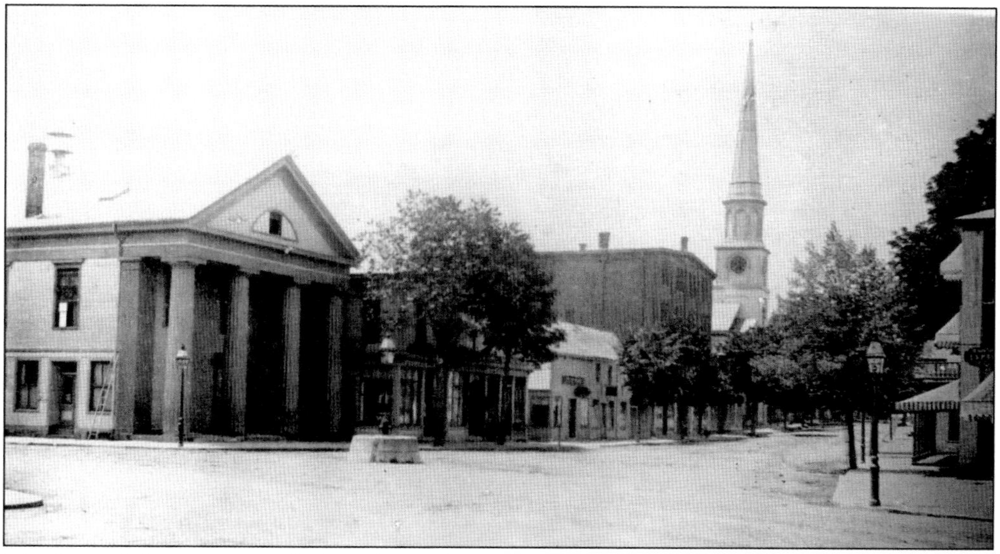

The Second Congregational Church was formed by members of the First Church in 1823, and in 1824 a church was built on High Street. When that structure burned in 1860, it was replaced with the building seen here next to the Masonic Apartments and the city hall. The church changed its name to the First Trinitarian Congregational Church in 1857. The building was later purchased by the Catholic church. (Courtesy of the Medford Public Library.)

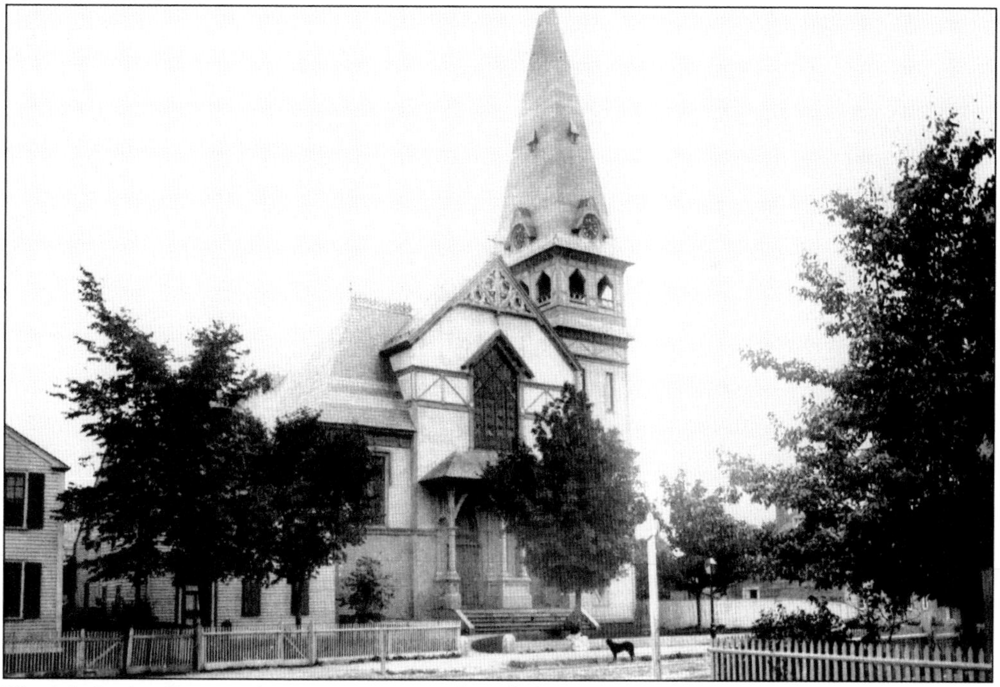

The Methodist Episcopal congregation was founded in 1822. Members met in a variety of places until 1845, when a small church was built, largely with volunteer labor by ship's carpenters. In 1873 the newer and larger church seen here, built in the Stick style of architecture, was erected on Salem Street. The building was destroyed by fire in 1905. (Courtesy of the Medford Historical Society.)

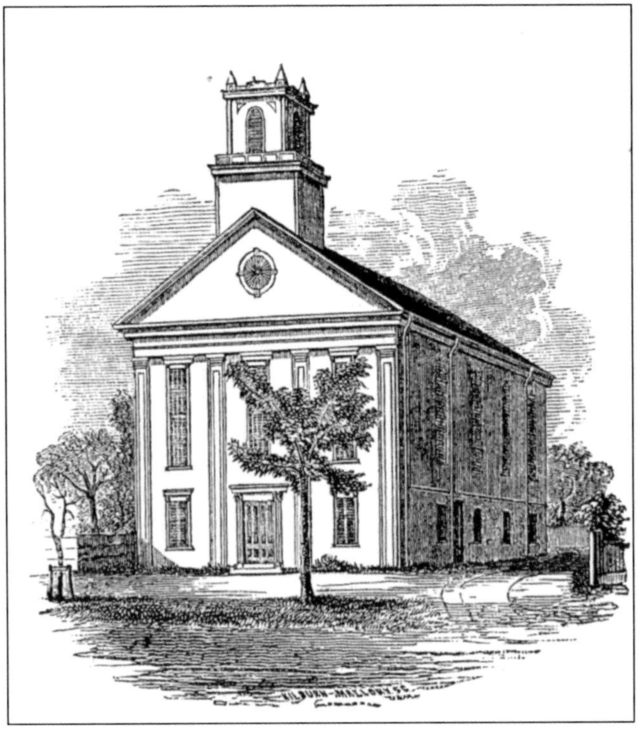

The First Universalist Church was founded in 1831. A small building was erected on Forest Street in 1832 and was substantially remodeled in 1850. The church is seen here after the remodeling. This church also showed elements of the Greek Revival style. (Courtesy of the Medford Public Library.)

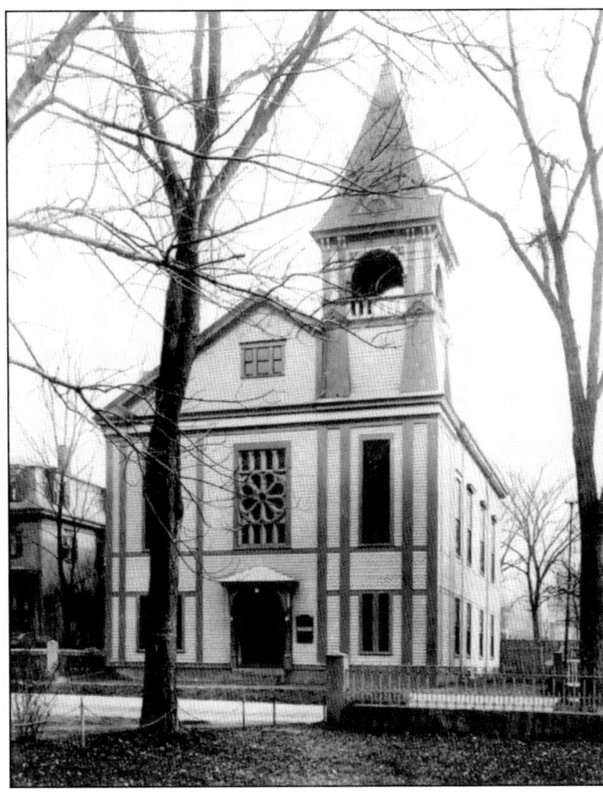

The First Universalist Church building was remodeled for a second time in 1886. The 1886 building featured a lovely mix of Victorian shingle patterns and decorative woodwork. Ministers of the church included Hosea Ballou, the first president of Tufts College. (Courtesy of the Medford Historical Society.)

The First Baptist Church of Medford was incorporated in 1842. A simple square church was constructed on Salem Street near the Cross Street Cemetery. Some members of the congregation gathered in front of the church for this photograph in the 1860s. (Courtesy of the Medford Historical Society.)

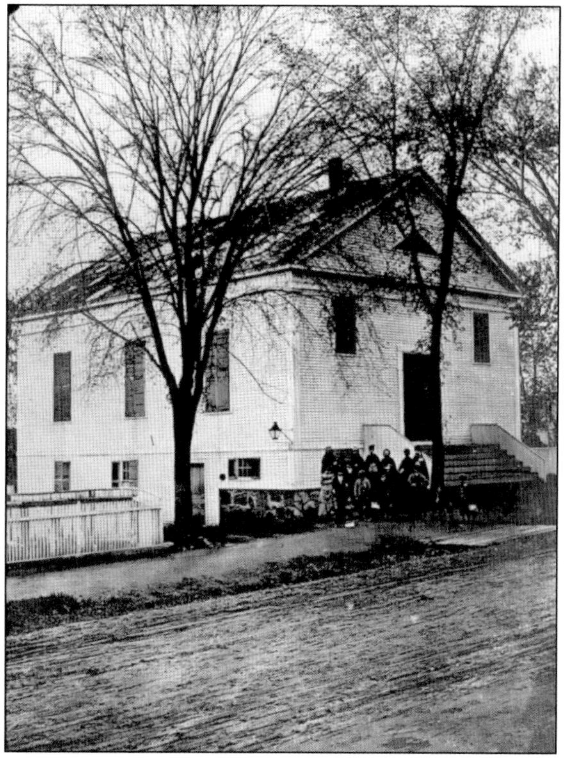

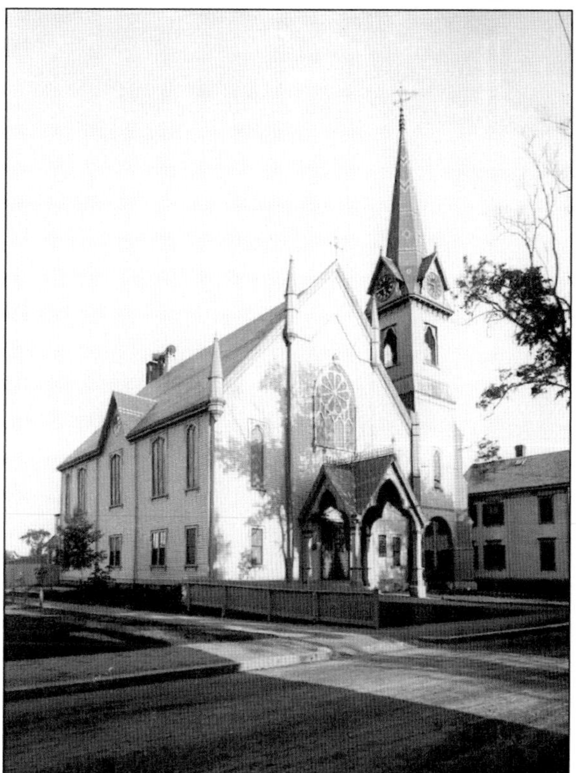

As the town grew, church congregations grew as well, and church buildings had to grow larger to accommodate them. When the First Baptist congregation outgrew the original small church, a large building was erected on Oakland Street in 1872. The Oakland Street church was another great Victorian eclectic structure; notice the Gothic arches and turrets and the slate patterns on the steeple. The building was destroyed in a spectacular fire in 1935. (Courtesy of the Medford Public Library.)

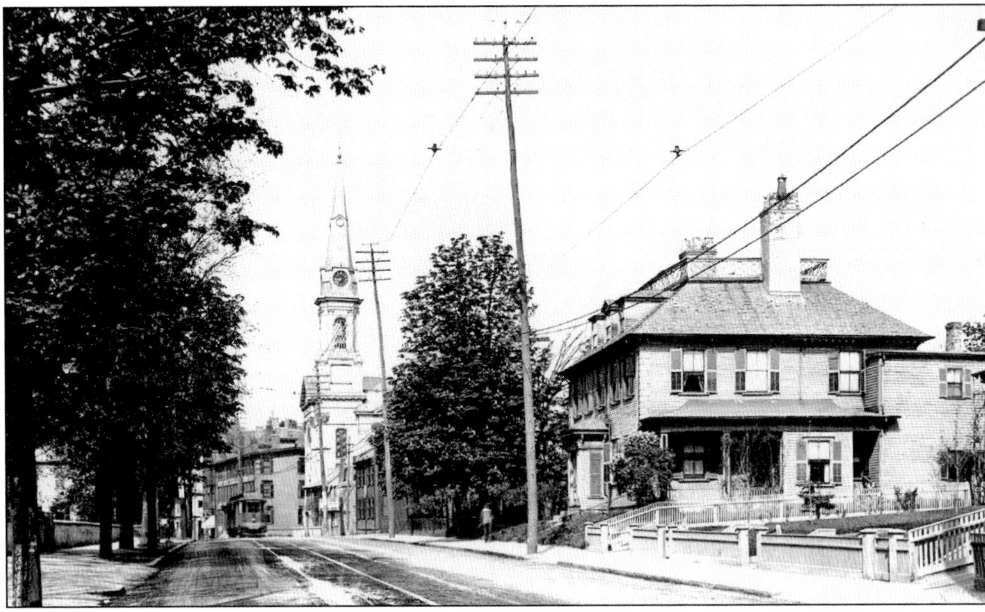

The Mystic Congregational Church split off from the Second Congregational Church in 1847. The members met in the town hall until 1849, when a church was built on Salem Street. The church building, which still stands, is pictured here in the 1890s. (Courtesy of the Medford Public Library.)

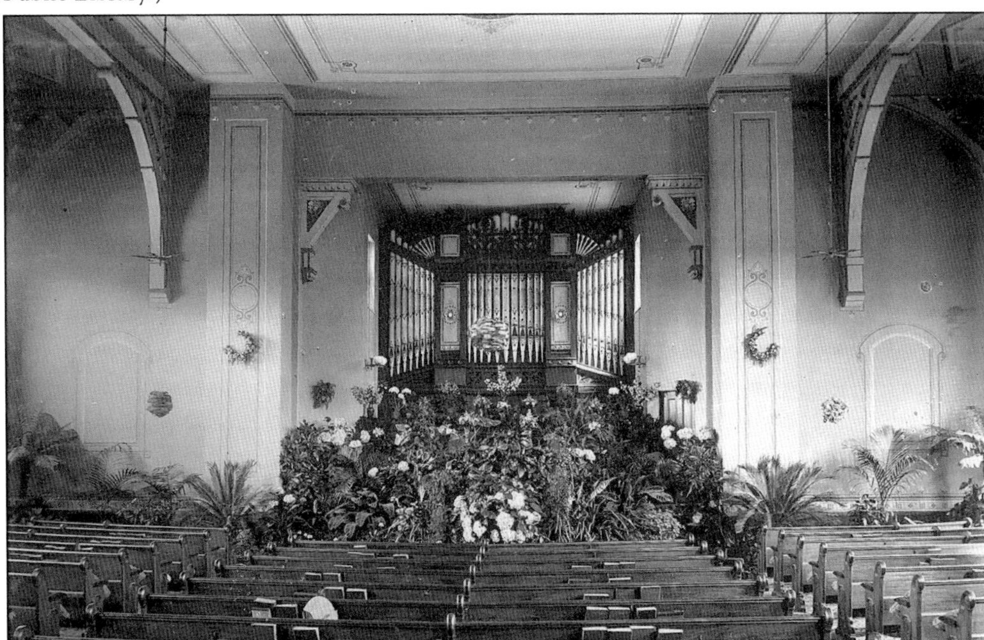

The interior of the Mystic church was graced by a substantial pipe organ, donated in 1854. The church was attended by many prominent citizens, including shipbuilder Galen James and abolitionist George Luther Stearns. The flowers decorating the church for Children's Sunday in 1888 probably come from the greenhouses on the Stearns Estate. (Courtesy of the Medford Public Library.)

Grace Episcopal Church was organized in 1848. The existing church, built in 1867, was an early work of H. H. Richardson. The distinctive exterior has glacial boulders set into the walls. The roof is of gray slate, with bands of red running the full length of the roof. The interior is of dark wood, with a stained-glass window designed by John LaFarge. (Courtesy of the Medford Historical Society.)

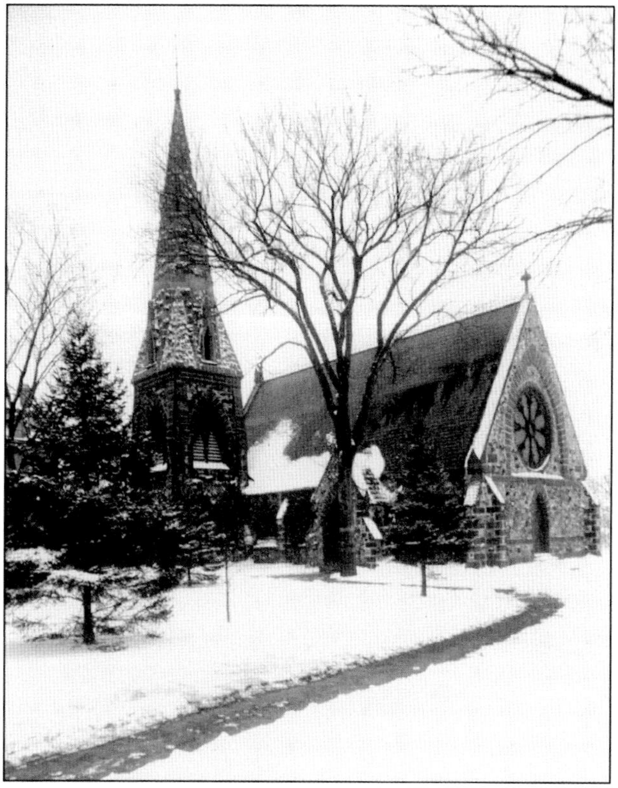

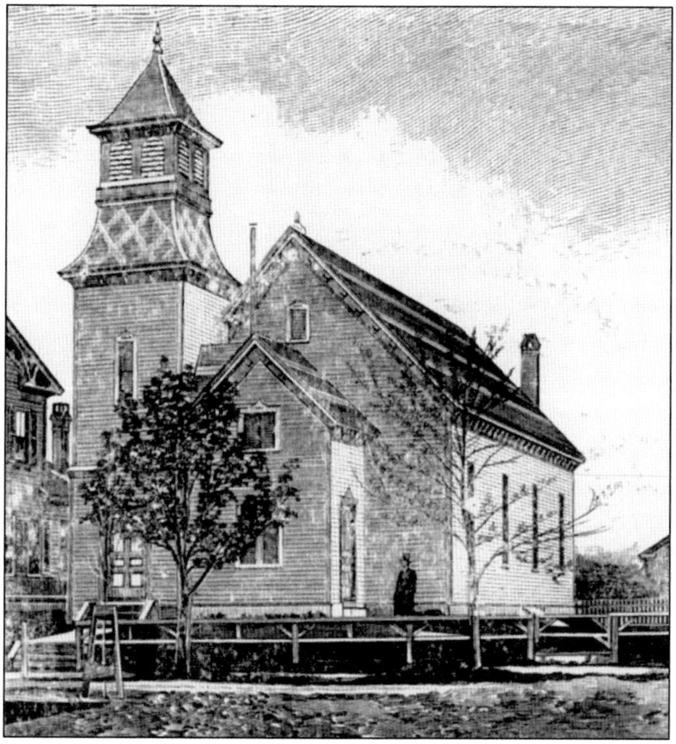

The Trinity Methodist Episcopal Church was formed in the 1860s by West Medford residents who wanted a church in their part of town. This church building, planned and built by local historian and contractor Moses Mann, was constructed on the corner of Bower and Holton Streets in 1873. It also shows elements of the Stick style in the wooden decorations under the eaves and on the steeple. (Courtesy of the Medford Public Library.)

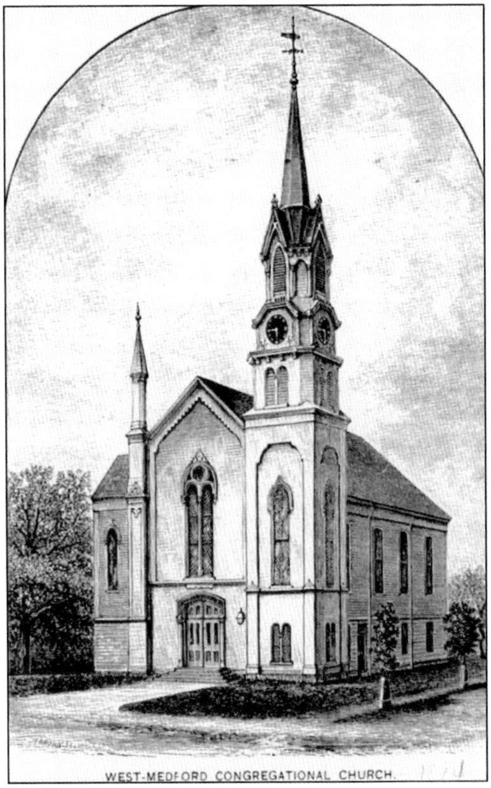

The West Medford Congregational Church was built in 1872, just as that part of the town began its major development. The first church building, on the corner of Harvard Avenue and Bower Street, was an elegant structure with a subtle Gothic influence in the architecture. (Courtesy of the Medford Public Library.)

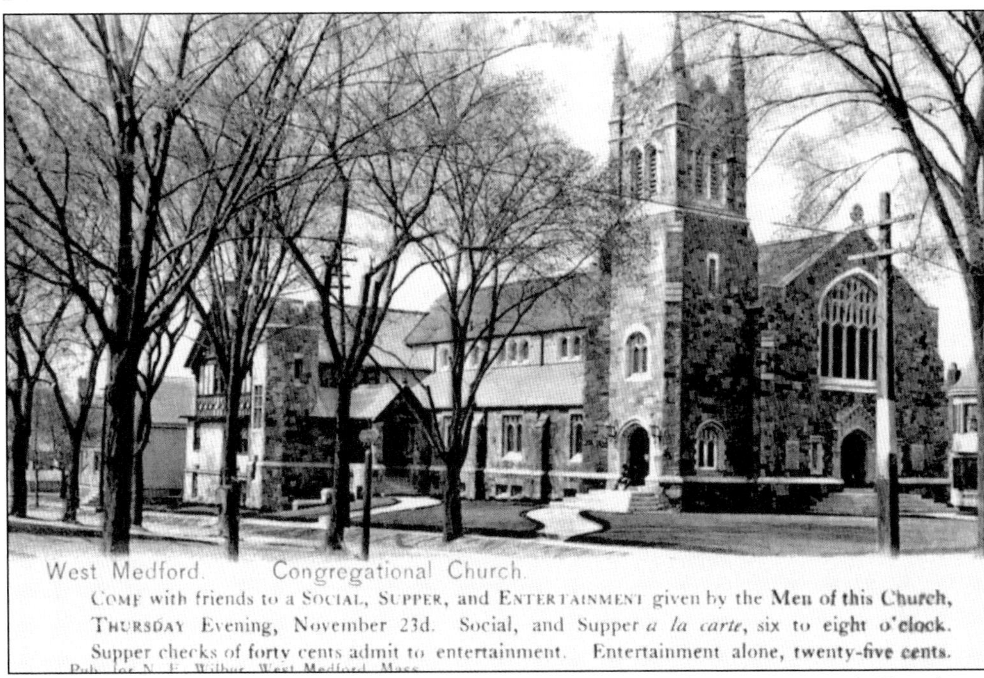

Like many Victorian Medford churches, the First West Medford Congregational Church was destroyed by fire in 1903. It was replaced by the present stone church, built in 1905 on the corner of High and Allston Streets. (Courtesy of the Medford Public Library.)

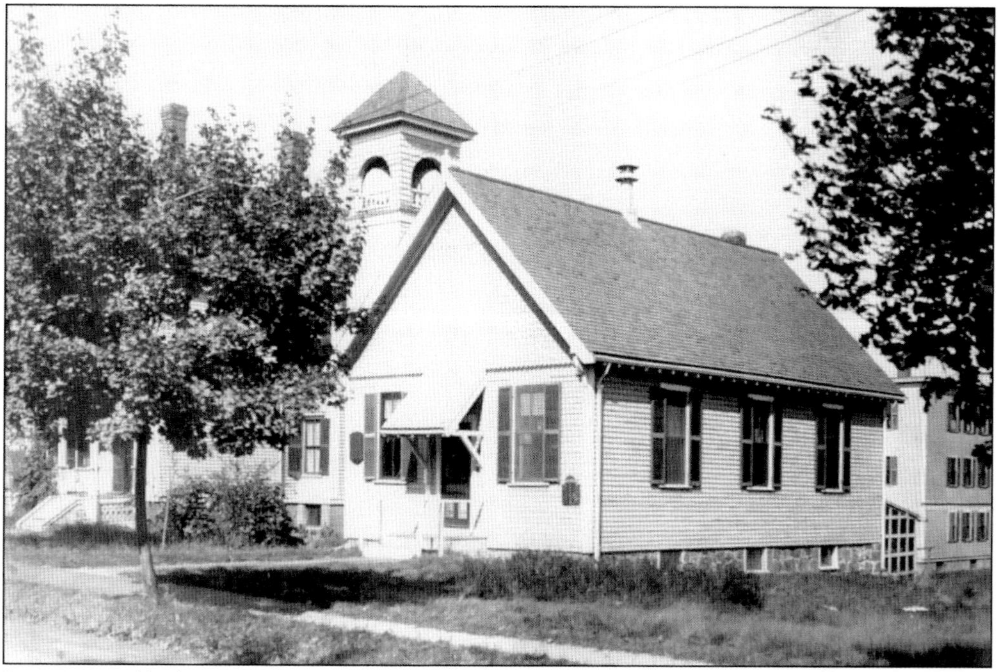

By 1880 Medford's citizens worshiped in almost a dozen churches, and new churches continued to open. The Bethany Methodist Episcopal Church in Wellington came into existence in 1888. The small chapel on Fourth Street was built by a congregation that had met in private homes and in the local school for a number of years. (Courtesy of the Medford Public Library.)

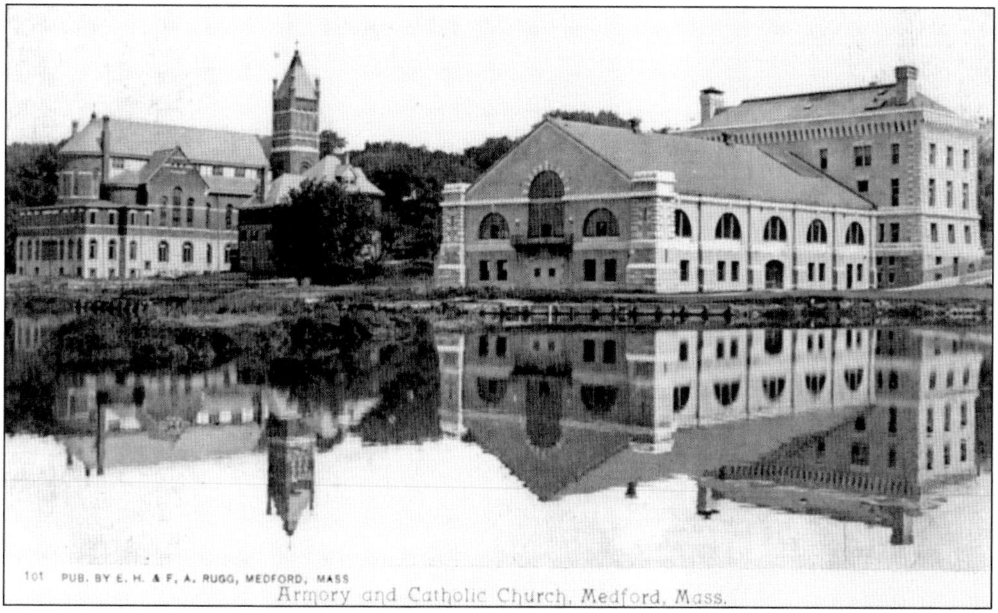

Until 1893 Medford's Catholics owned the church on High Street that had originally been the Second Congregational Church. St. Joseph's Catholic Church, opposite the library on High Street, was completed in 1900 on land that had formerly belonged to the family of shipbuilder Thatcher Magoun. St. Joseph's and the armory made a splendid sight along the river. (Collection of the author.)

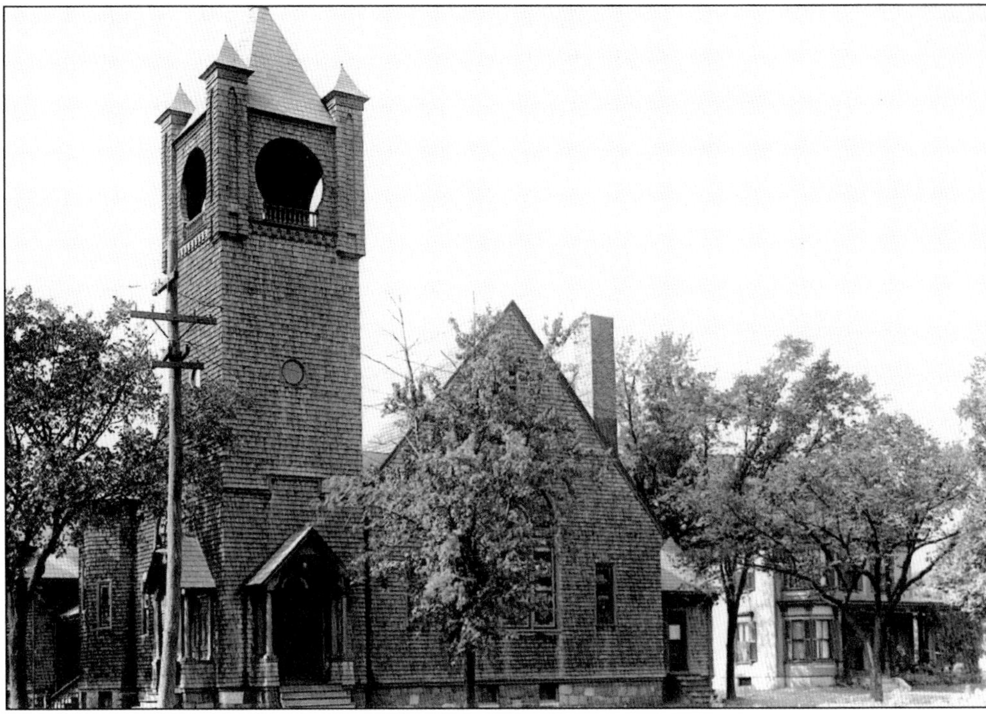

The Shiloh Baptist Church was established in 1898 by members of the African American population in West Medford. The first meetings were held in a private home on Lincoln Street, but a building was soon constructed on the corner of Lincoln Street and Fairfield Avenue. The original church was used until 1966, when the congregation purchased the building seen here, the former West Medford Methodist Church on the corner of Holton and Bower Streets. (Courtesy of the Medford Public Library.)

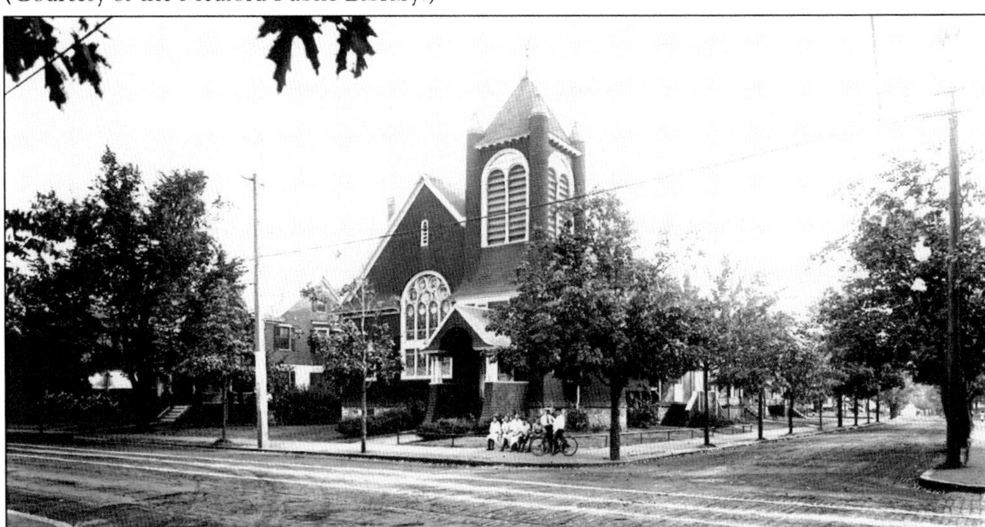

The West Medford Baptist Church came into being when the pastor of the First Baptist Church urged the West Medford members to form their own church. The congregation met in Mystic Hall until this church was built on the corner of Boston and Harvard Avenues in 1887. The building was dedicated on Easter Sunday of that year. (Courtesy of the Medford Public Library.)

Eight

Beautiful Houses

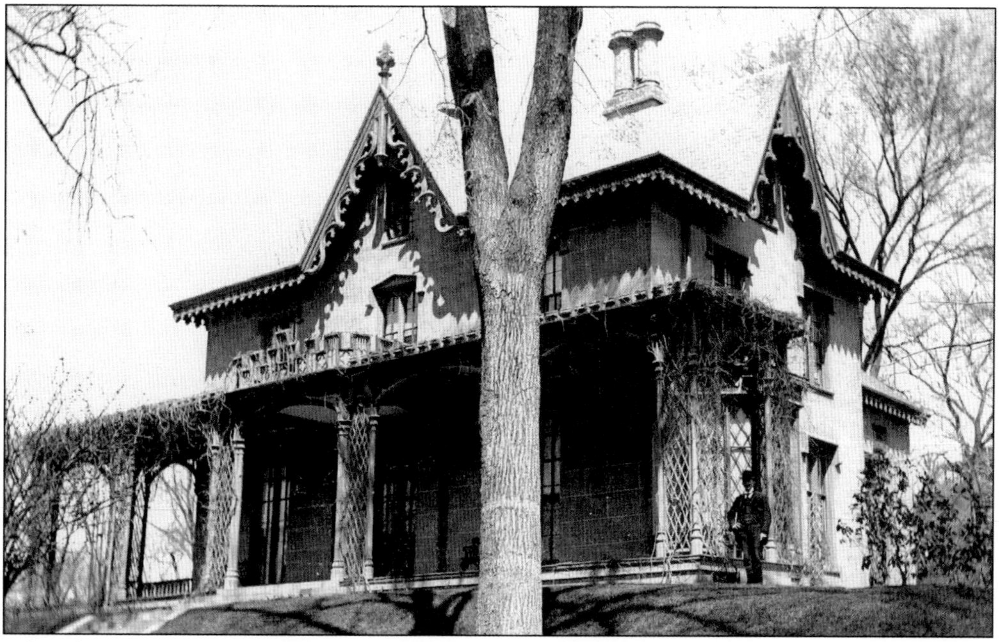

After the railroad made Medford accessible in the 1840s and 1850s, many new residents arrived and built houses. One of the first such homes, the Angier Boynton House on High Street, was built for John Angier in 1842 by Alexander Jackson Davis, who later designed the New York Customs House. The house is in the Gothic Revival style. Notice the wooden tracery and Gothic arches. (Courtesy of the Medford Public Library.)

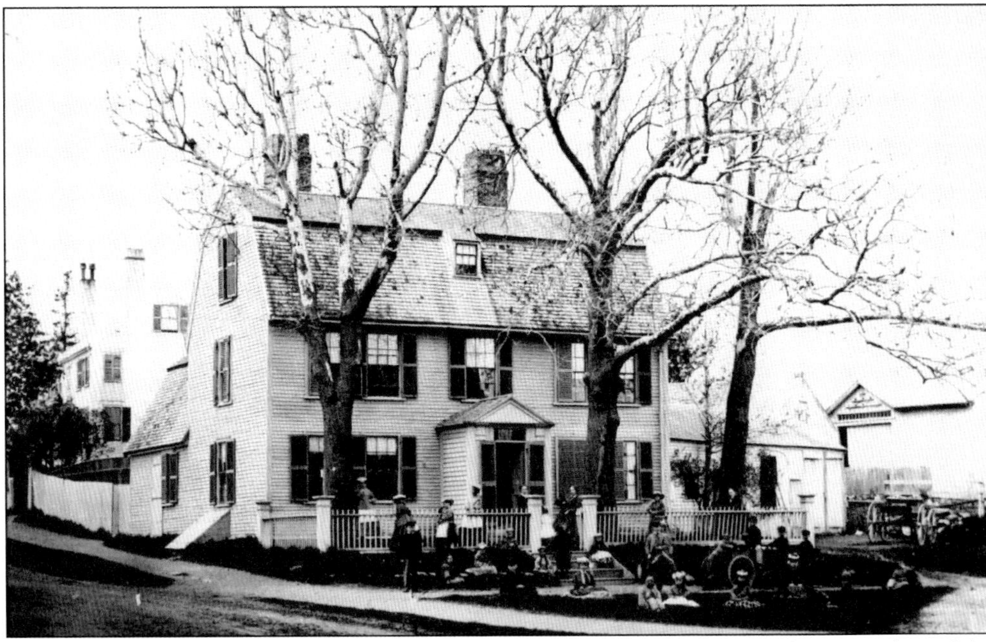

This is a 19th-century view of the 18th-century Jonathan Brooks House. The exact date of the house is not known, but its style was typical of the architecture most common in Medford in the early 1800s. The unadorned, square forms of the 18th century provided a striking contrast to the Victorian flights of fancy that were to come. (Courtesy of the Medford Historical Society.)

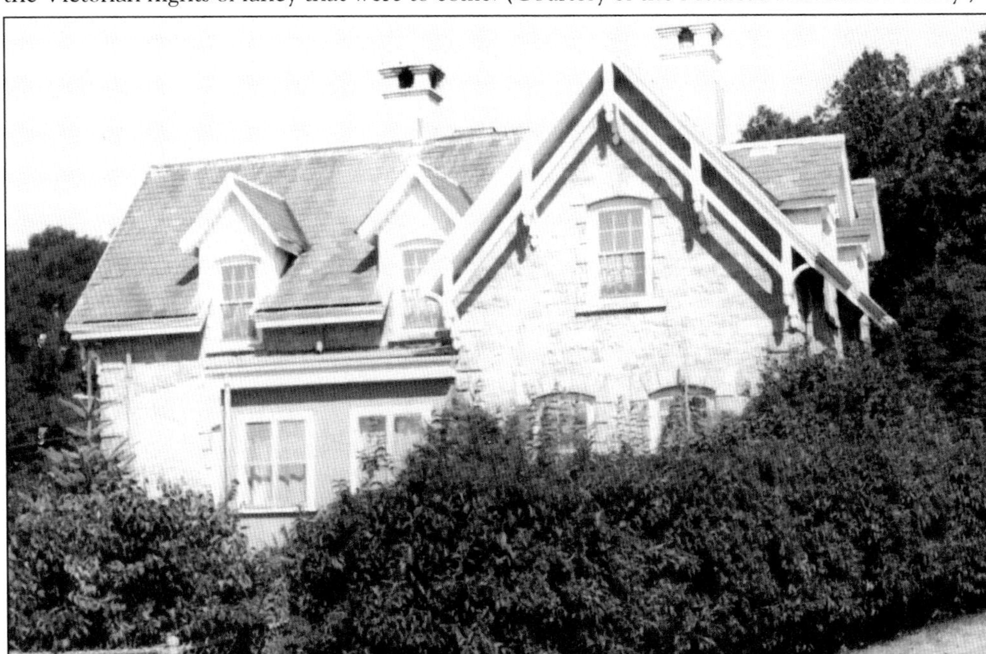

Peter Chardon Brooks III built a substantial summer home in Medford in 1860. This stone cottage on Apache Trail was part of the estate. The cottage is another example of the Gothic style. Like the Angier Boynton House, this house features gables with elaborate wooden tracery. (Courtesy of the Medford Public Library.)

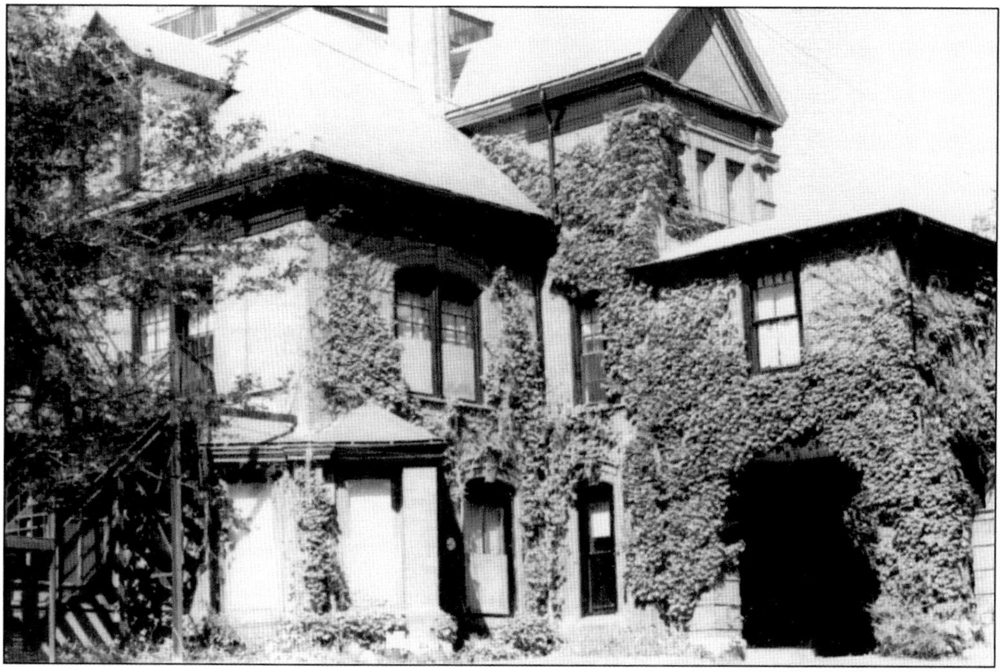

The Shepherd Brooks Estate was one of the most impressive summer residences built in Medford. Brooks, who had an interest in architecture, made the design of the estate part of his life's work. The manor house and carriage house were built in 1880. The manor house, seen here, is in the Queen Anne style, characterized by asymmetrical masses and large, complex forms. (Courtesy of the Medford Public Library.)

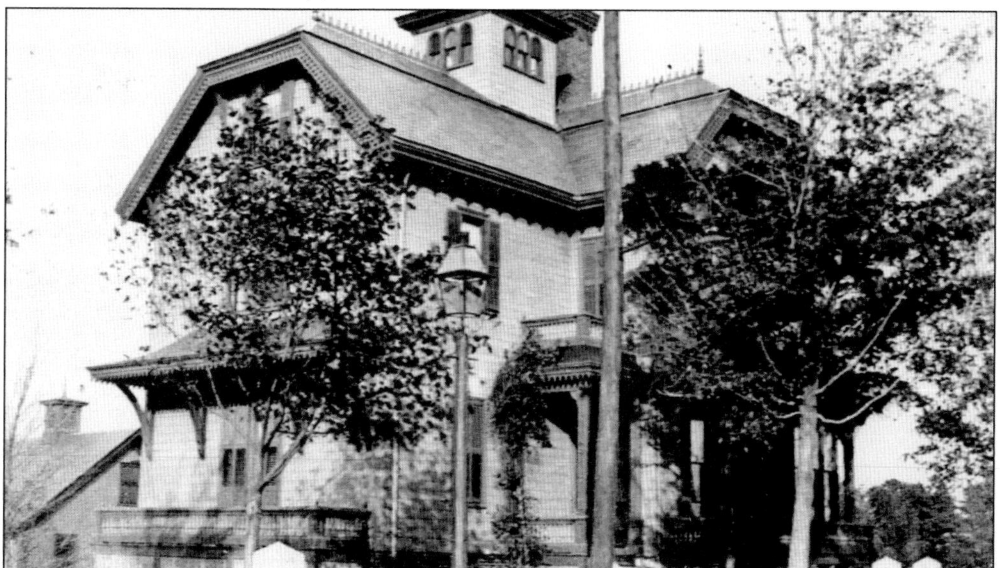

The George B. Green House on Powderhouse Terrace was built in the early 1870s in the Stick style. This style, popular from the 1860s to the 1890s, was characterized by the use of overhanging eaves, ornamental trusses, and decorative support braces. George B. Green was a flour merchant who owned the warehouse on Main Street next to the railroad station. (Courtesy of the Medford Historical Society.)

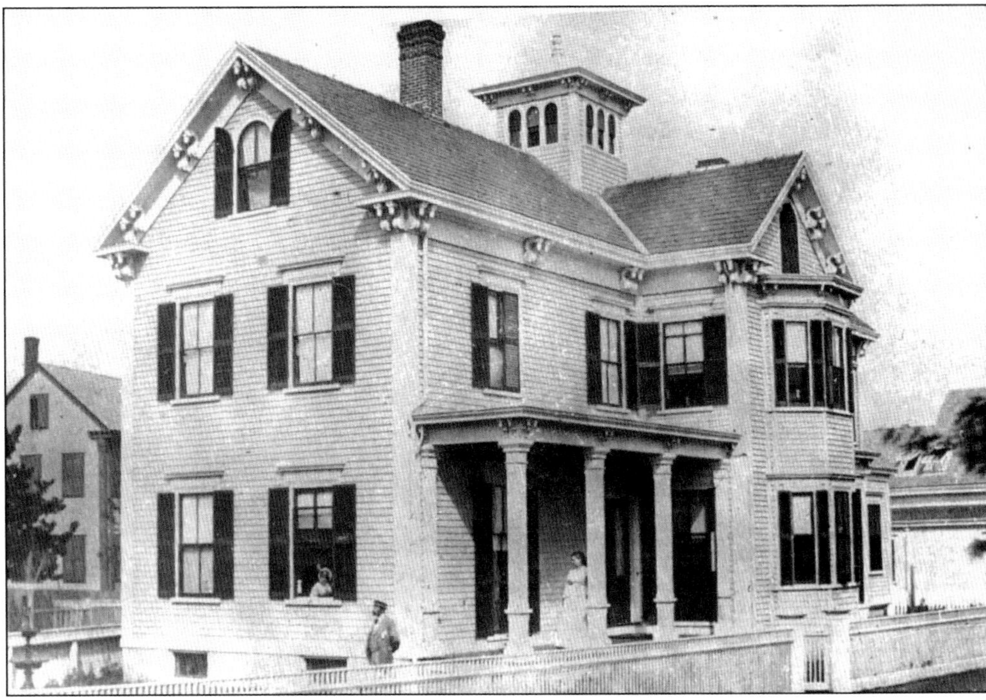

The Hersey House on Woodside Square, on the corner of Franklin and Washington Streets, was built before 1869 and has architectural details common to the Italianate style popular in the 1860s. Note the ornately carved brackets under the cornice, and also the cupola, a typical feature of Italianate houses. (Courtesy of the Medford Historical Society.)

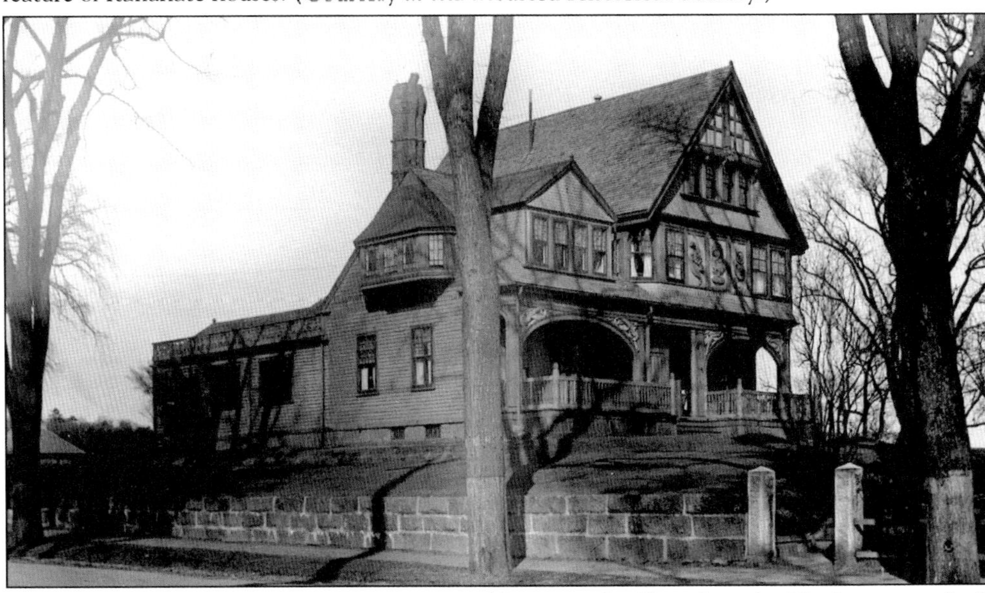

The Homer Estate on Forest Street was a grand house in the Shingle style. The house was built for William N. Homer, who was employed by the First National Bank in Boston. The Shingle style was so named because of the variety of shingle and siding patterns used on the exterior. In this example, the carved designs on the corners of the arches and on the front of the house are particularly dramatic elements. (Courtesy of the Medford Public Library.)

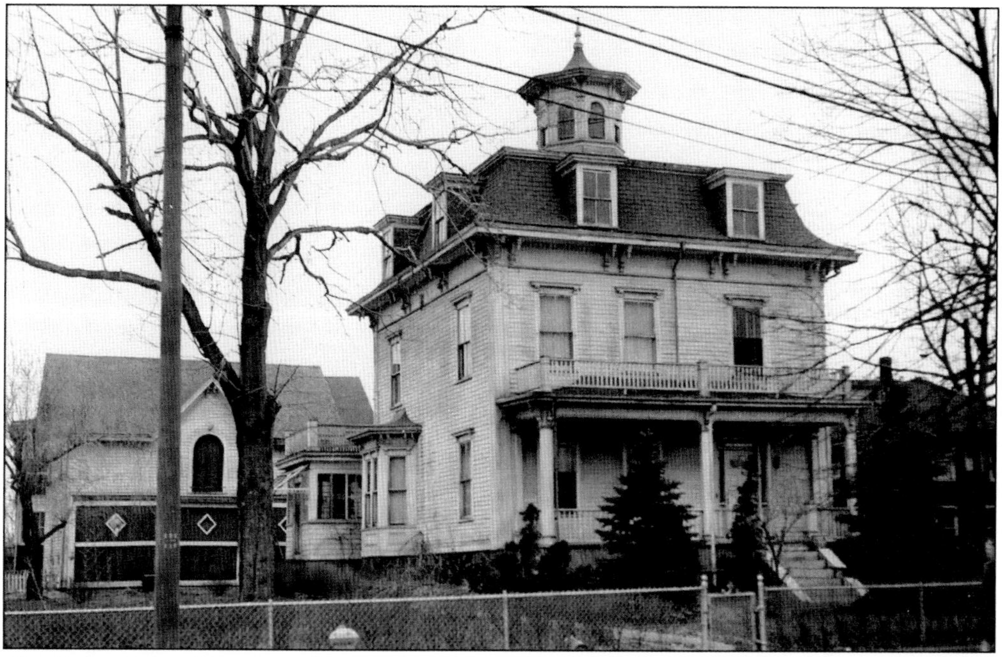

The Galen James House was located at the corner of Main Street and Stearns Avenue. James was one of Medford's shipbuilders; like many shipbuilders, he used the profits of the trade to build a mansion. The house was in the Italianate style popular in the 1860s and, like the Hersey House, features a cupola and ornate cornices under the roof. (Courtesy of the Medford Historical Society.)

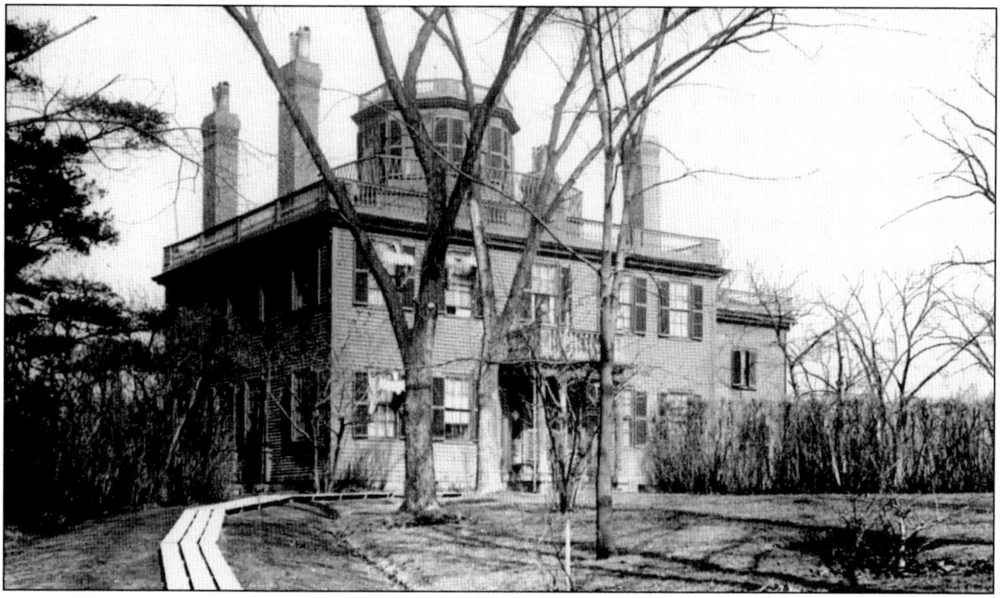

The Kidder Estate on Forest Street belonged to David Kidder, a merchant with offices in Boston, and his wife, Susan Magoun Kidder, daughter of Thatcher Magoun Jr. The house was built in the 1870s in an odd mixture of styles. Its simple, square body evokes the Colonial style and makes an interesting contrast with the Italianate railing and the unique octagonal cupola. (Courtesy of the Medford Public Library.)

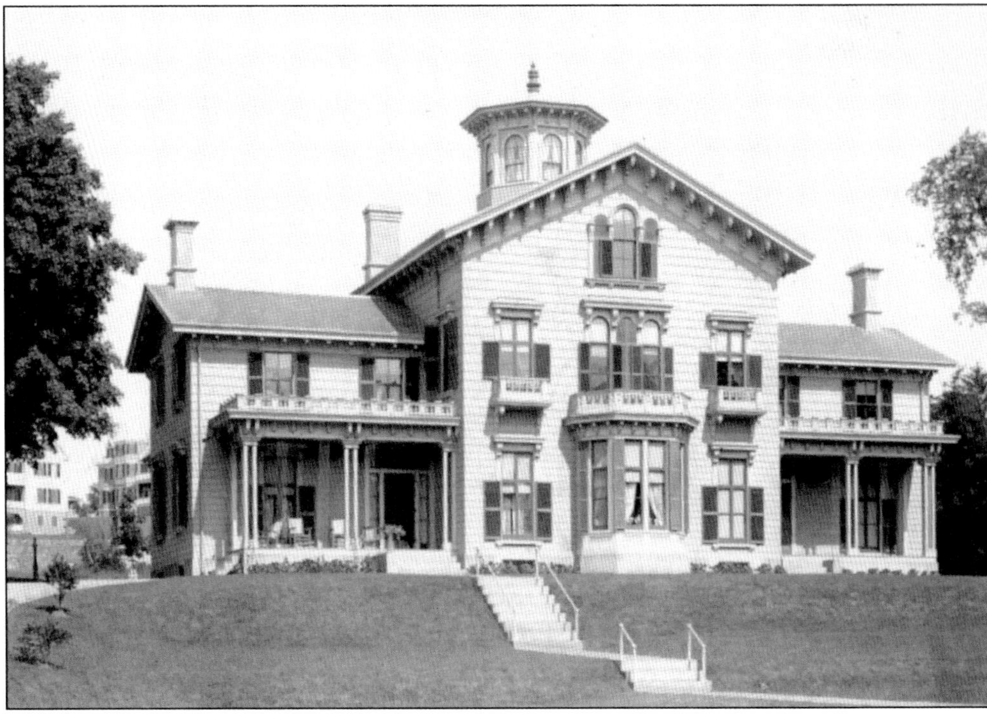

Daniel Lawrence founded the Lawrence Rum Distillery in 1830. He built this substantial house on Forest Street in the 1860s. The Lawrence house, a lovely, airy example of the Italianate style, stood on the site now occupied by the post office. (Courtesy of the Medford Public Library.)

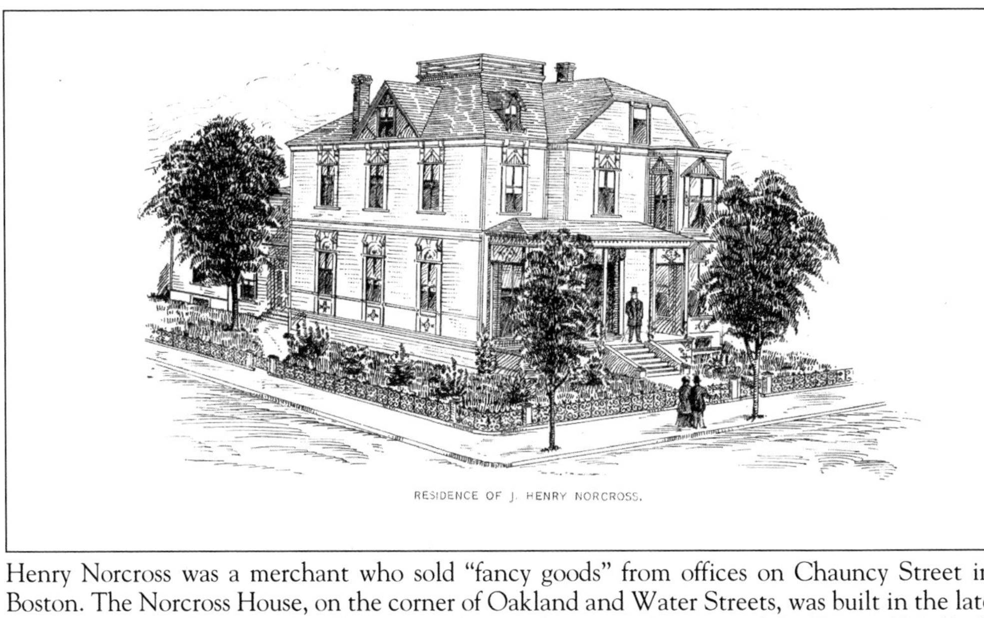

Henry Norcross was a merchant who sold "fancy goods" from offices on Chauncy Street in Boston. The Norcross House, on the corner of Oakland and Water Streets, was built in the late 1860s in the Stick style. This illustration, from Usher's 1885 *History of the Town of Medford*, shows off the elaborate decorative wooden trim and patterns typical of the style. (Courtesy of the Medford Public Library.)

Alvin Puffer was a partner in the American Soda Fountain Company, and he and his family owned a number of houses in Medford. This house was built in the early 1870s in the Second Empire style popular from 1860 to 1880. Houses in the Second Empire style usually had a mansard roof; the wooden ornamentation around the windows and doors shows influence of the Stick style. (Courtesy of the Medford Public Library.)

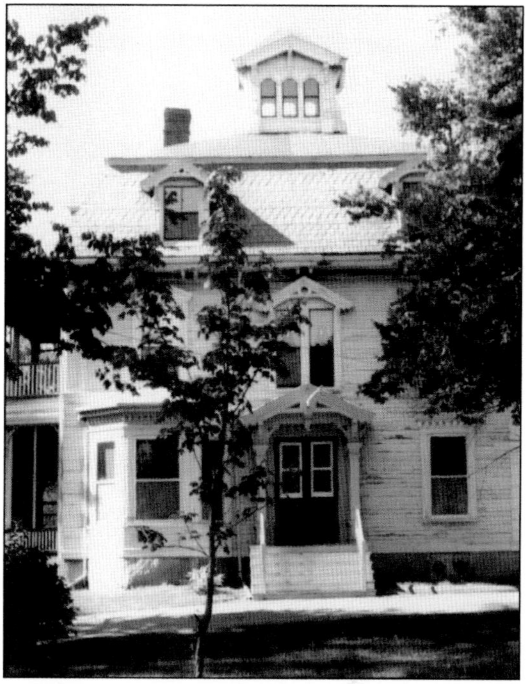

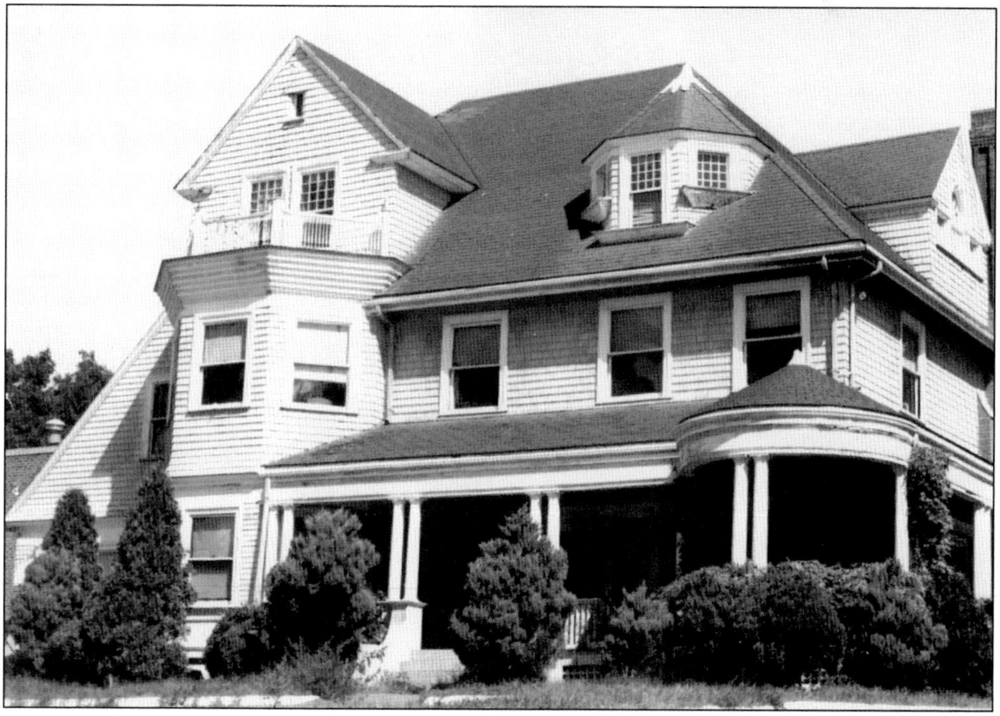

Luther Puffer continued the family soda fountain business. In the 1890s he built a substantial house on Winthrop Street in a combination of the Shingle and Queen Anne styles. Queen Anne buildings featured large, asymmetrical masses like the peaked roofs and circular porch seen on the Puffer House, while Shingle-style motifs are evident in the exterior decoration. (Courtesy of the Medford Public Library.)

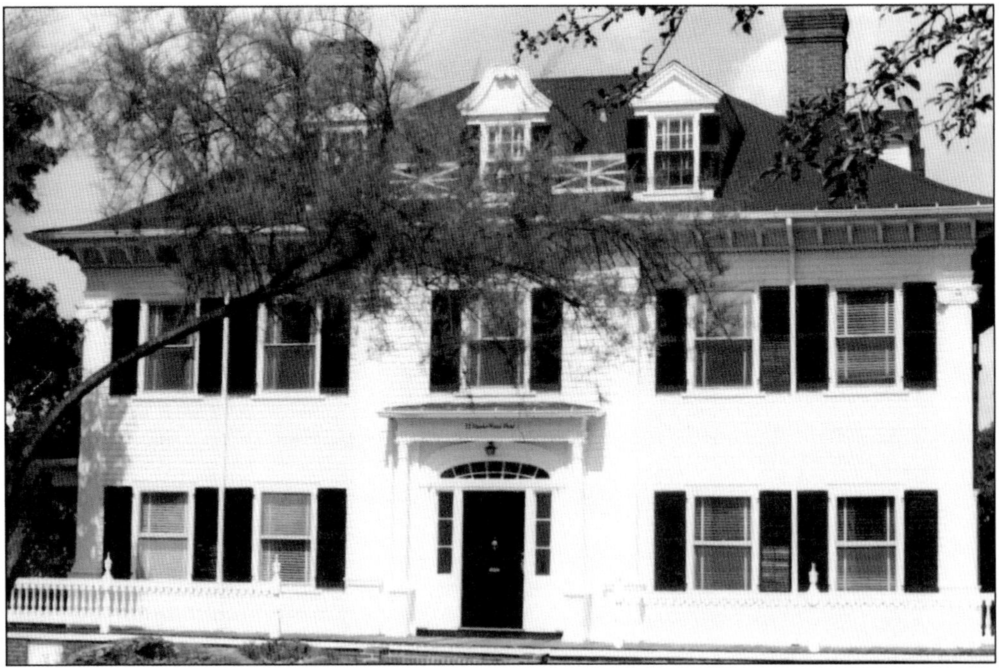

The James W. Tufts House on Powderhouse Road was built between 1890 and 1898 in the Colonial Revival style, which became popular at the end of the century. Colonial Revival houses were larger, more elaborate versions of the 18th-century originals. Like the 18th-century Jonathan Brooks House, the Tufts House had a simple square shape but was much larger, with more exterior ornamentation. (Courtesy of the Medford Public Library.)

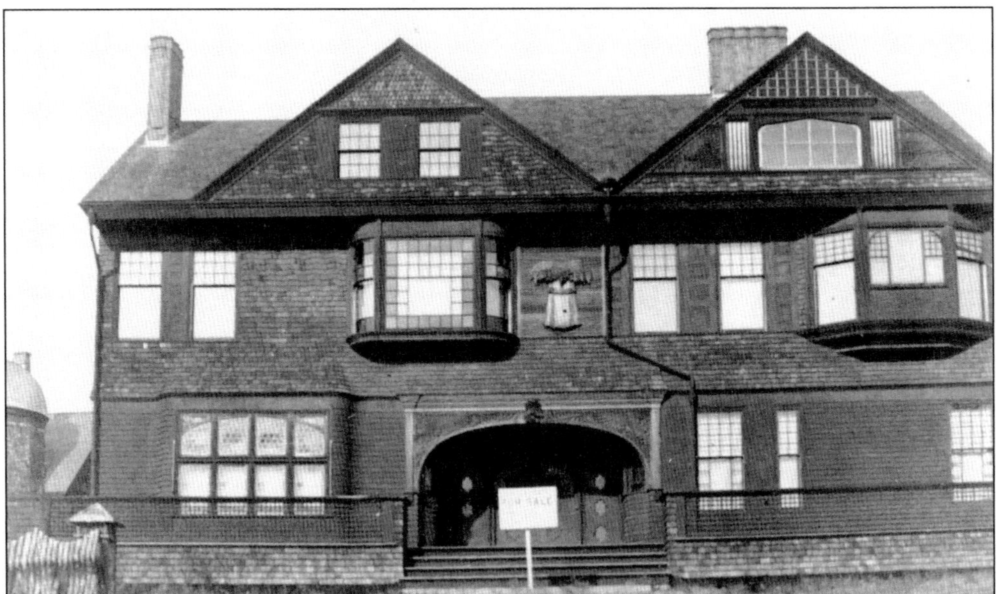

The Bela Warner House on Hillside Avenue was built in the 1880s. Warner was the president of the Eastern Salt Company. The house was a fine example of the Shingle style. Notice the varied textures of shingles and siding patterns that gave this style its name. (Courtesy of the Medford Historical Society.)

Nine

Bountiful Nature

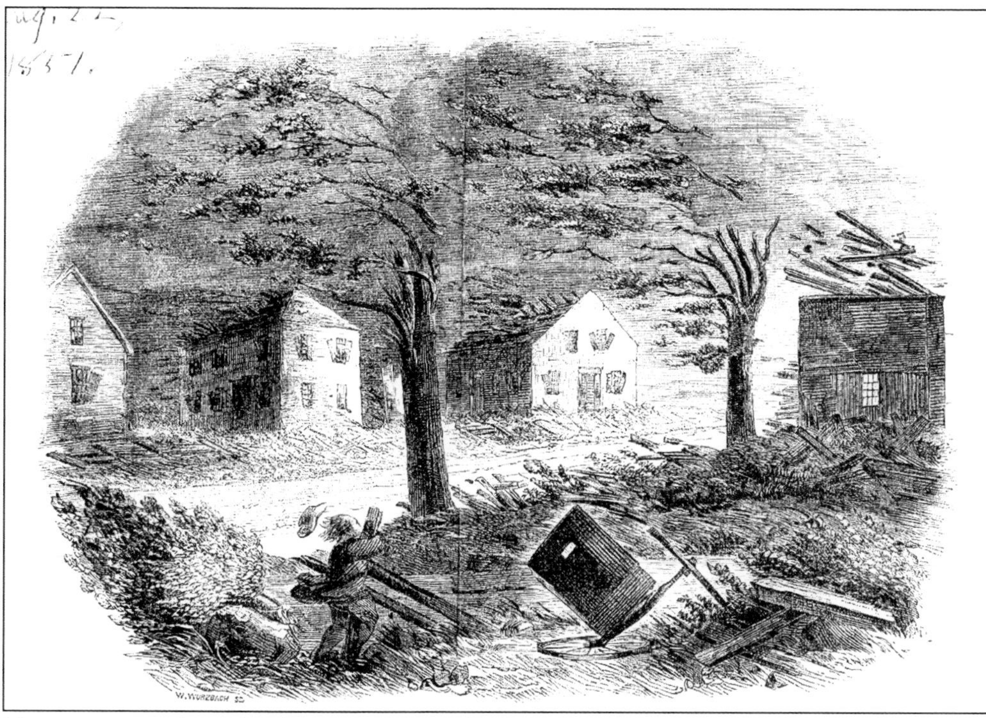

Nature was not always kind to Victorian Medford. On August 22, 1851, a tornado caused a great deal of damage in West Medford. Among the losses reported were 23 buildings, 22 fruit trees, and a Boston and Maine freight car that was blown off the tracks. (Courtesy of the Medford Public Library.)

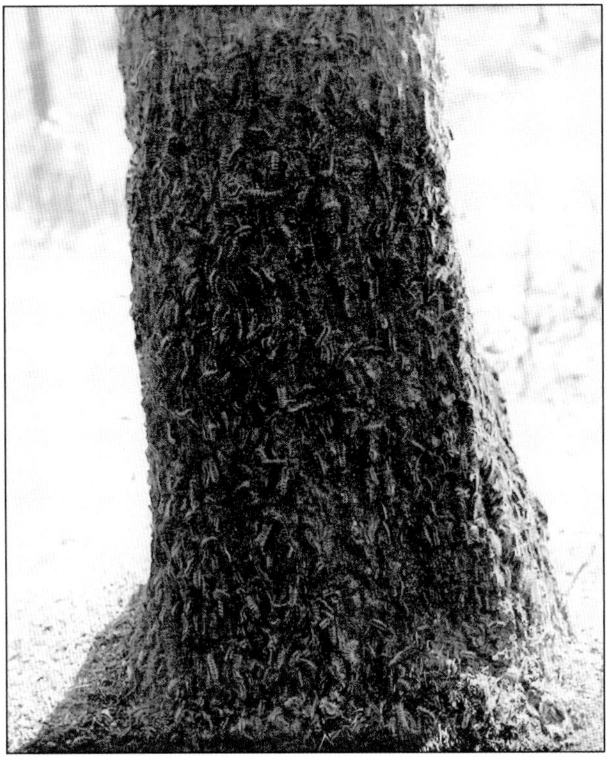

Nature struck again in the 1860s, when Medford became infamous for its infestation of gypsy moth caterpillars. If you look closely at the tree in this photograph, you can see that it is crawling with caterpillars. The tree was on the property of Samuel C. Lawrence on Forest Street. (Courtesy of the Medford Historical Society.)

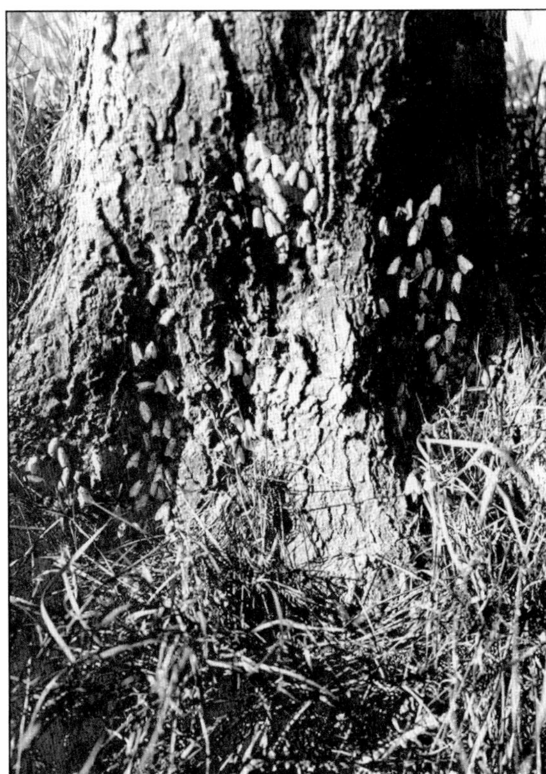

The gypsy moth came to Medford with Prof. Leopold Trouvelot, an artist and amateur naturalist. In 1868 Trouvelot was trying to breed a new species of silkworm by crossing silkworms with gypsy moths imported from Europe. At some point, a jar of moths fell out the window of Trouvelot's house on Myrtle Street, and the gypsy moths escaped into history. (Courtesy of the Medford Historical Society.)

By 1879 the moths were established, and by 1889 the first large devastations were occurring as the caterpillars devoured the leaves of trees and eventually killed the trees. This 1901 photograph of a willow on Forest Street shows a tree in big trouble. (Courtesy of the Medford Historical Society.)

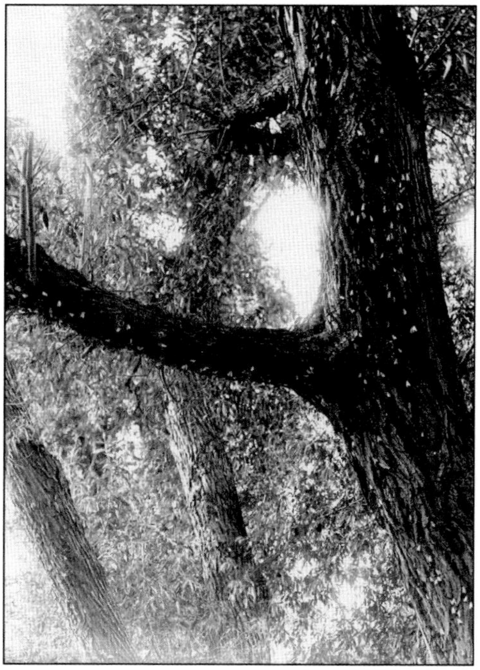

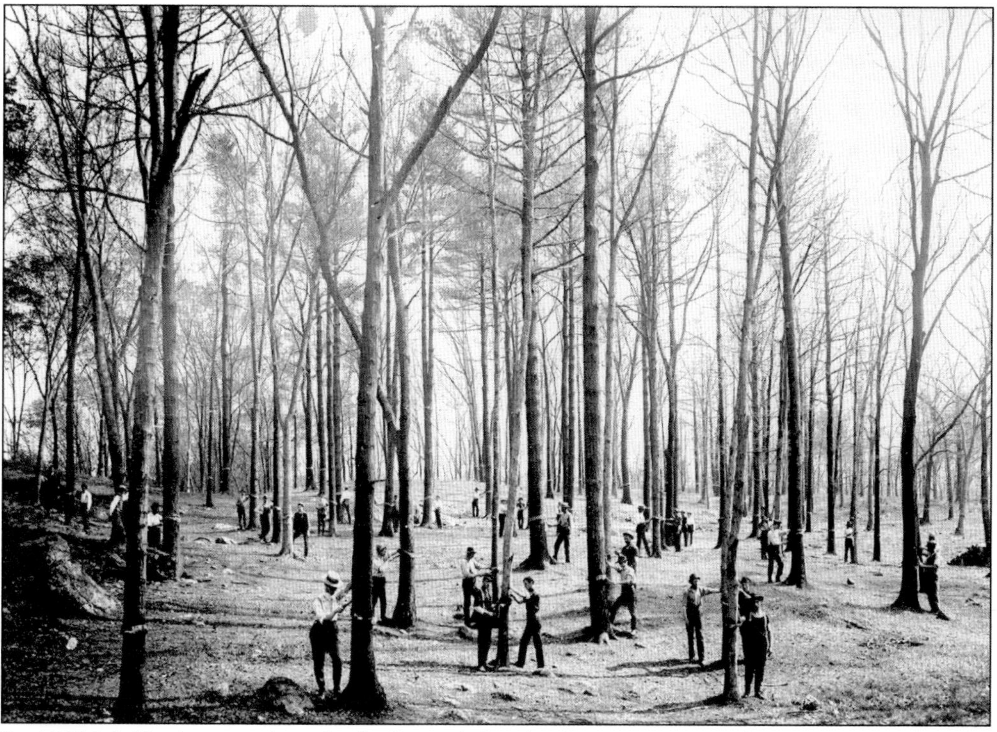

By 1905 Medford was striking back. Samuel Crocker Lawrence spent $500,000 to combat the infestation on his own land and on public lands. Over 100 men, armed with watering carts, pumping machines, and miles of hose, spread out to try to control the infestation all over town. Lawrence's crusade was successful, although the gypsy moth still occasionally comes to visit. (Courtesy of the Medford Historical Society.)

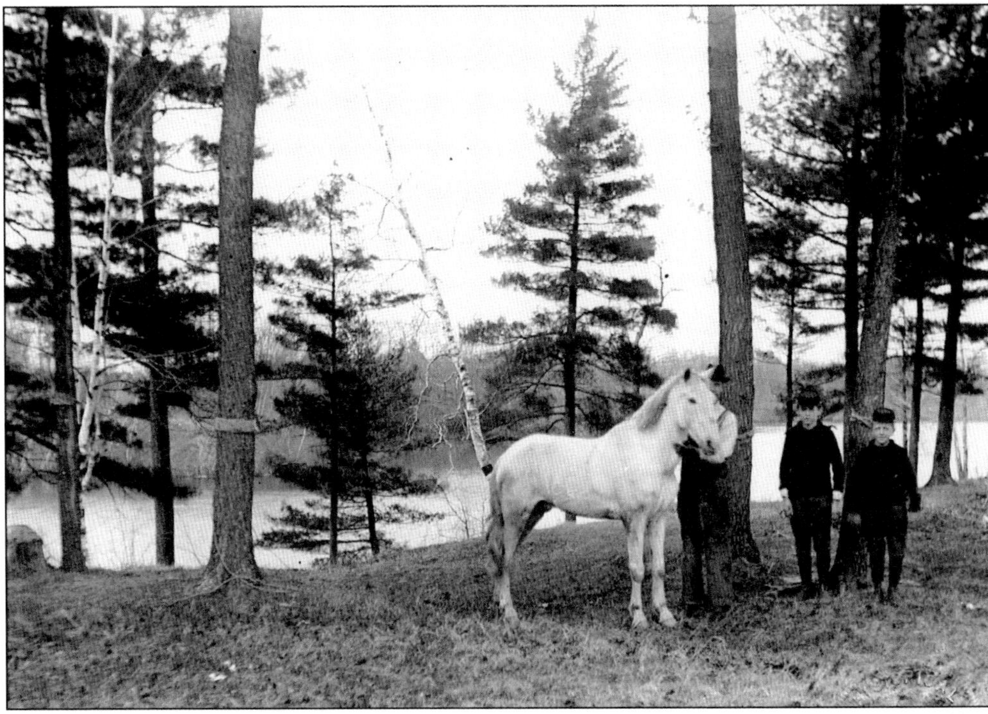

In spite of natural disasters and the rapid growth of residential areas, Victorian Medford maintained much natural beauty, particularly around the water. These young men and their horse are posed in the woodland by the upper Mystic River. The rings around the tree trunks were part of the battle against the gypsy moth. (Courtesy of the Medford Public Library.)

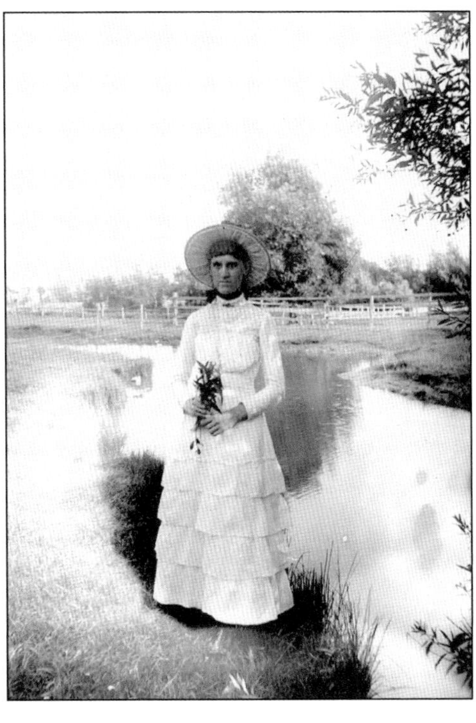

This winsome young woman is posing on the banks of Gravelly Creek sometime in the 1880s. Although the creek confounded city engineers for years, the landscape remained quite peaceful and bucolic. (Courtesy of the Medford Historical Society.)

Medford's most substantial natural area was the Middlesex Fells, which was divided between Medford and surrounding towns. In 1869 the insurance pioneer Elizur Wright began writing and agitating to turn the Middlesex Fells into a park in order to preserve its natural state. In 1880 the Middlesex Fells Association was formed. Work was under way to purchase much of the land when Wright died suddenly in 1885. (Courtesy of the Medford Historical Society.)

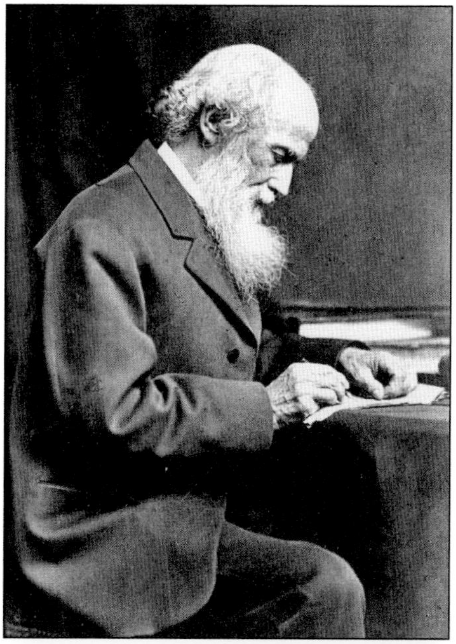

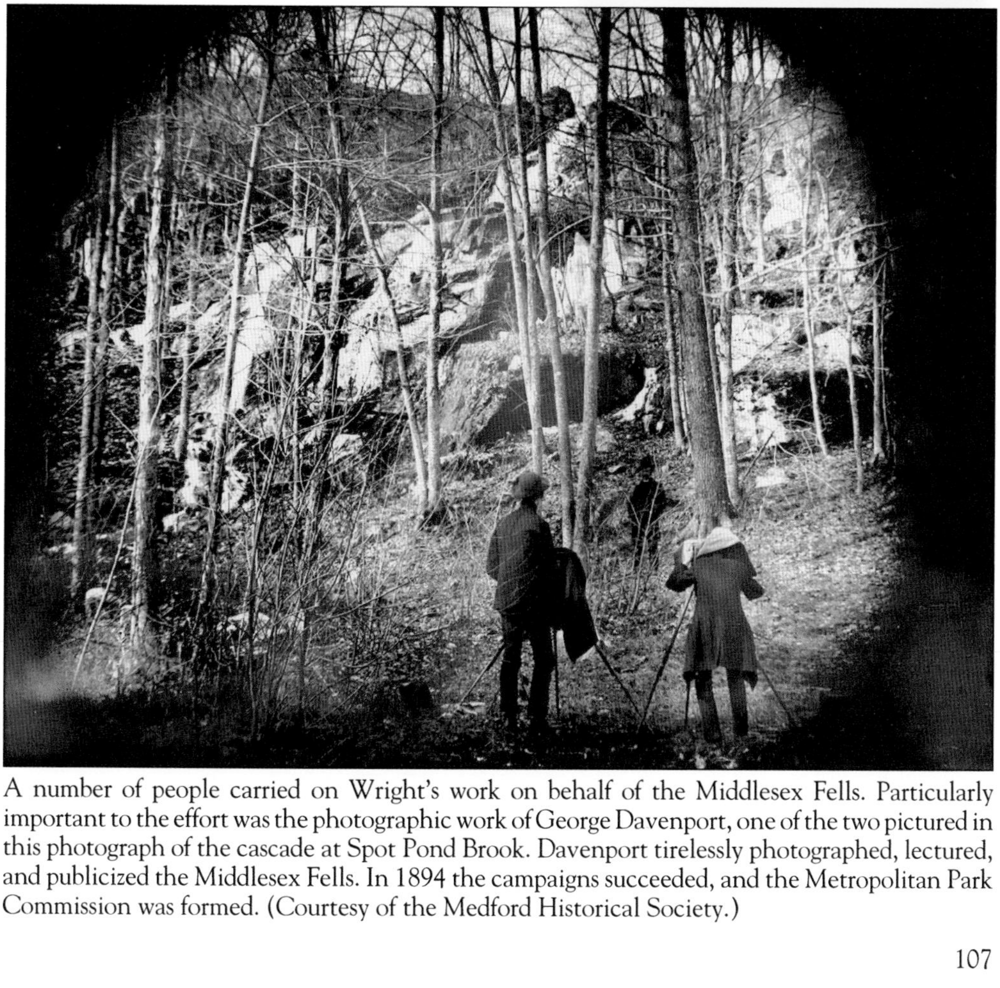

A number of people carried on Wright's work on behalf of the Middlesex Fells. Particularly important to the effort was the photographic work of George Davenport, one of the two pictured in this photograph of the cascade at Spot Pond Brook. Davenport tirelessly photographed, lectured, and publicized the Middlesex Fells. In 1894 the campaigns succeeded, and the Metropolitan Park Commission was formed. (Courtesy of the Medford Historical Society.)

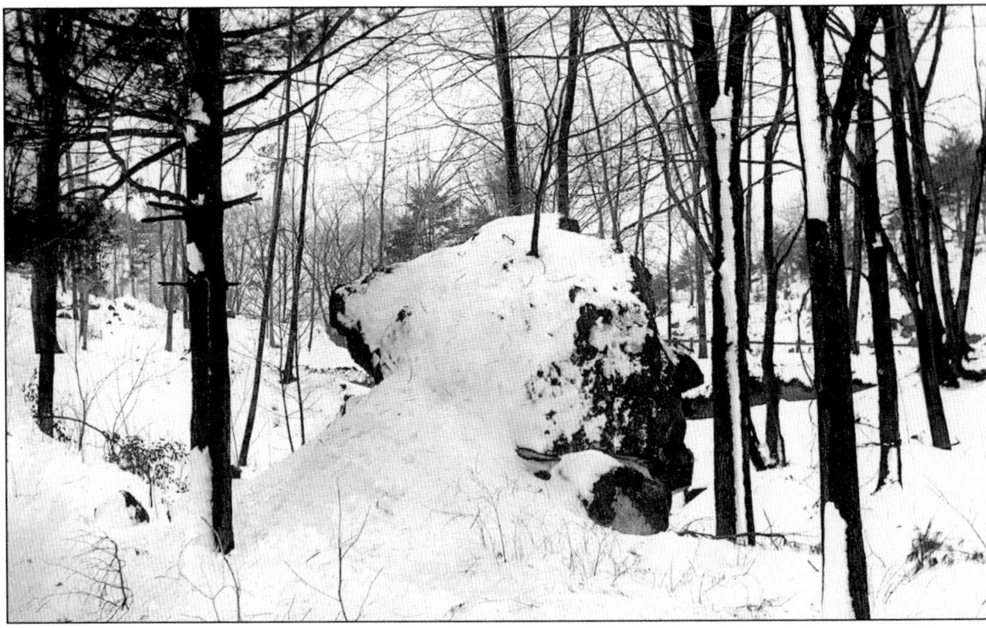

The Middlesex Fells was full of natural features that captured Victorian fancy. Pictured here is the Old Man of the Fells. The rock formation was considered to look his best when wearing a wig of snow. The Old Man was destroyed during the construction of Route 93. (Courtesy of the Medford Historical Society.)

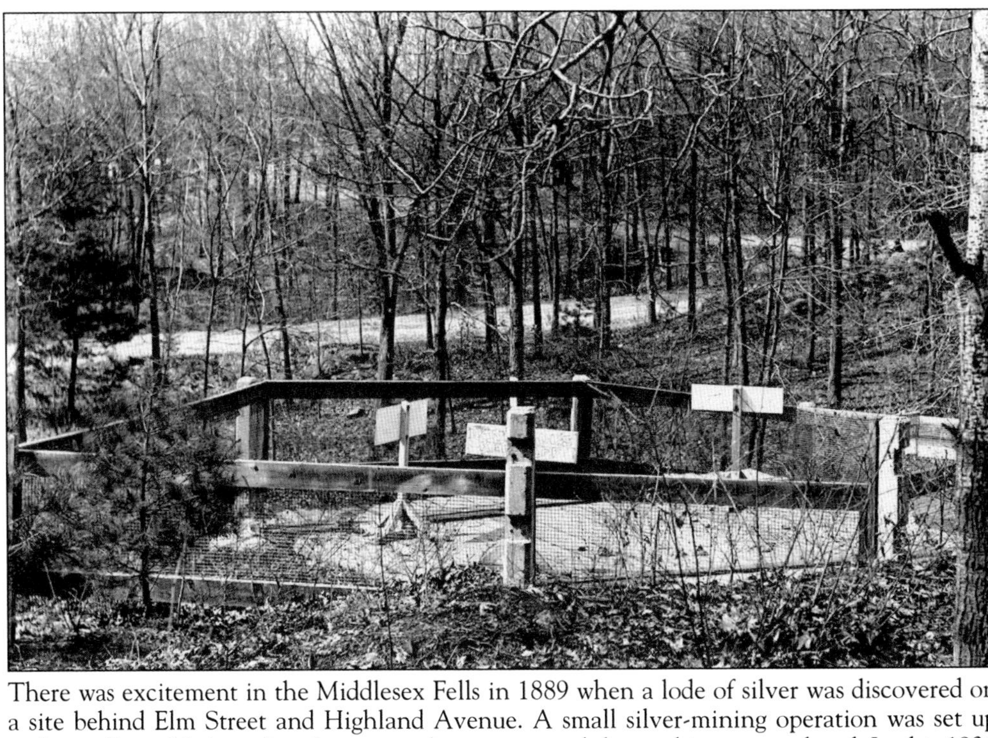

There was excitement in the Middlesex Fells in 1889 when a lode of silver was discovered on a site behind Elm Street and Highland Avenue. A small silver-mining operation was set up and actually yielded ore, but the owners lost money and the workings were closed. In this 1934 photograph, the workings are still visible. (Courtesy of the Medford Public Library.)

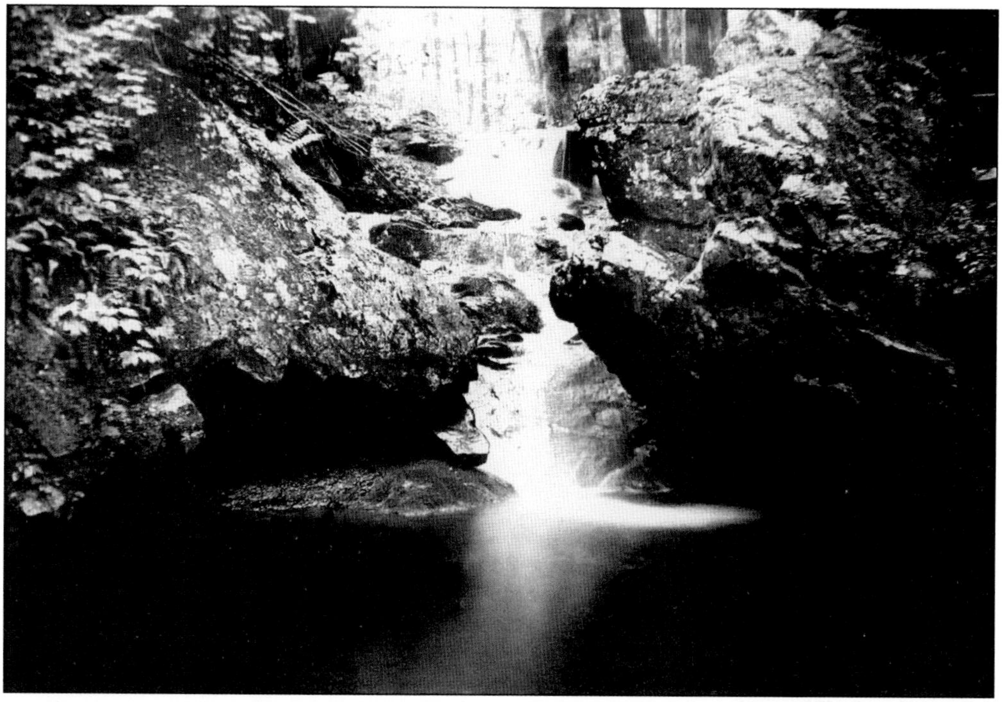

Brooks, streams, and springs created much of the ambient beauty of the Middlesex Fells. Among the affectionately named waters were Crystal Spring, Quarry Spring, and Meetinghouse Brooks. This striking cascade, photographed by George Davenport, flowed down from Shilly-Shally. (Courtesy of the Medford Historical Society.)

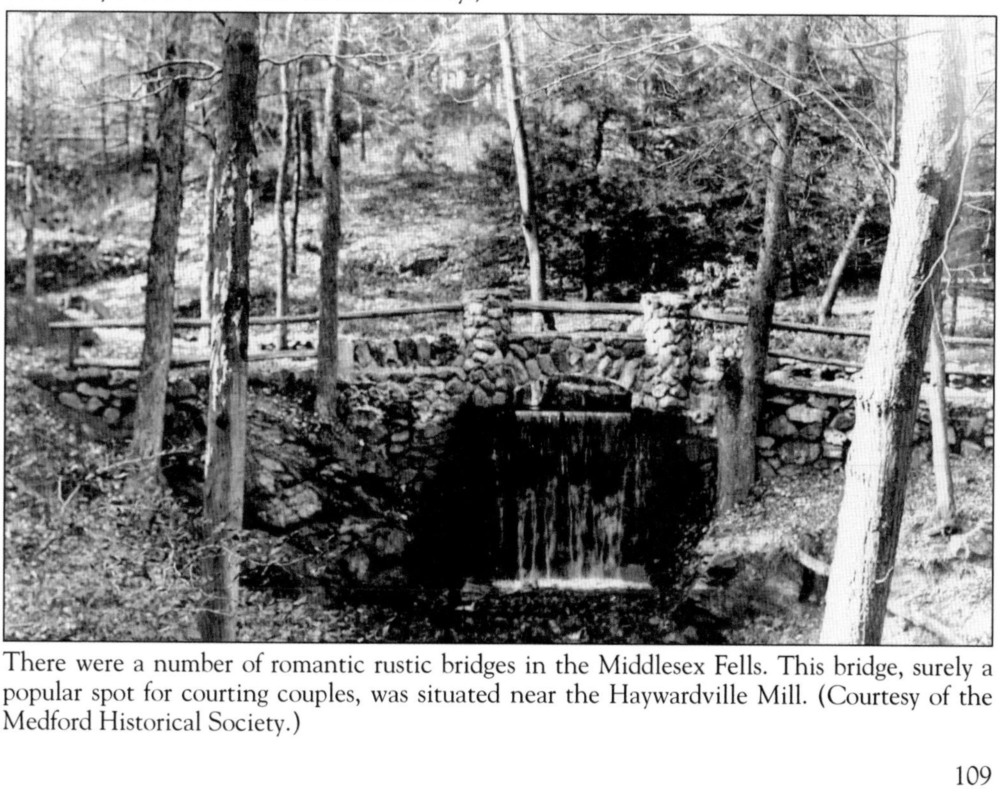

There were a number of romantic rustic bridges in the Middlesex Fells. This bridge, surely a popular spot for courting couples, was situated near the Haywardville Mill. (Courtesy of the Medford Historical Society.)

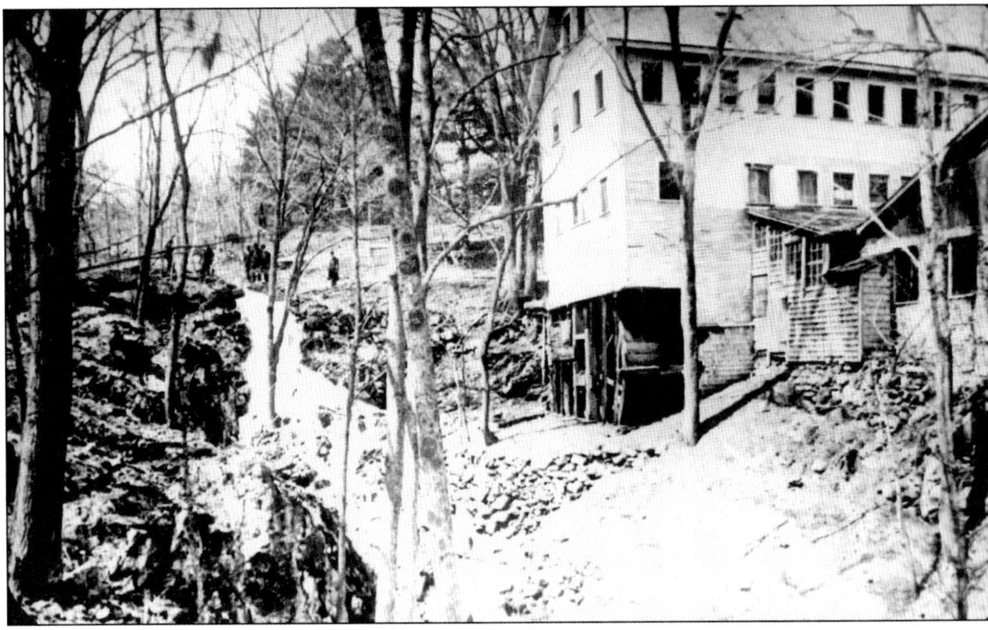

The village of Haywardville was located east of Spot Pond. In 1858 a Bostonian named Nathaniel Hayward built a rubber works on Spot Pond Brook, and a small village sprang up around the site. In 1867, when Spot Pond became the water source for Medford, the loss of water power ended both the rubber business and the village. Seen here is the Old Red Mill of Haywardville in the late 1860s. (Courtesy of the Medford Public Library.)

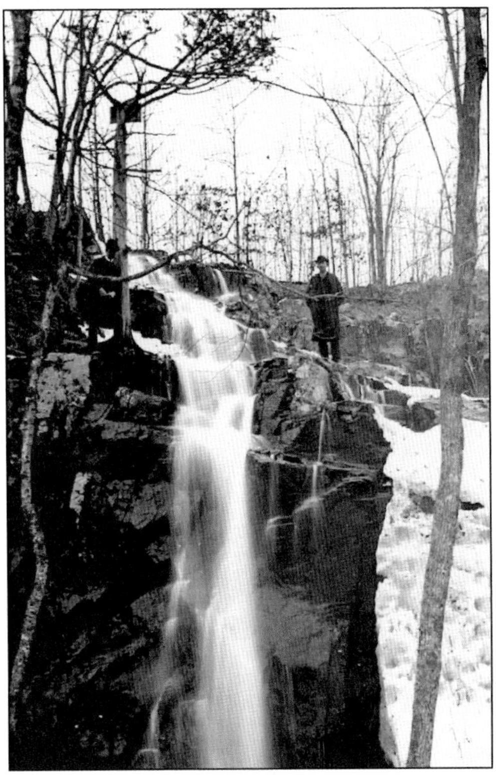

Until 1880 this cascade and the water from Spot Pond Brook furnished power for a number of mills and factories, including the Haywardville Mill. The photograph was taken in 1884 as part of George Davenport's campaign for the Middlesex Fells. (Courtesy of the Medford Public Library.)

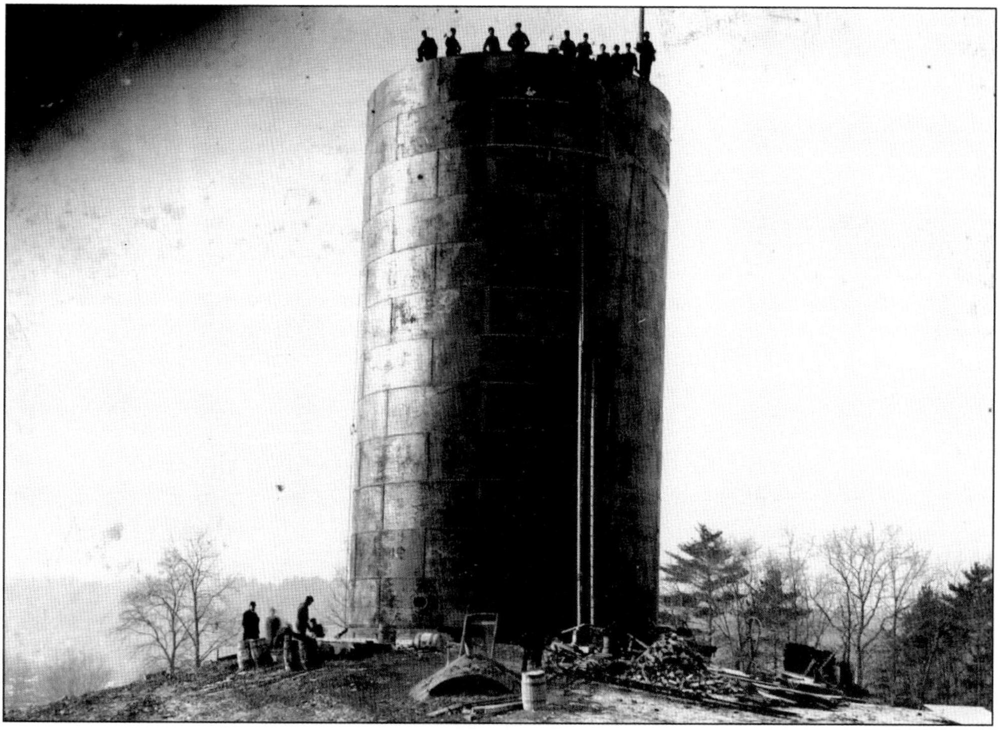

Wright's Pond was an artificial body of water initially created for the ice industry. Seen here is the water tank used during its construction in 1888. The pond, later acquired by Medford as part of the water system, was also a popular place for recreation. (Courtesy of the Medford Historical Society.)

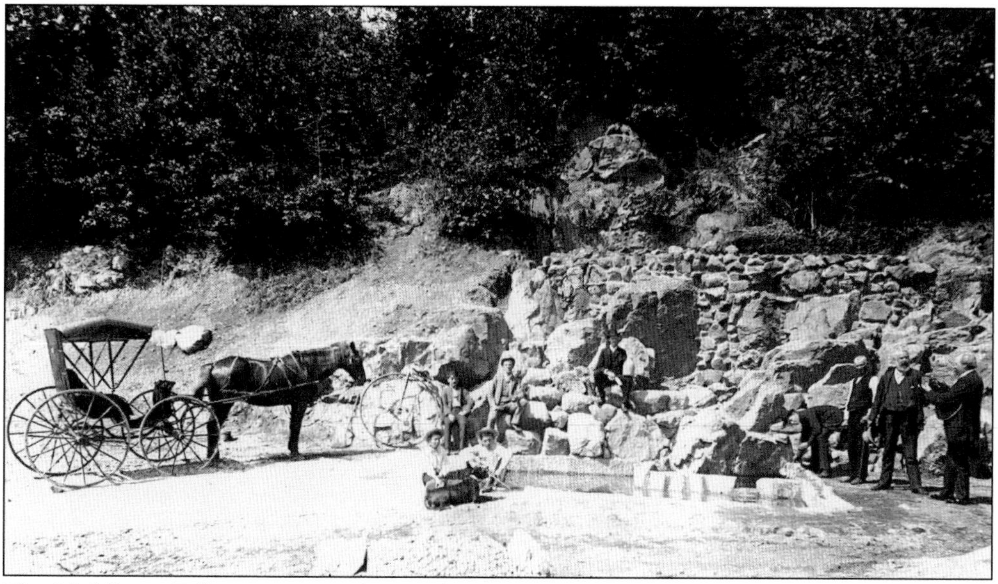

The Middlesex Fells was extremely popular with Victorian day-trippers. Here travelers of all shapes and sizes pose for the photographer at the Middlesex Mountain Spring. Note the high-wheeled bicycle to the right of the horse, and the man on the right washing the picnic dishes in the spring. (Courtesy of the Medford Historical Society.)

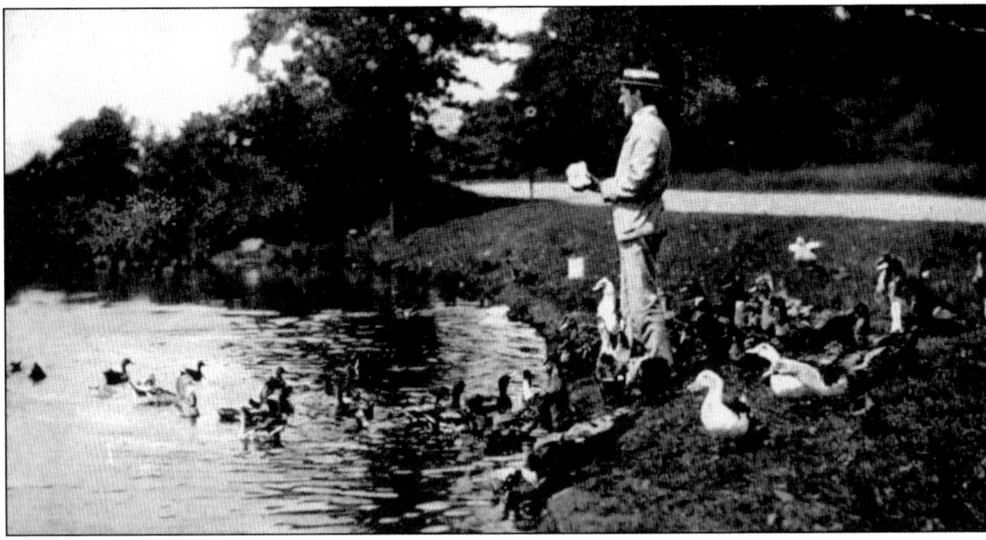

The Middlesex Fells offered many diversions. A small zoo was part of the attraction from 1900 until the 1920s, but wilder animals also roamed freely through the woodland. On this postcard, a well-dressed man is mobbed by ducks during his afternoon in the outdoors. (Courtesy of the Medford Historical Society.)

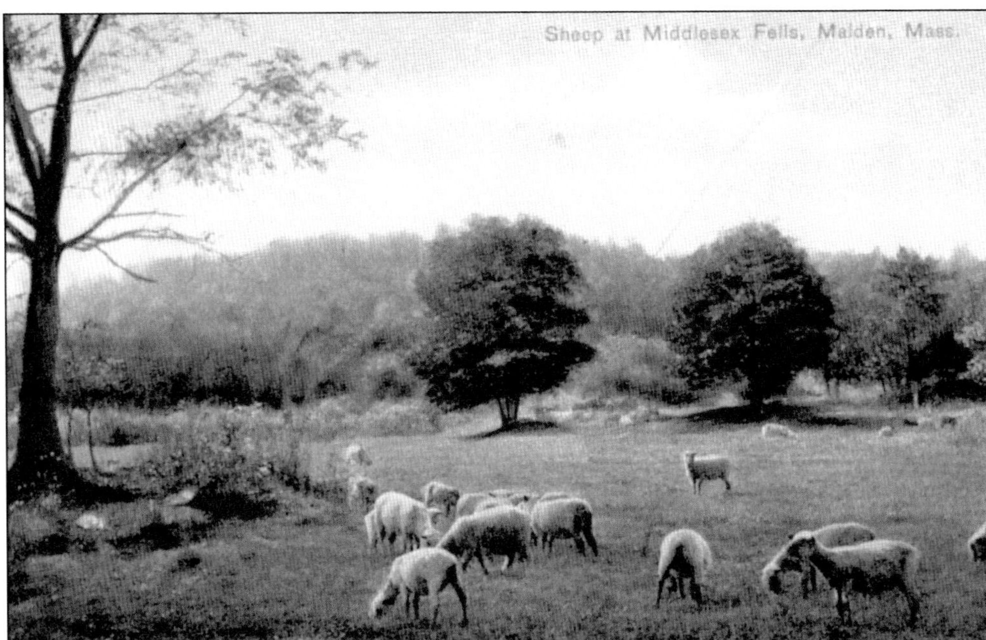

The Sheepfold was a popular place to visit. The open meadow had been part of a farm in the 18th century. In 1902 the park commission advised that the meadow be kept open in order to improve the landscape, and sheep were imported to keep the grass close-cropped. The meadow was a popular place for picnics. (Collection of the author.)

Ten

Passing the Time

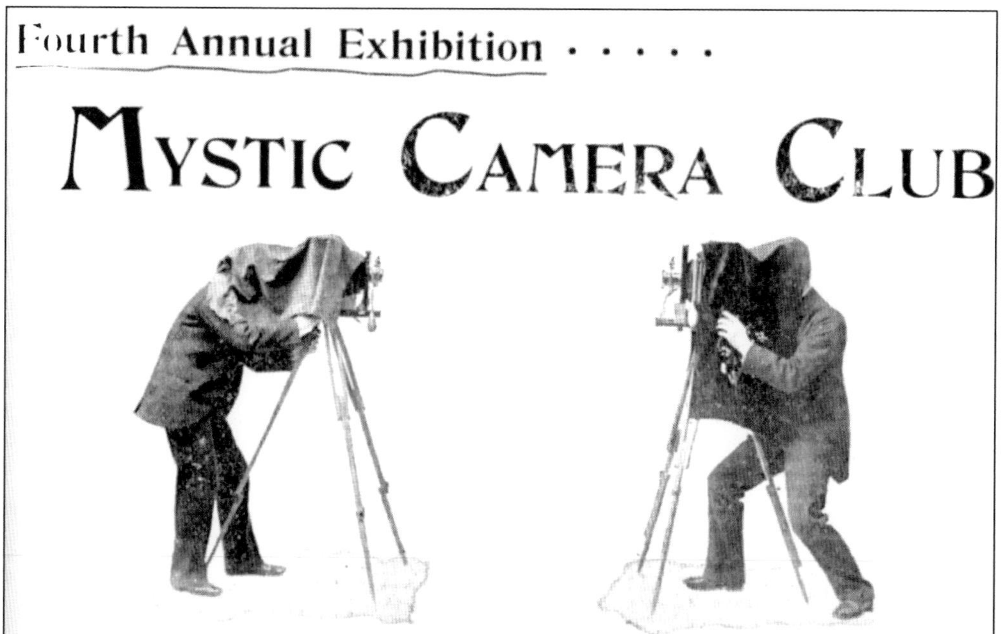

The residents of Victorian Medford found many ways to pass the time. In the 1870s photography became very popular. The Mystic Camera Club was founded in the 1880s and put on its first exhibition in 1889. The members held their exhibitions and meetings in their clubrooms on Main Street. (Courtesy of the Medford Public Library.)

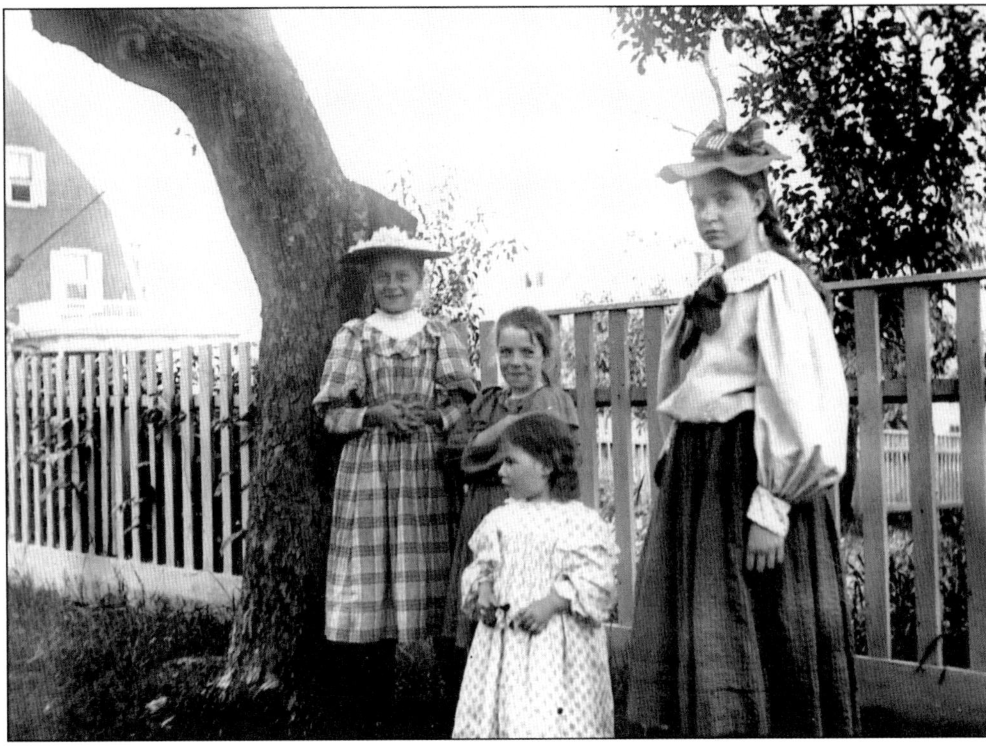

In the new age of photography, having your picture taken became a popular diversion. Pictured in this photograph are, from left to right, Myra Gage, Bernice Gage, the washwoman's baby, and Mildred Bigelow. (Courtesy of the Medford Public Library.)

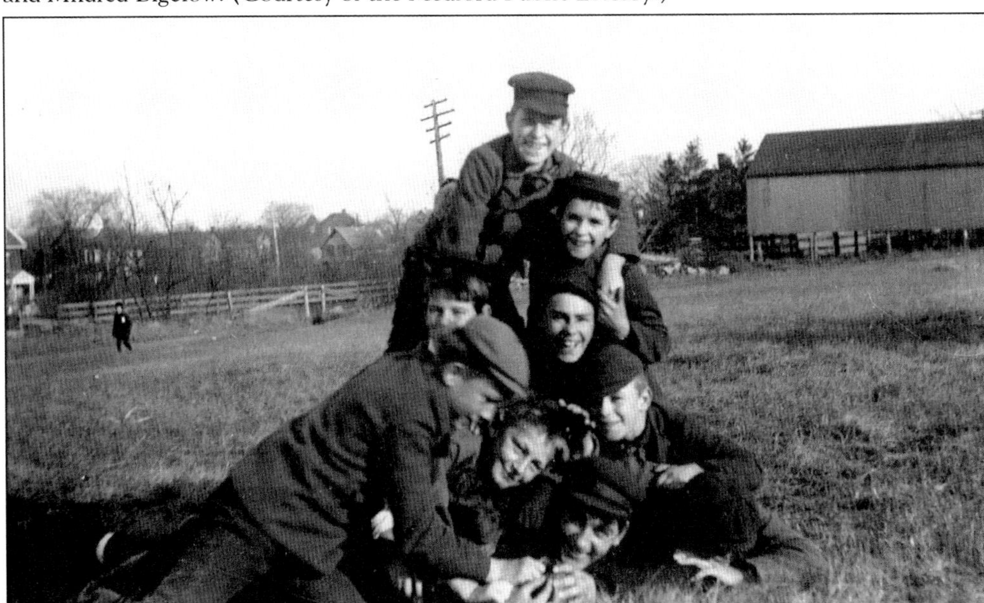

A football game turns into an impromptu pyramid pose for the photographer. The field and football players were photographed near the bowling alley on Boston Avenue on November 30, 1894. (Courtesy of the Medford Public Library.)

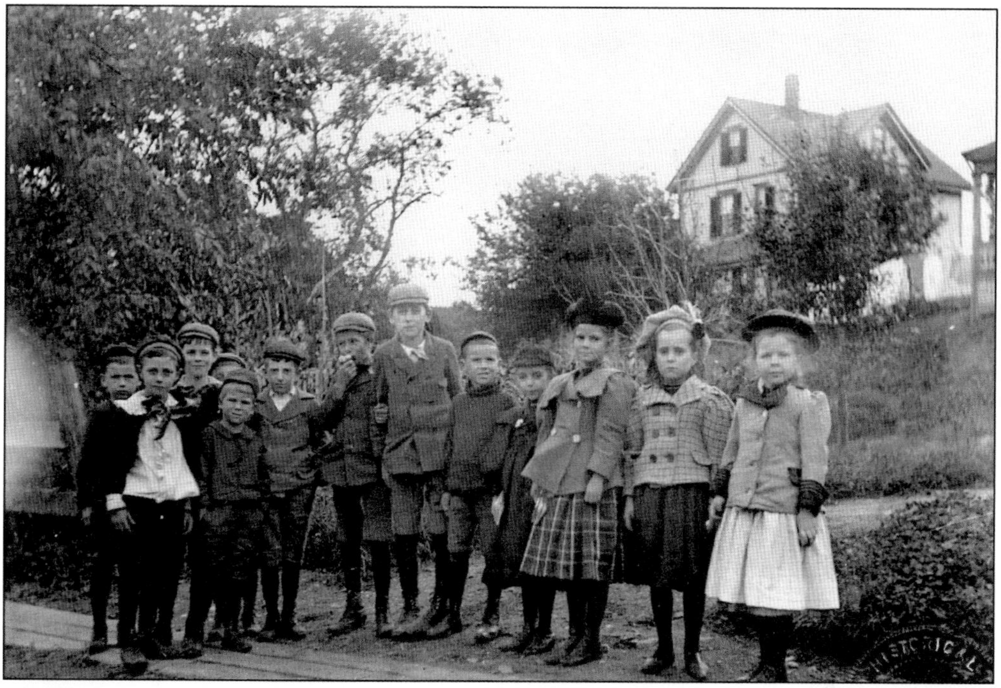

Children pose on Emery Street in October 1896. Notice the high-buttoned shoes and short pants on the boys. (Courtesy of the Medford Public Library.)

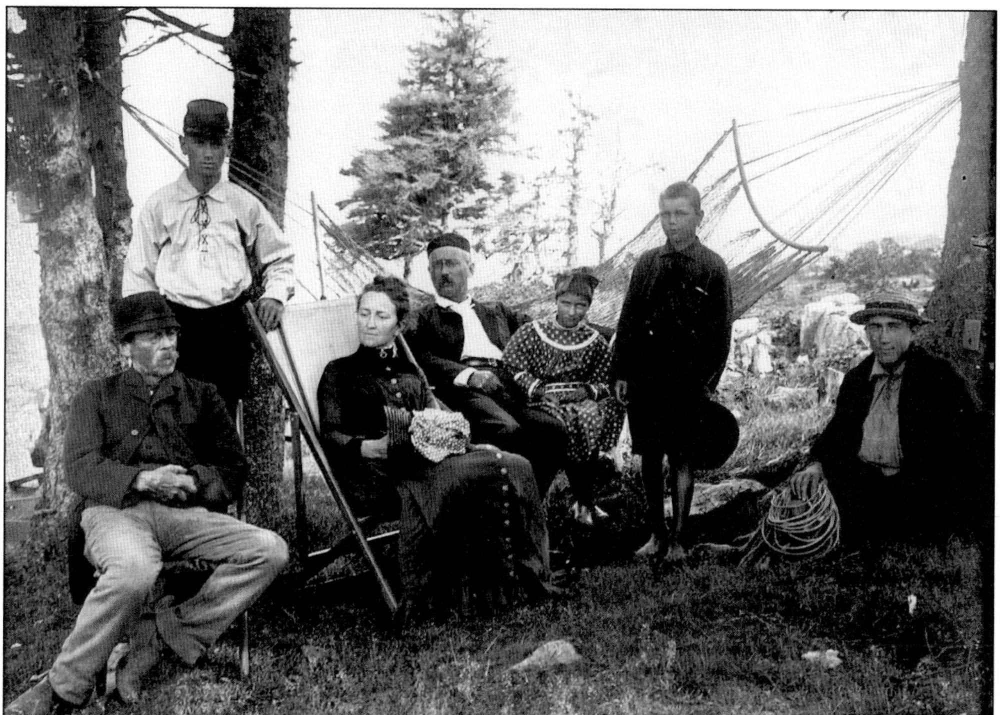

A well-dressed and well-equipped family poses during a day out in the Middlesex Fells. (Courtesy of the Medford Historical Society.)

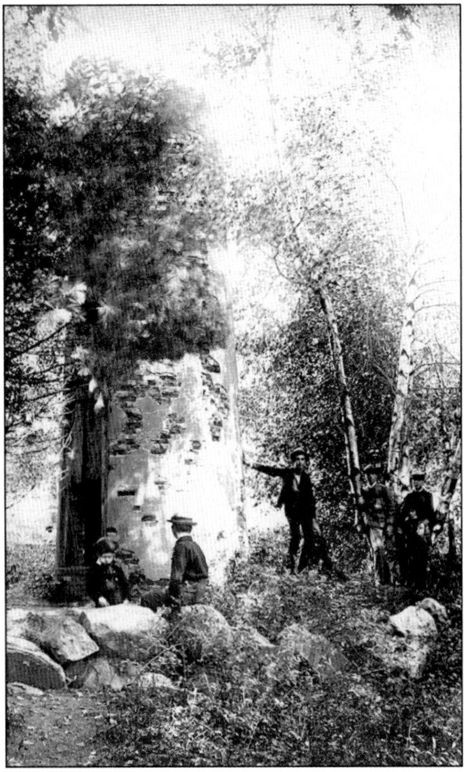

Photographer George Davenport captured this group in the 1880s at the old mill on the Stearns Estate. Rumor had it that the mill hid an entrance to a tunnel that was part of the Underground Railroad. (Courtesy of the Medford Historical Society.)

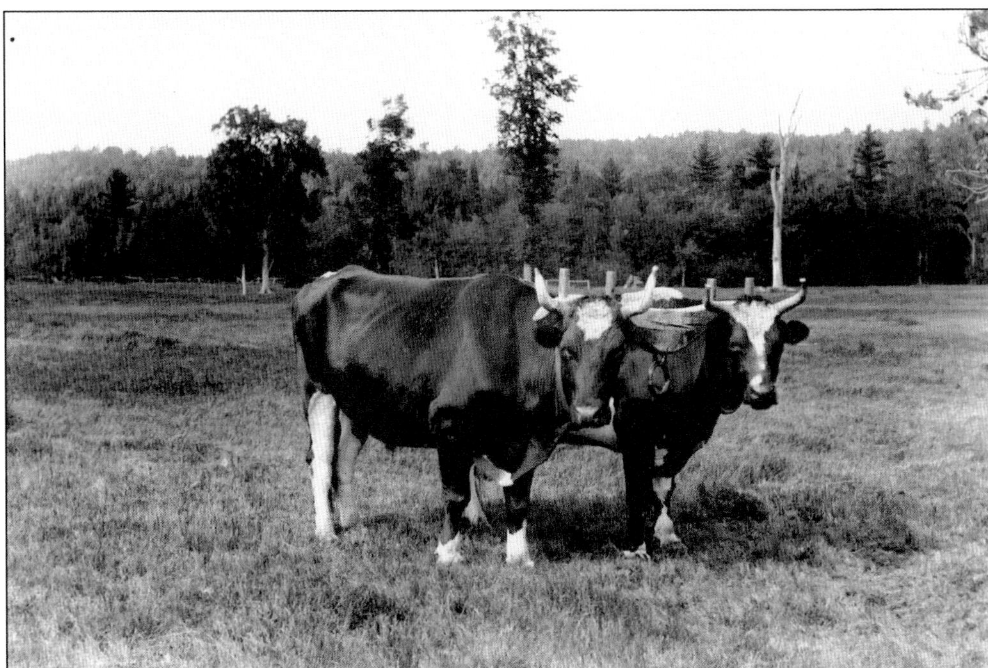

Posing for photographs was not only a pastime for humans. The photographer captioned this picture "Charlie Oxnard's Father's Oxen." Charles Oxnard's father, Frank, was a milk dealer, and the photogenic oxen worked on the family farm. (Courtesy of the Medford Public Library.)

Musical and dramatic performances were another Victorian pastime. The Medford Opera House was built in 1895 on High Street, next to the Masonic Apartments. The Gothic-style building was used for both professional traveling performances and local amateur productions. (Courtesy of the Medford Historical Society.)

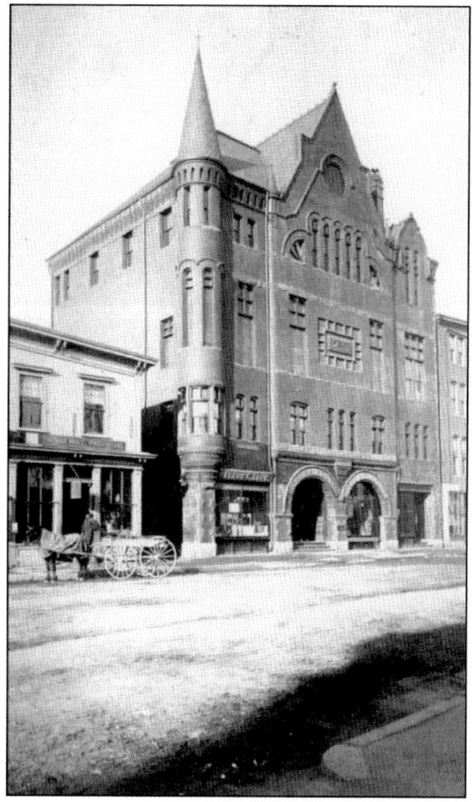

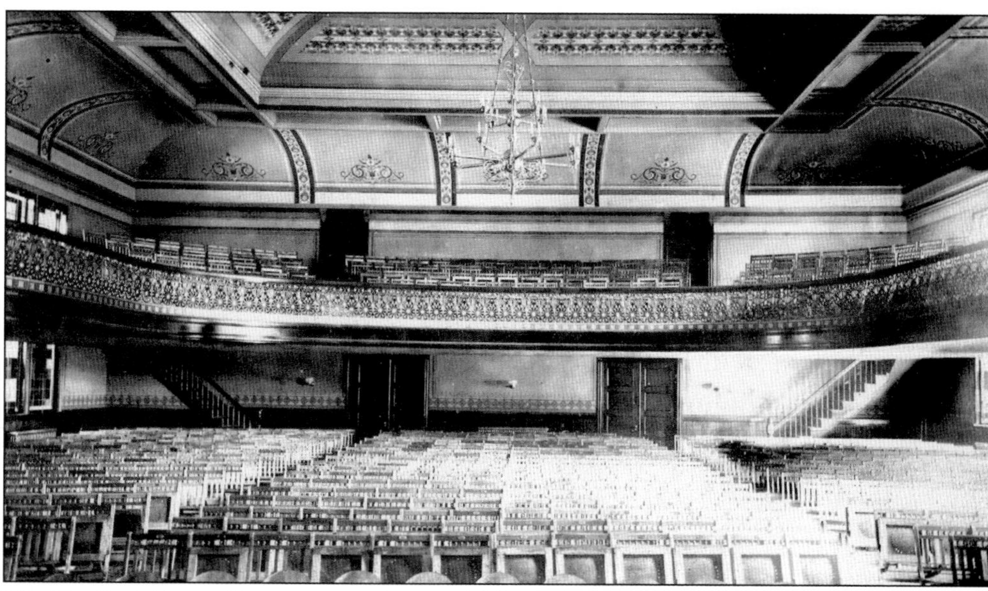

The Medford Opera House seated close to 1,000 persons. Built by the Medford Lodge of Odd Fellows, the building also included offices, clubrooms, a soda fountain, and several stores. The top story of the building was destroyed in a fire in 1911, but the theater remained in operation until 1916. (Courtesy of the Medford Historical Society.)

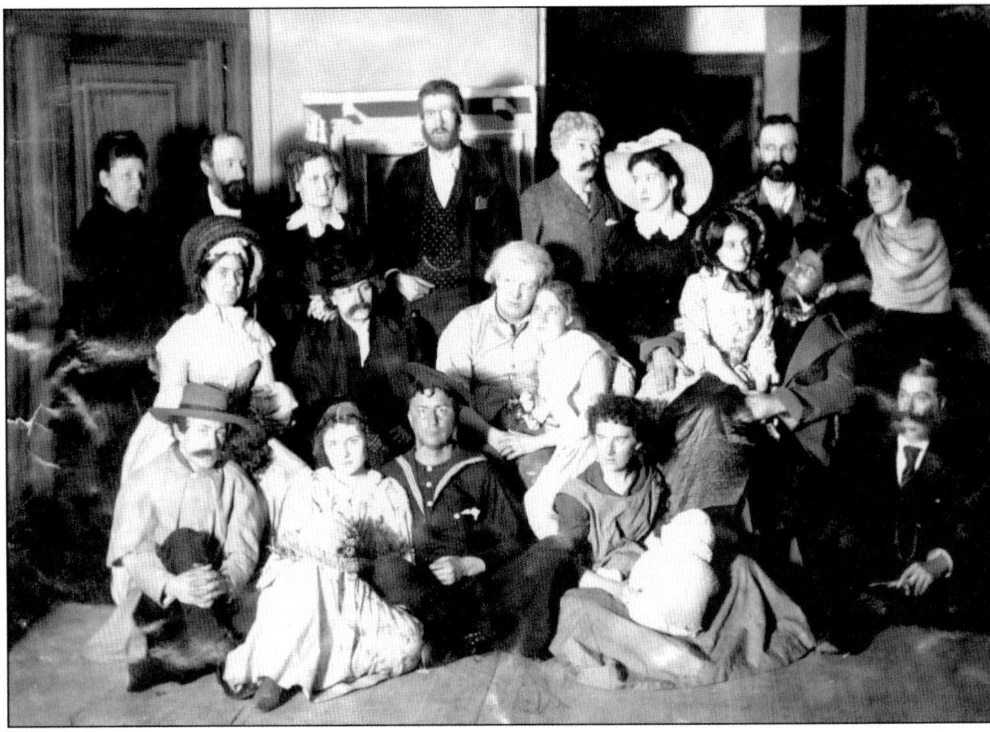

Amateur dramatic societies flourished in Victorian Medford. The Medford Comedy Club was organized in November 1890. The group presented several performances a year at the Medford Opera House and got rave reviews in the local newspaper. Pictured is the cast of *The Loan of a Lover*, performed on March 3, 1891. (Courtesy of the Medford Public Library.)

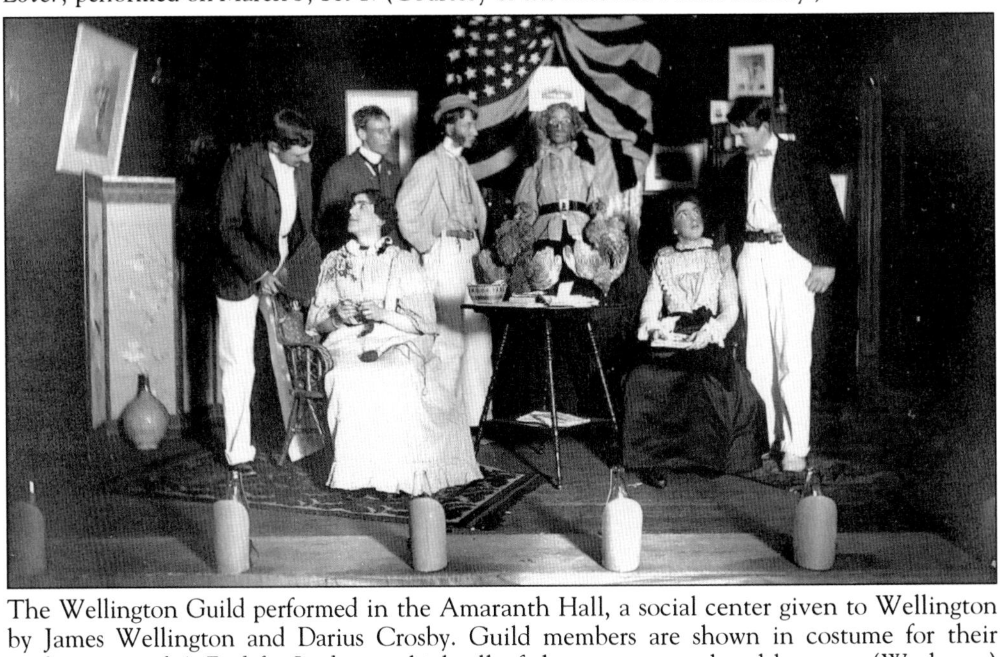

The Wellington Guild performed in the Amaranth Hall, a social center given to Wellington by James Wellington and Darius Crosby. Guild members are shown in costume for their performance of *A Fool for Luck*, in which all of the parts were played by men. (We hope.) (Courtesy of the Medford Public Library.)

Historical pageants were another popular pastime. The Medford Historical Society was organized in 1896 and was based in the Lydia Maria Child birthplace on Salem Street until 1916, when the current building was built. One of the society's first events was *On the Banks of the Mystic*, a pageant celebrating the founding of Medford. (Courtesy of the Medford Public Library.)

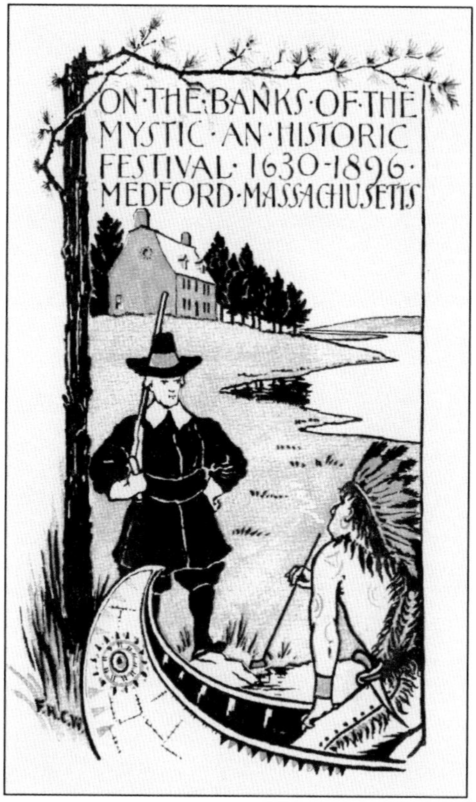

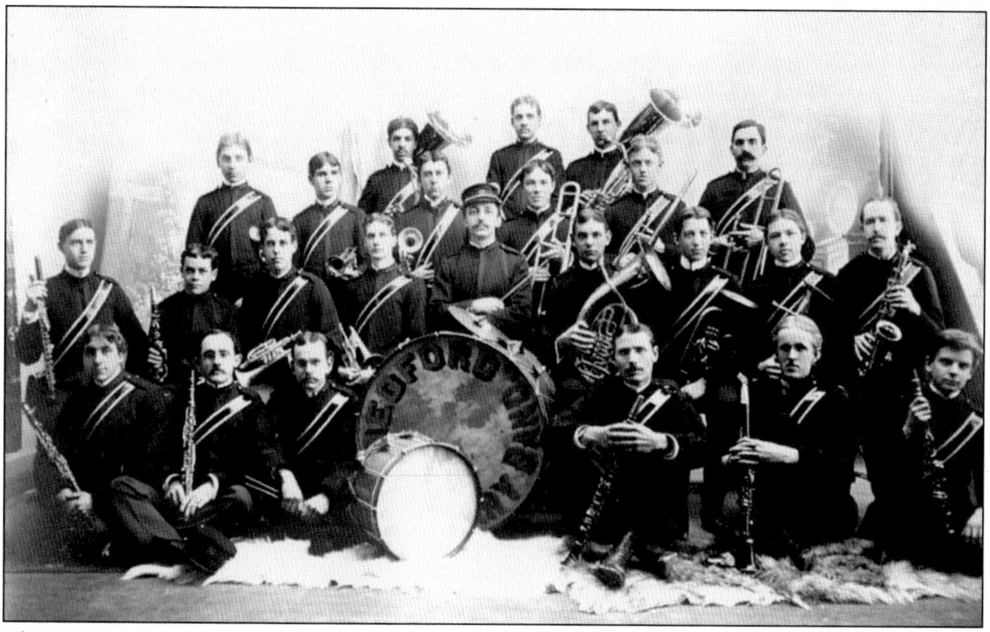

The Medford Band was one of the town's most honored musical groups. The band, formed in 1873 through the union of the Mystic Brass Band and the Medford Cornet Band, was invited to perform all over the country. It became the Boston City Band in 1882. (Courtesy of the Medford Historical Society.)

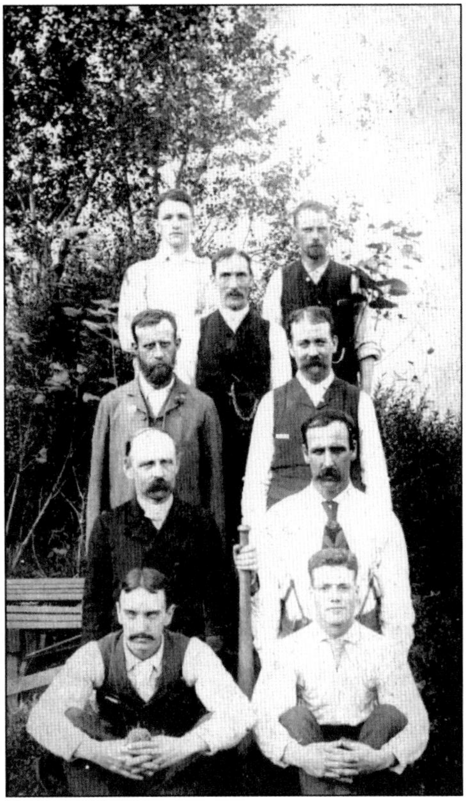

Many clubs and social events were connected with Medford churches. These men are fresh from a baseball game at the Baptist Labor Day picnic in 1889. (Courtesy of the Medford Historical Society.)

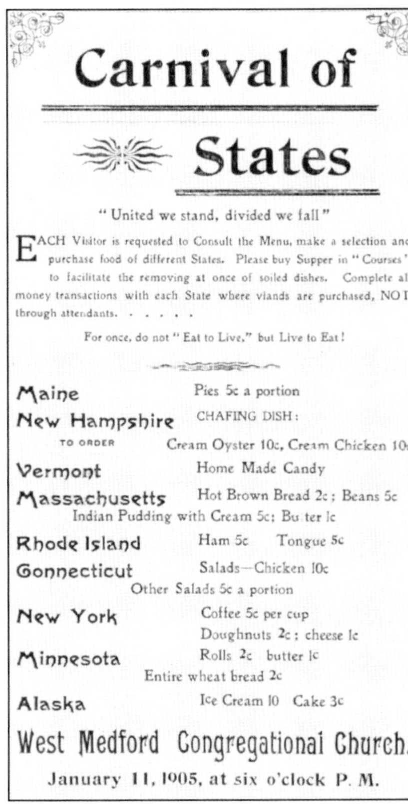

Carnival of States

" United we stand, divided we fall "

EACH Visitor is requested to Consult the Menu, make a selection and purchase food of different States. Please buy Supper in " Courses " to facilitate the removing at once of soiled dishes. Complete all money transactions with each State where viands are purchased, NOT through attendants. . . . . .

For once, do not " Eat to Live," but Live to Eat!

Maine	Pies 5c a portion
New Hampshire	CHAFING DISH:
TO ORDER	Cream Oyster 10c, Cream Chicken 10c
Vermont	Home Made Candy
Massachusetts	Hot Brown Bread 2c; Beans 5c
	Indian Pudding with Cream 5c; Butter 1c
Rhode Island	Ham 5c Tongue 5c
Connecticut	Salads—Chicken 10c
	Other Salads 5c a portion
New York	Coffee 5c per cup
	Doughnuts 2c; cheese 1c
Minnesota	Rolls 2c butter 1c
	Entire wheat bread 2c
Alaska	Ice Cream 10 Cake 3c

West Medford Congregational Church.

January 11, 1905, at six o'clock P. M.

Church suppers were popular social events and fund-raisers for church groups. This clever idea was a benefit for the West Medford Congregational Church in 1905. (Minnesota seems a bit outnumbered by the East Coast states.) (Courtesy of the Medford Public Library.)

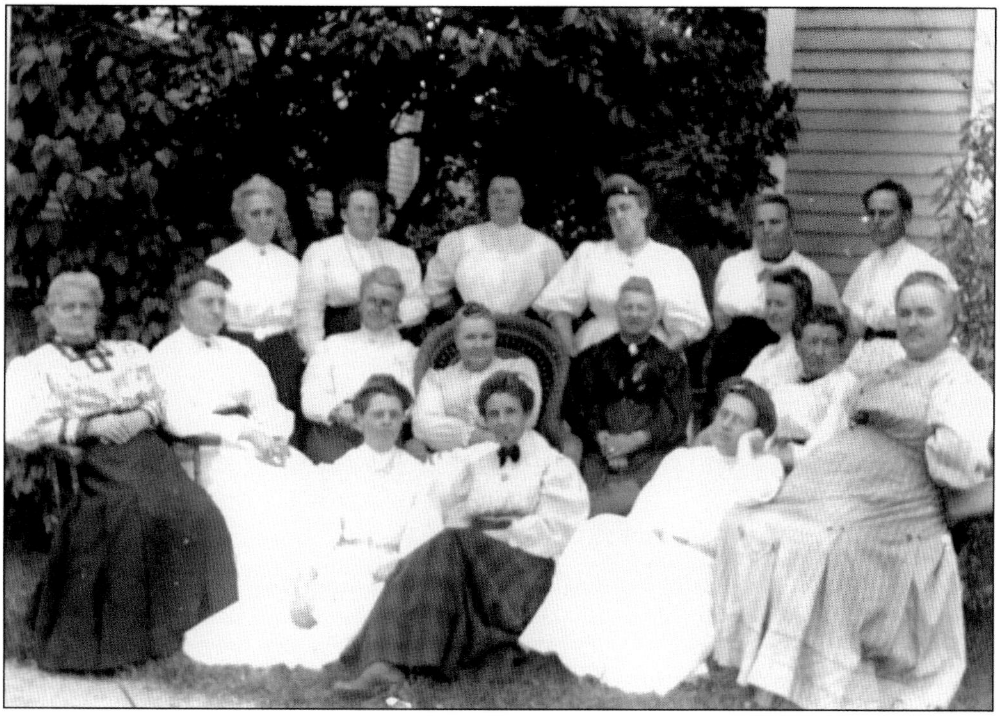

Medford's Victorians were active in clubs and charitable organizations. Here members of the Ladies Aid of the Hillside Methodist Church gather in the garden in the early 1900s. The church was founded in 1895, and the building on the corner of Winthrop and Dearborn Streets was dedicated in 1900. (Courtesy of Beth Fuller.)

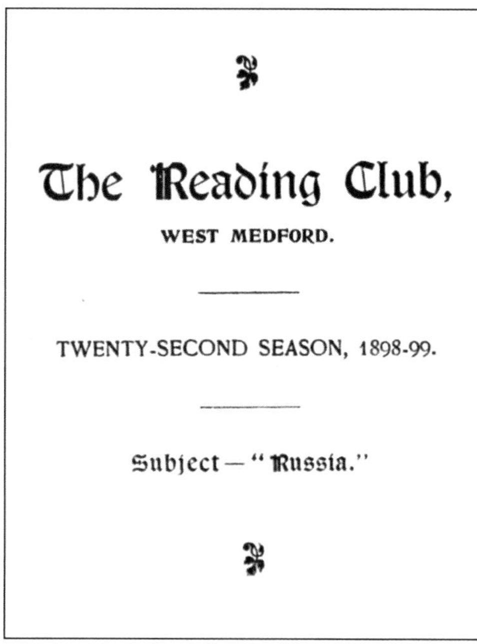

The Reading Club,

WEST MEDFORD.

TWENTY-SECOND SEASON, 1898-99.

Subject — "Russia."

One of the oldest clubs was the West Medford Reading Club, which met for the first time in December 1877. The club met several times a month for discussions and presentations on many topics. Featured topics in the 1898–1899 series on Russia included Napoleon, the partition of Poland, and socialism. (Courtesy of the Medford Public Library.)

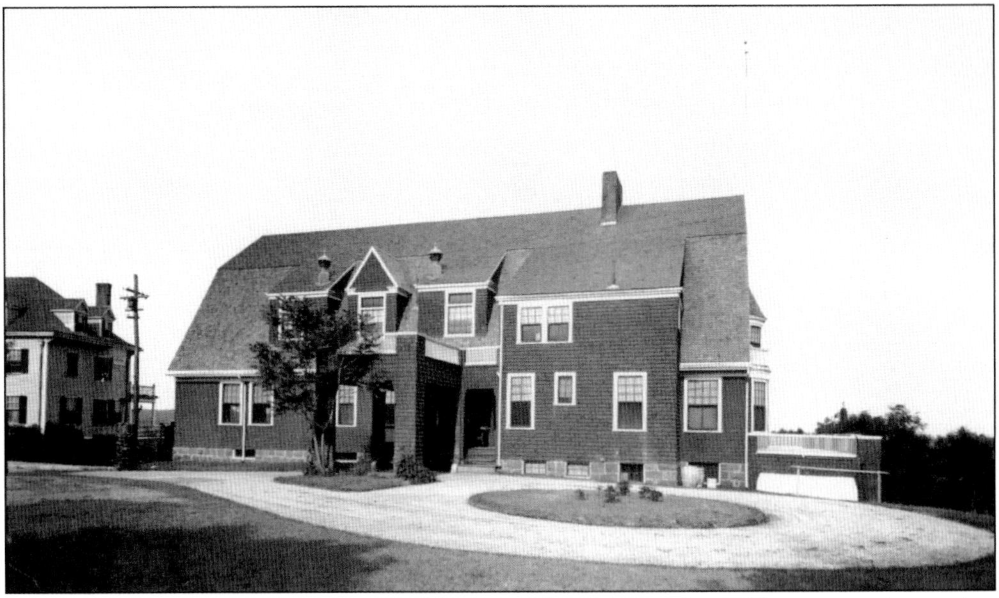

The Medford Club was proposed in 1893 by Samuel Lawrence, Henry Norcross, and a number of other prominent citizens. A club building was constructed at the top of Summit Road and was opened in June 1893 with a membership of 200 men and women. The club offered pool, billiards, cards, bowling, and a ladies' parlor. (Courtesy of the Medford Public Library.)

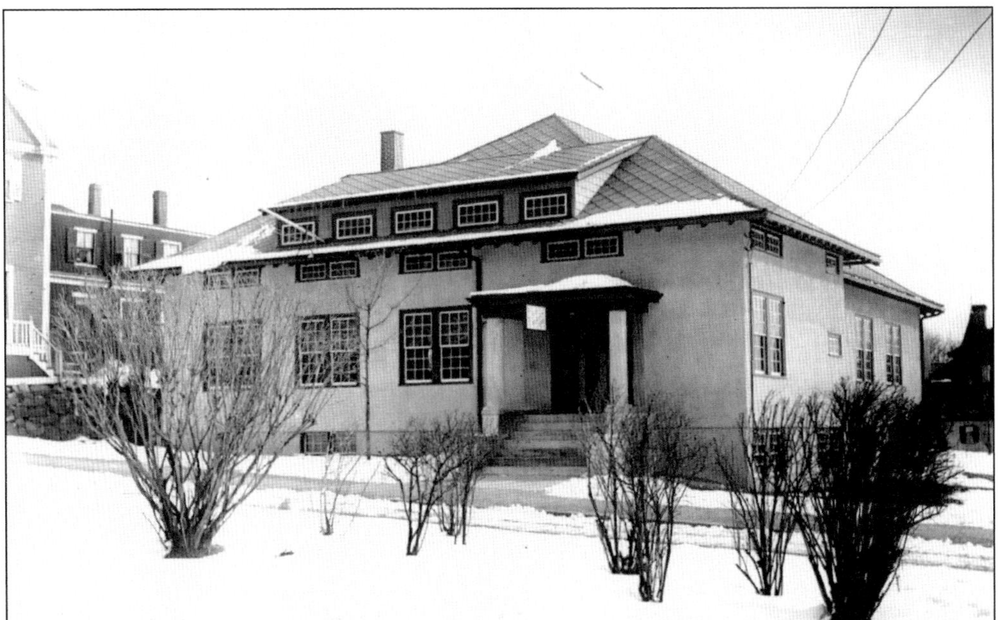

The Medford Women's Club was also organized in 1892 and was incorporated in 1897. The club met monthly to discuss literary and scholarly topics. The meetings were held in private homes until this clubhouse was built on Governor's Avenue sometime after 1905. (Courtesy of the Medford Public Library.)

In addition to clubs and societies, many athletic pursuits were available in Victorian Medford. In the 1880s bicycles were all the rage. This high-wheeled model, called an ordinary in America, was known as a pennyfarthing in Britain because of its small and great wheels. Take note of the riding outfit. (Courtesy of the Medford Public Library.)

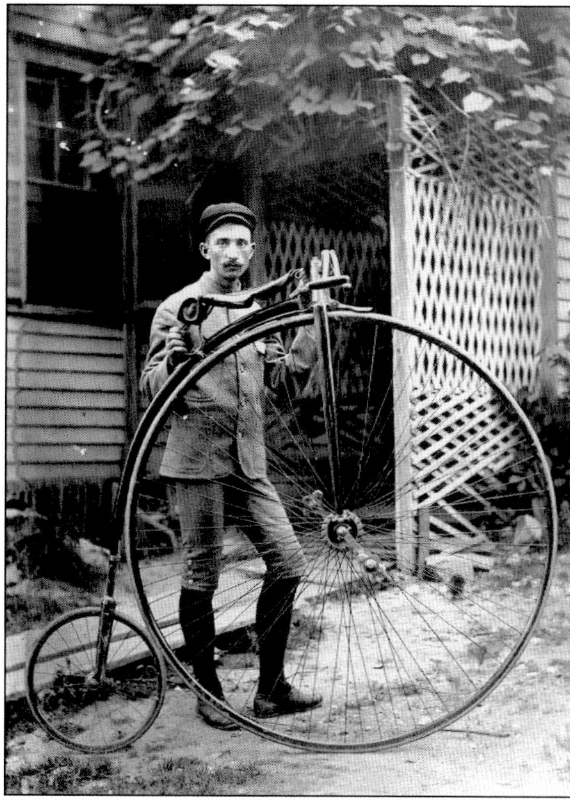

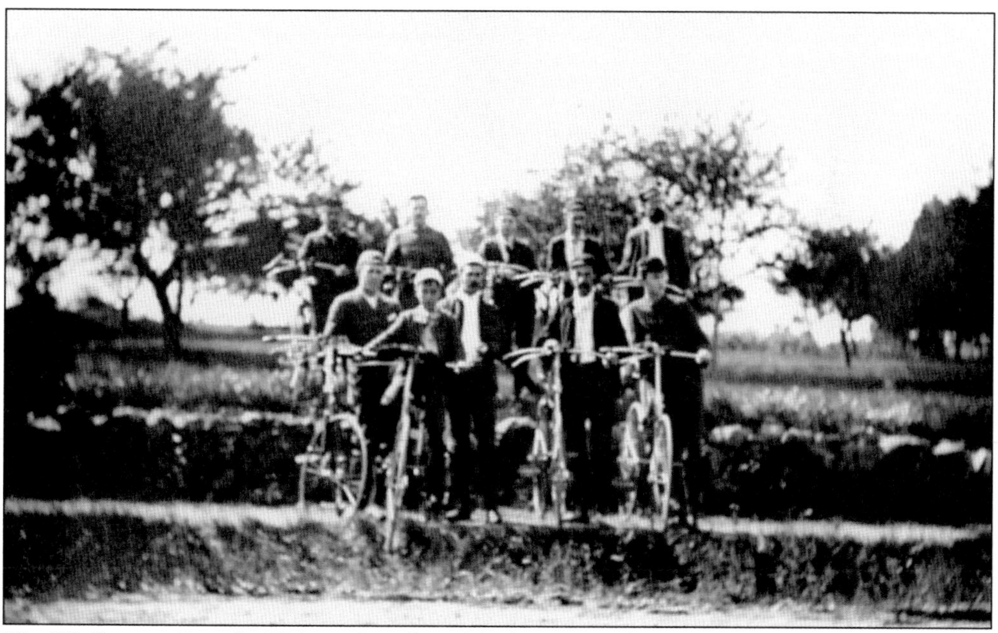

The Wellington Bicycle Club preferred models that were a little closer to the ground. In 1890, when this picture was taken, bicycles of a more familiar style had taken the place of high-wheelers. (Courtesy of the Medford Public Library.)

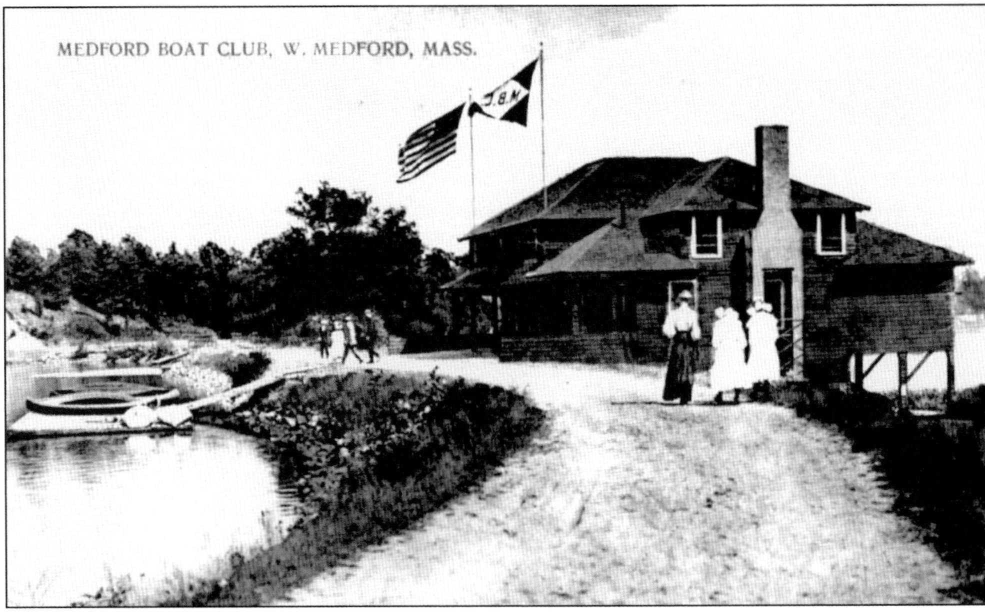

The aquatic set passed the time in and around Medford's many bodies of water. The clubhouse of the Medford Boat Club, on the Mystic Lakes, opened in 1898. By 1904 the club boasted 136 canoes, and club members participated in races and regattas in the Boston area. (Courtesy of the Medford Historical Society.)

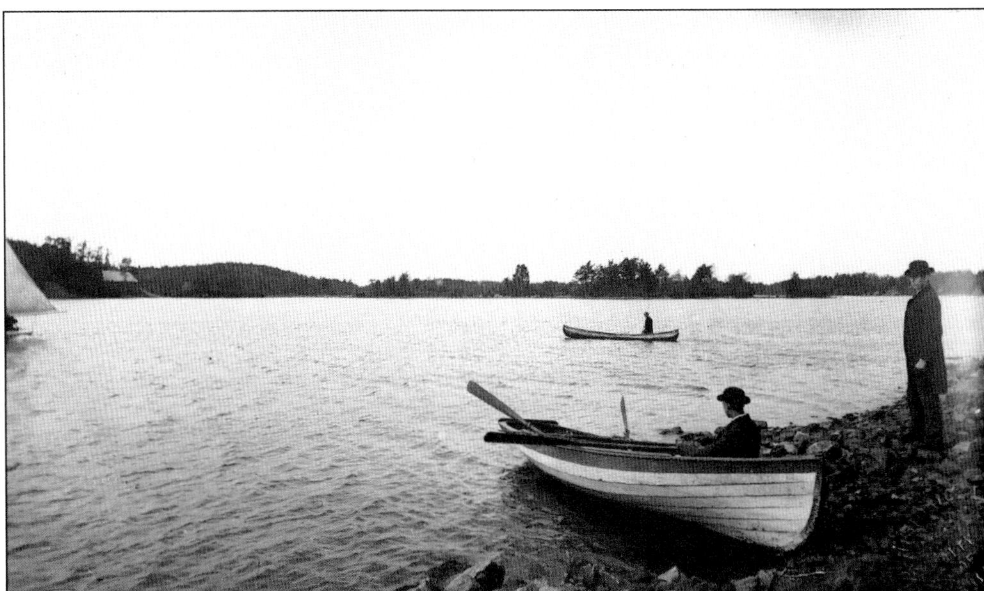

Spot Pond was also a popular place for boating. This 1880s view includes a sailboat, a canoe, and a rowboat—and well-dressed pilots in all of them. (Courtesy of the Medford Historical Society.)

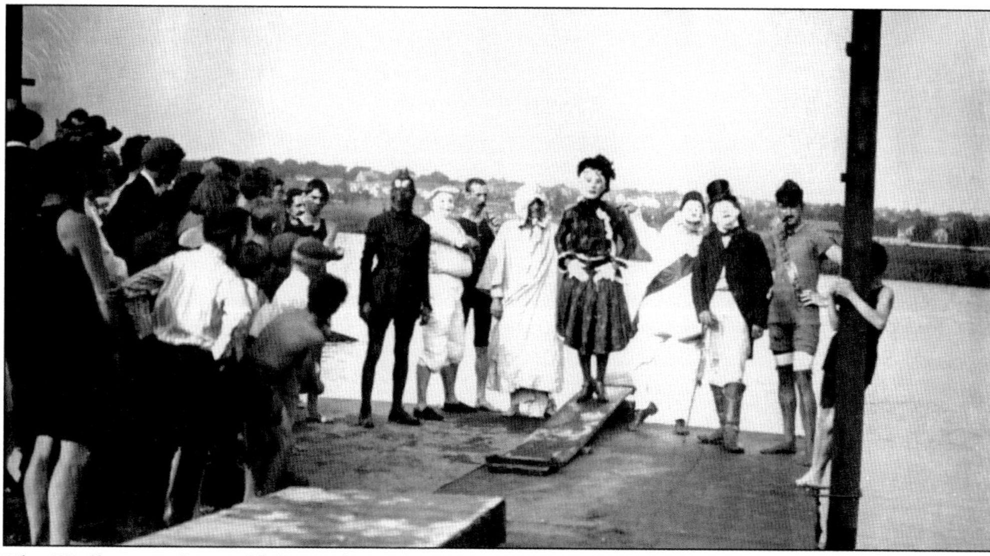

The Wellington Swim Club was formed in 1902 and was a popular social club for Wellingtonians of all ages. The scary-looking characters were part of the Fourth of July celebration in 1903. (Courtesy of the Medford Public Library.)

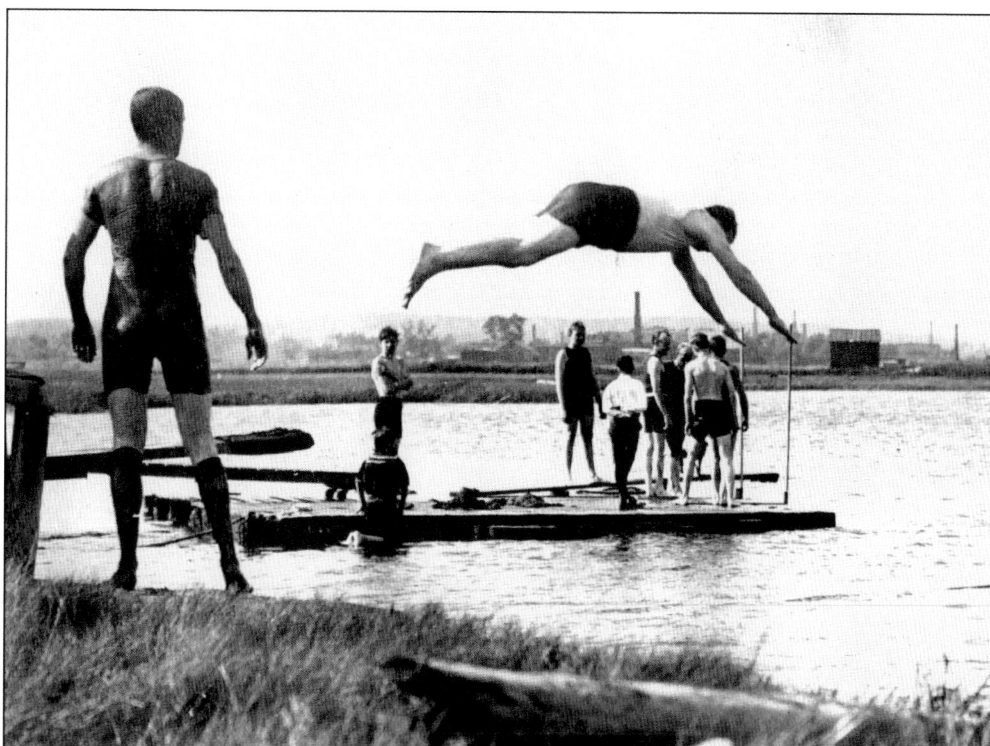

The Swim Club dedicated its new bathhouse in 1904. For the occasion, professional swimmers Glenister and Peter McNally (shown here) gave an exhibition. The story goes that within a week, every one of their stunts had been duplicated by some member of the club. (Courtesy of the Medford Public Library.)

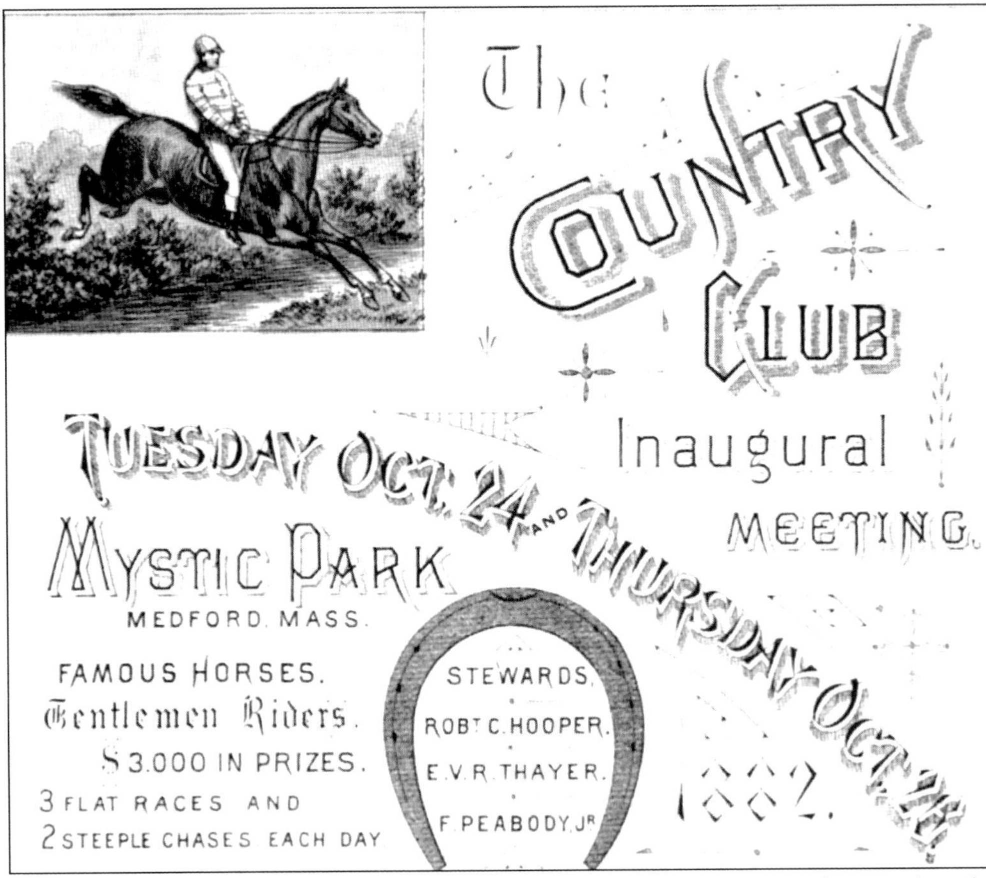

Horse racing came to Medford in the 1870s, when the Mystic Trotting Park opened in the area between Main Street and Mystic Avenue. Combination Park opened in 1893 southeast of Mystic Park. The tracks flourished until the early 1900s, but by 1903 both tracks were closed and the land was divided into house lots. (Courtesy of the Medford Historical Society.)

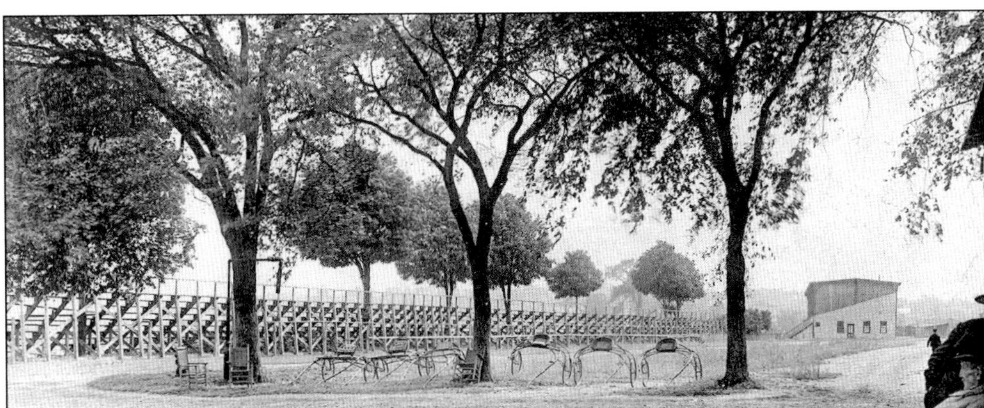

The racetracks drew large crowds of spectators, as seen from the size of this grandstand at Mystic Park. The races were harness or trotting races, in which the horses pulled a rider and a cart, and the prizes were large. The horse Smuggler won $10,000 in a race at Mystic Park in 1874. (Courtesy of the Medford Historical Society.)

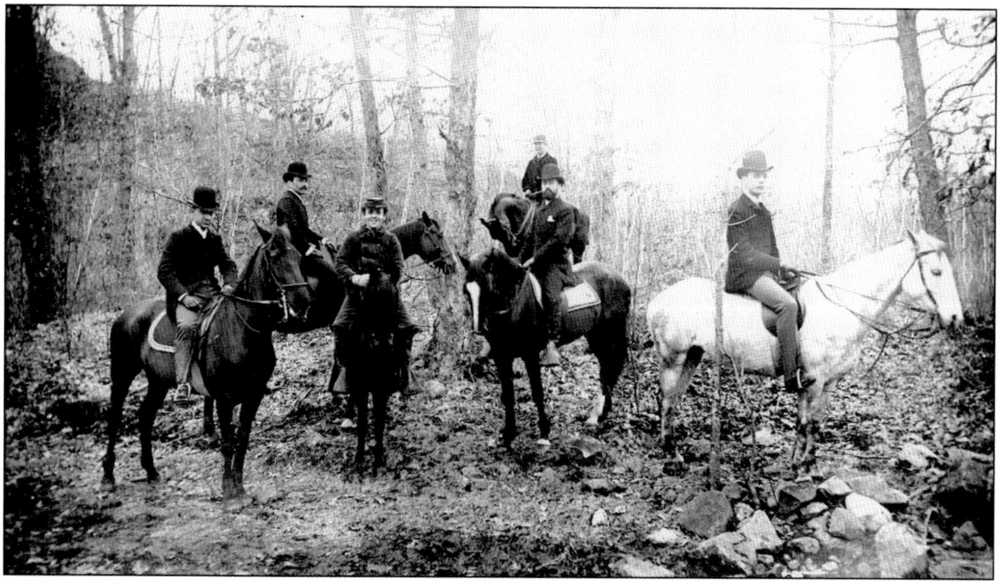

Although horses were necessary for transportation in the Victorian era, they were also used for sport and pleasure. These men, all going in different directions, are on an outing in the Middlesex Fells, which offered a variety of bridle paths and trails. (Courtesy of the Medford Historical Society.)

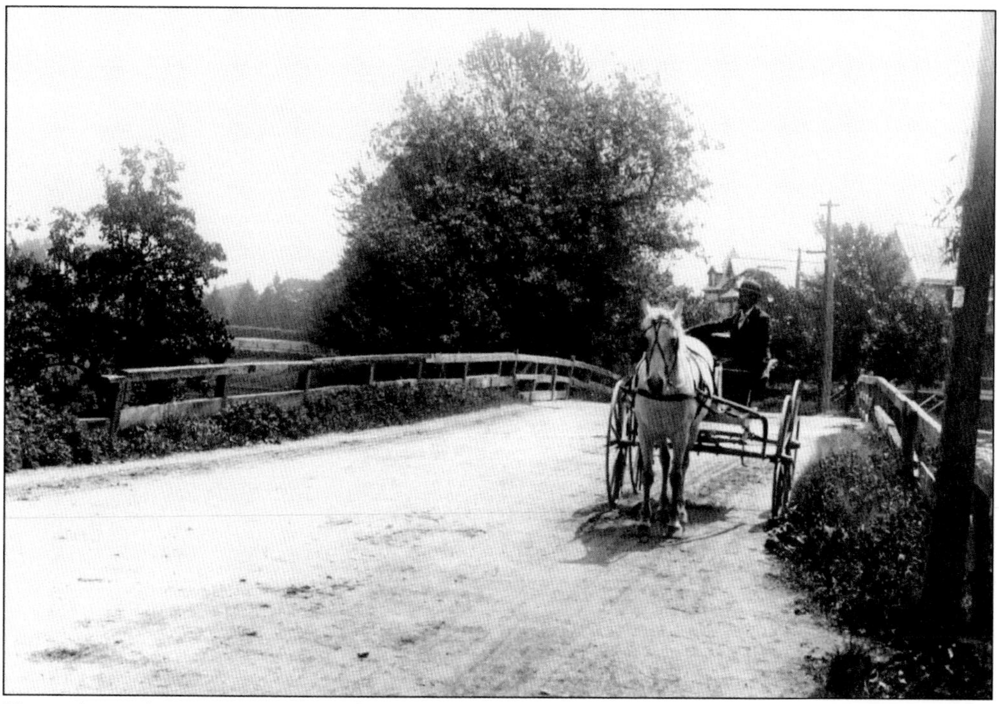

Horse-drawn buggies, carriages, phaetons, and traps were the sports cars of the 19th century. This man, out for a ride in a smart trap, pauses to enjoy the view on Weir Bridge. (Courtesy of the Medford Historical Society.)

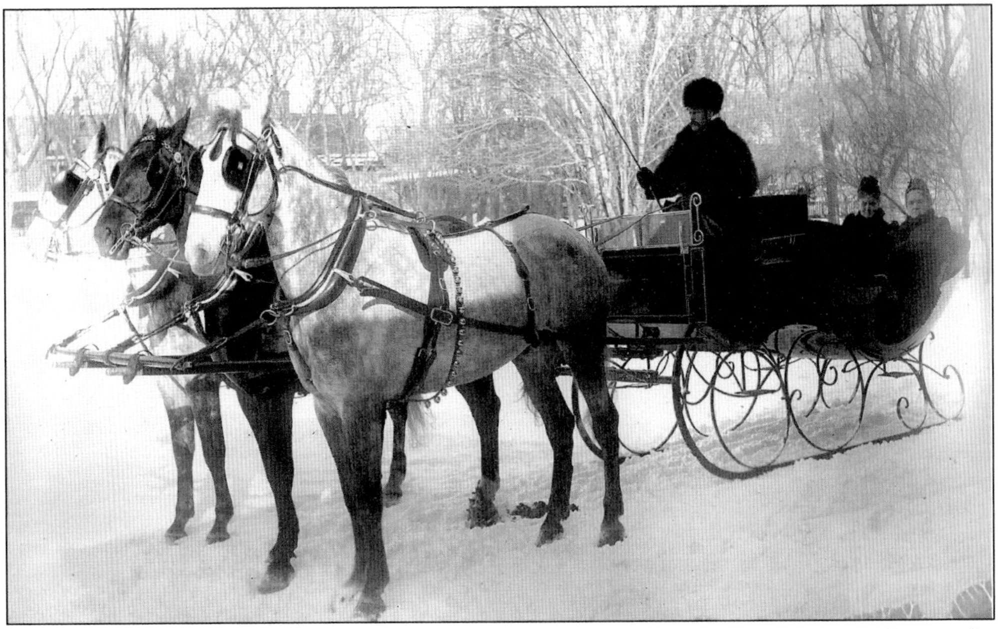

Sleighs provided an elegant way to get around in the winter. They were common sights on the streets of the town in snowy seasons. The women in this substantial three-horse model are probably the wife and daughter of George Luther Stearns. (Courtesy of the Medford Public Library.)

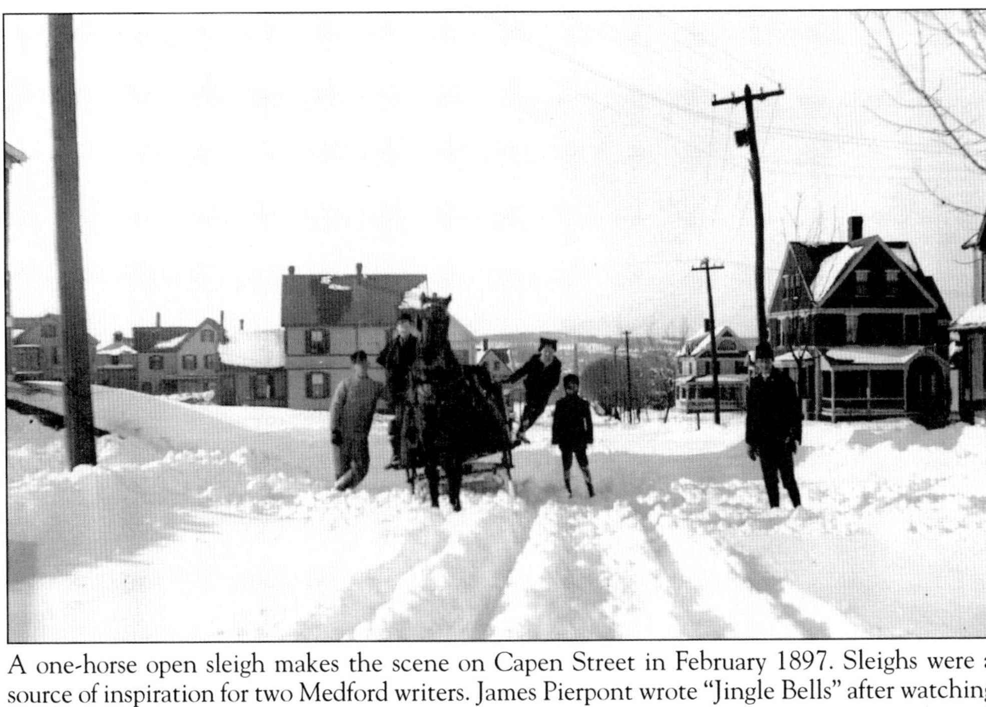

A one-horse open sleigh makes the scene on Capen Street in February 1897. Sleighs were a source of inspiration for two Medford writers. James Pierpont wrote "Jingle Bells" after watching sleigh races on Salem Street, and Lydia Maria Child penned the famous verse that begins, "Over the river and through the woods" after a Thanksgiving ride to her grandmother's house on the other side of the Mystic River. (Courtesy of the Medford Public Library.)